# "Lady in the Locker Room"

Susan Fornoff

SAGAMORE PUBLISHING
Champaign, Illinois

Production Manager: Susan M. McKinney
Cover and photo insert design: Michelle R. Dressen
Editors: Sara Chilton, Russ Lake
Proofreader: Phyllis L. Bannon

*All insert photos are from the personal collection of Susan Fornoff unless otherwise indicated.*

Library of Congress Catalog Card Number:92-63139
ISBN: 0-915611-70-8

Printed in the United States.

*To my parents, Bill and Romaine Fornoff, and my fellow Junior Orioles, Tom, Carl, and Bob; to my best friend, Debbie; and to every woman who ever heard, "You can't come in here," and replied, "Oh yes, I can."*

———————————————

# Contents

# Acknowledgments

I would like to thank Melissa Ludtke for opening the locker room doors to women in sports journalism. Thanks to Betty Cuniberti for ushering me inside.

Many thanks to the cofounders of the Association for Women in Sports Media (AWSM) — Nancy Cooney of the *Philadelphia Inquirer*, Michele Himmelberg of the *Orange County Register*, and Kristin Huckshorn of the *San Jose Mercury News*. I don't remember what we ate that night at the Fisherman, but I'll never forget what we accomplished. An additional thank-you to Kristin for lunch at La Colline, and to her husband, Tim Larimer, for the rejected title, "Ms. October."

AWSM's newsletters were a valuable source of history and anecdotes, and I thank Jane Hughes-Yeung, Tracy Dodds, Julie Cart, Celeste Williams, Johnette Howard, and Leslie Gibson for their work over the years.

Thanks to my always amiable friends on the baseball beat — Dusty Baker, Don Baylor, Kim Boatman, David Bush, Dick Draper, Dave Duncan, Dennis Eckersley, Bud Geracie, John Hickey, Kathy Jacobson, Bruce Jenkins, Brian Martin, Wally Miller, Jackie Moore, Dwayne Murphy, Gene Nelson, Ray Ratto, Glenn Schwarz, Dan Shaughnessy, Larry Sheets, Claire Smith, Dave Stewart, Kit Stier, Carl Young — for trying to preserve my sanity. And thanks to Ron Kroichick for getting me out of there in the nick of time!

Special thanks to Mickey Morabito for turning me into a road warrior, to Jay Alves for keeping me informed, and to Tony La Russa for so patiently teaching me his game. Thanks to Roger Craig for giving me a "Humm Baby" even on my "worst-hair" days.

Thanks to Cheryl Stotler for the move north and to Serge Etcheverry for the Silver Oak cab at Bix. Thanks for the guest room and good cheer provided by Barry Locke and Robin Carr. Thanks also to Kelly Kosinski for making Spring Training seem so short.

Thanks to the men who hired me—Russ Brown, Henry Freeman, Stan Johnston, and Jim Dawson.

Thanks to my agents, Jack Hailey and Jim Levine, and to Joe Bannon, Jr., and the people at Sagamore for providing me with so many blank sheets of paper.

And thanks, finally, to Dave Kingman, for removing me from his gift list.

# The Lineup

**Sandy Alderson.** A's president, Sandy was general manager the year that Dave Kingman sent me the rat. Sandy, an Ivy League-educated lawyer, is liked and respected by many, but I always remember him telling me that he didn't give a shit about me and Dave Kingman. I did dance with him a few times, though — once to a bad Lionel Ritchie song in the bar of the Minneapolis Hyatt.

**Christine Brennan.** Sportswriter for the *Washington Post*, Chris's path never crossed mine until the formation of the Association for Women in Sports Media in 1986. We disagreed philosophically and ethically in many departments, and maybe that's why she's working at the *Post* and I'm not. She's an enthusiastic politician and served AWSM well as president.

**Jose Canseco.** Right fielder for the Texas Rangers, Jose played for the Oakland A's from September of 1985 through August of 1992. His teammates considered him a selfish player and the law considered him a menace to the highway, but—maybe because he was always good for a story—I always liked him. He's such a pet lover, though, that if Kingman had sent him a rat, he'd have played with it.

**Dennis Eckersley.** The best relief pitcher in baseball, Eckersley won the American League's Cy Young and Most Valuable Player awards for his 1992 season. In my book, he's also the best-looking player in baseball and an all-around great guy. Knowing Eckersley kept me from believing, as many sportswriters do, that all baseball players are automatically jerks.

**Bud Geracie.** A sports columnist for the *San Jose Mercury News*, Bud began covering the Oakland A's the same year I did, 1985. He's well-liked by the people he covers (and also his fellow sportswriters),but the 24-hour-a-day potential of the baseball beat instilled in him such a fear of missing a story that he happily left after the 1988 season. He was one of my favorite drinking buddies.

**Michele Himmelberg.** A sportswriter for the *Orange County Register*, Michele is a battler for equal access and against sexual harassment in clubhouses. She was president of the Association for Women in Sports Media the year that Zeke Mowatt exposed himself to Lisa Olson and Sam Wyche kicked Denise Tom out of the locker room.

**Kristin Huckshorn.** A reporter for the *San Jose Mercury News* Washington bureau, Kristin is a former sportswriter who was there the day I bought my first leather skirt. (She already had one.) She helped form AWSM and continues to design our annual T-shirt and administer our scholarship program.

**Reggie Jackson.** A Hall of Fame player who hit lots of homers and struck out even more frequently, Reggie was almost as big a pain in the ass as Dave Kingman. I admired the way he played the game, even in his final season, 1987, but I didn't admire the way he'd strut around naked in the clubhouse afterward.

**Bruce Jenkins.** A sports columnist for the *San Francisco Chronicle*, Bruce was the guy who said, "I'm writing this," the night I received a boxed rat. He's an absolute sports nut and the fastest, loudest typist I've ever seen. "Pounding" referred either to sportswriters drinking or Jenks typing.

**Dave Kingman.** An all-around weirdo not unlike Reggie Jackson, except that Kingman didn't break a sweat on the field — much less bleed, the way Reggie would. He played for the A's from 1984 through 1986, when he sent me the present that ultimately ended his career.

**Tony La Russa.** Manager of the Oakland A's, Tony is one of the few people I find impossible to reduce to just a sentence or two. I don't think there's a better manager in baseball, yet, I wouldn't want to play for him. I loved sitting down for dinner with him, yet, he's not someone I'd put on my party list. Let's say that Tony is either incredibly complicated or utterly simple, and I could never manage to figure out which. At least he's not a male chauvinist pig.

**Robin Carr Locke.** Publicity manager for the San Francisco Giants, Robin taught me that the male chauvinist pigs didn't stay in the clubhouse—sometimes they got powerful positions in the front office of baseball. She's loved sports since her father, a sportswriter for the *San Francisco Chronicle*, let her tag along to tennis matches, and she's married to sportswriter Barry Locke of the Alameda Newspaper Group.

**Melissa Ludtke.** Former sportswriter for *Sports Illustrated* magazine, Ludtke and *SI* sued the New York Yankees for equal access after she couldn't get into the clubhouse during the 1978 World Series. Since then, she has been a Nieman Fellow at Harvard and a writer for *Time* magazine. Ludtke no longer covers sports.

**Mark McGwire.** The A's first baseman, McGwire provided a great example of the personal cost of baseball fame and fortune. I really liked him in 1987, his rookie year, and I always enjoyed talking to him. But it was apparent that all of the attention ultimately made him wary, and all of the money ultimately made him uptight. And I hope he shaves off that awful goatee.

**Jackie Moore.** Third-base coach for the Texas Rangers, Jackie is a much-traveled baseball man who stopped to manage the A's for two seasons—including my first on the beat, 1985. He tried so hard to please everyone—from management to players—that his own managerial style never emerged. But his personal style is all class.

**Mickey Morabito.** The director of team travel for the A's, Mickey took me everywhere I needed to go (particularly to the hotel bars) for five years. The hardest part of his job, I learned, is keeping his players — and their wives and imports — happy on the road. Mickey was one of the best friends of the late Billy Martin, manager of many teams, and he remains one of mine, too.

**Lisa Olson.** Feature writer for the *Daily Telegraph-Mirror* in Sydney, Australia, Lisa was the *Boston Herald* football writer who accused Zeke Mowatt of the New England Patriots of sexual harassment for exposing himself to her crudely in the locker room in September 1990. By then, women sportswriters had actually begun thinking, "This is no problem anymore—we're just plain old sportswriters." We were wrong.

**Glenn Schwarz.** The sports editor of the *San Francisco Examiner*, Schwarzie was the dean of the A's writers when I joined the beat in 1985. He's an approachable guy who shared his baseball wisdom generously, although I think he was still a Kingman fan then. He had moved to the Giants beat in 1986, and King Thompson replaced him.

**Claire Smith.** A sportswriter for the *New York Times*, Claire was covering the Yankees when I began covering the A's. She's off the beat now — worn down, like me, by the daily grind and constant battles. But Claire showed me you could make friends on the beat without compromising your professionalism.

**Dave Stewart.** A starting pitcher for the Toronto Blue Jays, Stew was a four-time 20-game winner for the A's during their heyday. He's opinionated about the game and its players, and that's gotten him in trouble at times. He's really hardheaded, too, and I can say that because I consider him one of the best friends I made covering baseball. I love this guy.

**Kit Stier.**     The A's beat writer for the Westchester-Rockland Newspapers, Kit covered the A's for the only daily paper in their town, the *Oakland Tribune*. That may be why he seemed so territorial about the beat and secretive about even the most insignificant stories. The players don't like him much and he doesn't like them much, but he's great at what he does and I grew to enjoy his company at the post-game bar scene.

**Lesley Visser.** Sports reporter for CBS-TV, Lesley was already a sportswriter for the *Boston Globe* when I was breaking into the business.   Now she's hit the big time, and it couldn't have happened to a nicer (or funnier, or more professional or enthusiastic) woman sportswriter.   Her husband, Dick Stockton, was signed on to do A's TV broadcasts in 1993.

# Prologue

## One of the Guys

This is not one of those "balls" baseball books. Ball Four
... Balls ... Foul Ball ... No Balls ... You Gotta Have Balls. I spent
13 years poking around in locker rooms and learned exactly one
thing about balls: The umpires break in the new ones with a
coating of mud.

No, I don't know much about balls.

And, no, I don't know the size of Jose Canseco's penis.
I don't know how long it is, how thick it is, how functional it is,
or how pulchritudinous it is.

I never saw Jose Canseco's penis.

In 13 years of covering sports and interviewing men in
locker rooms, I learned one thing about penis exposure: men
look, women look away.

Wait a minute, you say. No balls? No penises? But, lady,
you *must* have learned something useful, something compelling,
from 13 years in men's locker rooms, five of them spent exclusively covering the Oakland A's.

So what did I learn?

I learned all about what it's like to be one of the guys,
whether I wanted to be one of them or not.

I was a living lab experiment on what would happen to a
child raised to dress, think, and act like a woman but sent to live
in a world of men. Only, the world I was sent to live in was not

inhabited by mere men, but men of muscle and machismo. One could argue that every woman lives in a man's world: I was living in the quintessential man's world.

I wasn't living there alone. There are several hundred women working in the sports media today, all across the country and in other parts of the world. But when I first started covering the Oakland A's in 1985, only two other women writers were traveling with major-league baseball teams. By 1987, no other women were traveling with major-league baseball teams. More appeared briefly, later. But, by the winter of 1992-93, not one woman writer had been assigned to a traveling baseball "beat" for the 1993 baseball season.

The numbers render me a freak. One player, Dave Kingman, may even have called me that. But most of his teammates came to think of me as "one of the guys." Mickey Morabito, the travel director of the A's, once told me, "You fit."

This was, to these men, the supreme compliment. In their world, to "be a man" meant to be strong and swift, to be smart and successful and sportsmanlike, to play through pain, and to always do your best.

I learned it also meant being stubborn and self-absorbed, with an ample shot of swagger and strut. But when these men said, "Sue, you're like one of the guys," I was supposed to say, "Thank you."

After all, their world didn't say things like that in the beginning. A woman doesn't become "one of the guys" without a long, sometimes unending, initiation period.

Says *New York Times* baseball writer Claire Smith: "I've always said that you could take a bum off the street, shave him, clean him up, and put a pad and a pencil in his hand, and he could walk into a clubhouse you or I have worked for five years, and he will be *instantly accepted* — in a way that you or I will *never* be."

The road to acceptance for women is lined with the men declaring, "We don't want you here." Men in sports did this through the ages, taking their sons to the ballgames, keeping the remotes from their wives, barring women sportswriters from their playhouses — oops, I mean, clubhouses — even into the otherwise progressive 1970s and 1980s. One baseball player, Bob Knepper, said that God did not mean for women to be sportswriters or umpires.

When the women respond, "Too bad, I'm here," then the tests of manhood begin. Michelle Kaufman of the *Detroit Free Press* had to tolerate a dancing football player who gyrated naked behind her back as she conducted an interview. Lisa Olson of the *Boston Herald* was dared to touch the penis of football player Zeke Mowatt. Rachel Shuster of *USA Today* recalled a Green Bay Packer "vigorously fondling himself" — Rachel's family-newspaper euphemism for masturbating — as she tried to interview him. I received a gift-wrapped rat.

Those were the tests. Some of us would answer by silently turning away. Others would reply by screaming and then leaving.

Me, I belonged to the holler-and-stay school. Nobody was going to jerk off in front of me or expose himself to me or do a little dance around me and expect to get away with it without a lot of yelling — from me, and my boss, and sometimes even the culprit's boss. And then I'd come back tomorrow and see if we could please get it right this time, or I'd start yelling again and come back and try again the next day, and the next, and the next, until we got it right.

When the initiation period ended in 1987 — after *eight* years in the business — I found the biggest surprise of all awaiting me: We *could* get it right! We could do our work in spite of the gender gap. The Oakland A's and the writers who covered them realized I didn't have to peep at the men in the locker room or cramp their social styles. I realized they didn't have to hit on me in the bars or send me nasty gifts.

I learned that if I approached them with knowledge, compassion, and humor, they would overlook my disconcerting presence in their dressing area and accept me as a human being. On the job, they looked me in the eye and answered my questions as they would anyone else's.

But they also flattered me, bought me drinks, and danced with me. I think they knew I wasn't "one of the guys."

And I think, after that long initiation period, that it was OK not to be one of the guys. I could accept every advantage of being a woman in a man's world and fight every disadvantage. I could be myself, and this business of being a woman in a quintessential man's world could work.

I just wish it didn't have to take so long.

# The Big Locker Room

Eluding security, the rat made its way to the press box in the second inning, disguised in a corsage box as a friendlier gift. The letters printed on the top of the box formed the words, "Sue Fornoff, Sac Bee."

I went by "Susan." My newspaper was the "*Sacramento*" *Bee.* I guess I could have told the courier, "No sir, you've got the wrong Fornoff." But there was no denying that this gift was clearly intended for me.

As I removed the lid, the tissue paper inside rustled.

"It's alive," I said, quickly closing the box.

"It's a rat," surmised the security guard who had unknowingly acted as its deliverer.

Oh. Snicker. Hee hee. Ha ha.

Did you get it?

The rat was baseball player Dave Kingman's "gift" — his idea, he said, of a hilariously clever practical joke — for a woman sportswriter who covered his team, the Oakland A's. He didn't want that woman in the clubhouse, didn't think any women belonged where players might be undressing. And that was Kingman's way of expressing his opinions.

The joke bombed, though. I didn't get it. The Oakland A's didn't get it. Not even Kingman's teammates seemed to think it was very funny.

And the joker was out of the game, involuntarily retired, by the end of that year, in spite of his statistically respectable season.

That was when I finally started thinking, "Maybe that joke was funny after all." I remained for many more laughs, traveling with the Oakland A's into their glorious seasons of the late 1980s, through their visit to George Bush's White House in December of 1989. It was an unexpectedly bumpy ride for me, that sportswriter, but I do gloat now because it was also a joyride.

I got to know Jose Canseco and Mark McGwire and Dennis Eckersley. I learned baseball from Tony La Russa. I shopped and dined from coast to coast.

I lived the baseball life, and I enjoyed it.

I sunbathed on Dave Stewart's boat, such an opulent vessel that a less modest man than Stewart would have called it his yacht. I breakfasted at Denny's at 3 a.m. with some A's players and the ladies they'd been dancing with. I went out to dinner with Tony La Russa and his coaches, and once I even danced with the manager.

I had a lot of fun and made a lot of friends in 13 years of sportswriting. Serious journalists will say I had too much fun and made too many friends.

But I decided, over a dinner with John Feinstein many years ago, that they were going to say that anyway.

I don't remember why I was having dinner with Feinstein that night in North Carolina. We were probably just killing time in the hotel restaurant before some University of Maryland sporting event, and he probably thought it would be big of him to entertain a 21-year-old rookie sportswriter. I know I thought that he, being three years older and working for the God almighty *Washington Post*, knew everything about sportswriting while I knew nothing.

That premise certainly set the mood for the dinner chit-chat — so one-sided, I should perhaps stop at "chit" — that evening. Feinstein would later become rich by writing a book about Indiana basketball entitled *A Season on the Brink*, but this talk was cheap. He embarked on a train of sexual tittle-tattle about Betty Cuniberti, a sportswriter at the *Post* who considered John to be her friend and whom I considered to be my mentor.

As a nervous journalism major at Maryland, I had watched Betty, the only woman sportswriter I knew then, go about her business in a pleasant manner that seemed to successfully tiptoe the fine line between professionalism and intimacy. The football coach, Jerry Claiborne, called her "Miz Betty" in his Southern drawl. The basketball coach, Lefty Driesell, lit up whenever Cuniberti showed up.

The subjects of her stories seemed to feel compelled to give her the kinds of "come-on-in" details about their lives that made for some of the most revealing profiles ever to fill sports pages. I'll never forget a story she wrote during my junior year about Ted Klaube, a fun-loving, inspired defensive guard on Claiborne's football team. Betty wrote about why he had named his car "The Blue Bullet" and how he had developed an appetite for pie-eating contests. Klaube had been my collegiate heartthrob since our eyes met at a mixer my freshman year, yet Betty's story told me things I had never known.

She had an eye for detail and a knack for exposé, and she could write. The *Los Angeles Times* would eventually lure her away from sports and the locker room wars to write about the life and people of the nation's capital for its features section. It was sportswriting's loss.

But perhaps Betty did her job too well, so well that she inspired vicious rumors about her methods. Or maybe she suffered for her young, attractive, blond looks, or her friendly demeanor. Perhaps professional jealousy explained why Feinstein deemed himself licensed to tattle on Cuniberti that night in North Carolina, I don't know.

And I certainly don't know that any of Feinstein's allegations were true, so I will not bother to list specifics, as he did that night. Why, if any were true, did he feel compelled to share her confidences with me, a fledgling scribe who found Betty to be an admirable role model and John to be a pompous know-it-all? Why, if any were true, should it have mattered to John Feinstein or to me? This was none of his business and certainly none of mine.

So I never asked Betty about Feinstein's rumors, and I wouldn't be bringing them up now, except for this: They taught me the double standard that is applied to women sportswriters.

I already knew that Betty was a pretty terrific writer who happened to be a pretty woman. And, that night, I realized that no matter how diligently or professionally she conducted her business, no matter how long she wore her skirts or how high she wore her necklines, there would always be someone who would say, "She got that story because she was pretty and sexy," while there might never be somebody who would say, "I wish I could write like that."

This was what I could look forward to, if I overcame the odds and the sexism and my own ignorance to somehow make a go of a sportswriting career. I had known that if you failed, the men would say that women couldn't cover men's sports. Now I knew that if you succeeded, the men would say it didn't mean that women could cover men's sports; it only meant that you had gained some other unfair advantage because you were a woman.

And after 13 years in sportswriting, I say, "So what if we did?" I say, "So what if any woman sportswriter batted her eyelashes or flashed her teeth or used any reporting tactic that worked?"

I say this because I believe in special parking permits for the handicapped. I say this because I know now that Betty—who started in this business in 1973, six years before I did — and her contemporaries had to overcome many, many disadvantages simply because they were women who dared to become sports-writers.

And I say this because I know there's some guy out there right now saying, "Fornoff found out about the A's playoff pitching rotation because she went out to dinner with Tony La Russa and his coaches last night."

I say, so what if I did? Who cares? What difference does it make how I knew what I knew or how I spent my free time?

I decided, that night in North Carolina, that I could:

A. Wear a nun's habit and drink milk and hide in my room—in other words, be someone I wasn't—in order to appear personally and professionally beyond reproach in my dealings with male athletes and sportswriters, or

B. Dress fashionably and drink beer and socialize with the people I covered, with the aim of having a good time getting paid doing something most people pay to do... going to ballgames!

Many self-described serious journalists chose A. I chose B.

I would almost always pay a price for being a woman in that huge men's locker room that is sports and sports journalism.

There would be gifts I didn't want, attention I didn't solicit, harassment I didn't deserve.

So, damn it, I was going to have a good time and someday write a journalistically un-serious, personally one-sided, and subjectively truthful book about the big locker room.

And if I am no longer welcome in the business, I will consider my journey a circular one.

After all, I wasn't welcome there in the first place.

**2**

# *Barging In*

I'll bet hardly anyone ever asks John Feinstein why he became a sportswriter. And I'll guarantee nobody ever asks in that surprised/suspicious tone that I always heard.

The double standard requires that question to be asked of a woman sportswriter. It is easy for people to understand why a man would want to be a sportswriter.

"He wasn't good enough to play sports so he had to write about them." Or, "He wanted free meals and free tickets." And, "He just wanted to schmooze with all of those superstar athletes."

The man may have disguised these typical explanations with alibis like, "I blew out my knee playing college (fill in the blank with a sport), I've always loved to travel, and I wanted to penetrate the inner layers of the world of (fill in the blank with a sport)." And the listener nods, with the vacant look of one hearing the answer to a question she needn't have bothered to ask.

Most people, confronted with a real, live, male sportswriter, ask, "Do you really think the Giants are going to move?" Or, "What did you think of the Canseco trade?" Confronted with a real, live, female sportswriter, they ask, in that surprised and suspicious tone of voice, "What made you want to be a sportswriter?"

I always felt that the asker would then give me the once-over, zipping down the "Is she desperate/Is she gay/Is she perverted" checklist. I always felt that Joe Sportsfan concluded, "Well, she's not that bad looking so she can probably meet men without looking in a locker room. And her hair's not real short so she's probably not a lesbian. And those clothes are way too conservative for a sex machine. Hmm, why WOULD she want to be a sportswriter?"

I confess, I always evaded the hidden "Is she desperate/gay/perverted" question. I said nothing about my sexual preferences or tendencies. Instead, I told my clarinet story.

It wasn't so much that I failed to become a great clarinetist and had to turn to sportswriting instead. It was the choice I made on that day near the end of second grade when the music teacher gathered a group of us in the Frankford Elementary School auditorium. We each tried our talents at several instruments. I had the rhythm for the drums. And I made the violin whine and the flute toot. Then I tried the clarinet. The darned thing produced nothing more musical than a terrifying shriek.

"And which instrument," the teacher asked, "would you like to learn to play?"

No contest. I replied, "The clarinet."

My poor family. I practiced and practiced, and played that darned clarinet all the way through to the sixth grade spring musicale, when I shrieked for the final time in my duet with flute player Rae Mason. Fortunately for my poor family, reed players weren't cool at the junior high school level, so I retired after graduation from Frankford.

The clarinet story partly explains why I spent 13 years banging my head against closed doors. Even at the age of seven, I had acquired a predilection for challenge. At seven I thought, "What do you mean I can't play the clarinet? I can so." At 21 I thought, "What do you mean I can't be a sportswriter? I played the clarinet, didn't I?"

But a challenge-driven woman can opt to become a doctor or a lawyer and make a vault more money than she can at sportswriting. The real answer to the inevitable question of, "You, a sportswriter? Why?" is, I confess, much more complicated than, "I played the clarinet."

It begins in 1959, when my mother, Romaine, entered in my baby book, under the "Favorite Toys" heading:

Not too interested in any (toys), even at one year. Except books, paper greeting cards ... At two years, not interested in anything but what you're doing. Still loves books.

Taking advantage of the solo time before my three brothers arrived in the household, I learned to read on the lap of my Polish-born grandmother, Jennie Collins, before I went to kindergarten. My head start also served me in another way: My father, a big fan of the Baltimore sports franchises, took me to games as soon as I was old enough and before my three younger brothers became game-literate. Dad, a foreman at the Domino Sugar refinery, took me to my first baseball game when I was about eight years old. I remember inverting my popcorn box so that I could holler directly at Oriole shortstop Luis Aparicio. I remember screaming a lot, sure as I was that the players could hear me. And I think I ate a lot of junk food. We sat in the mezzanine that day, along the third-base line. How my father came up with seats like these I'll never know because he doesn't remember.

Another of the most unforgettable days of my youth was October 6, 1973, one of those autumn Saturdays when the sky and the air are so sharp and clear that you just can't stay indoors. I awakened and trotted downstairs for breakfast, thinking, "What a great day for a baseball game." And there on the countertop were two tickets for that afternoon's playoff opener between the Orioles and the Oakland A's—Jim Palmer vs. Vida Blue. My eyes widened, but my mother let me sweat for a few minutes before she told me my father was taking me to the game. We sat in the second row along the first-base line, and Palmer shut out Blue and the A's, 6-0.

"Dad, how did you get those seats?" I asked him recently.

"Don't remember," he said.

He remembers how he got his 35-yard-line Colts seats, though. Every year, he found the money to buy two upper-deck season tickets so that he could watch his hero, Johnny Unitas. Sometimes, he took me along. At those games, with my freezing feet wrapped in newspaper and my face muzzled in a scarf, I learned to be an all-weather fan. Those were the days when athletes remained loyal to one team, come frostbite or sweat. Their loyalty inspired us fans.

One night in 1988 after the Orioles had lost a record 21 straight games, fans packed the house at Memorial Stadium to show their support. When asked why he was there, one of them told a television interviewer, "This is our team. And no matter how bad it is, we have to support it. Because it's our team."

I learned to be a fan in that town, and even when I covered those great A's teams of the late 1980s, I made no secret of the object of my steadfast loyalty. I was so excited by the possibility of an A's-O's playoff series in September of 1989, I cried the night Toronto eliminated my hometown team.

Naturally, the journals I began to write in 1970 invariably included a note or two about my favorite teams. They also recounted the fights I was having with my mother over such things as how often I would be able to wear pants to junior high school, where the other kids were all wearing jeans, while my mother insisted that I continue to wear skirts and dresses. She grudgingly conceded me one day a week. Mom was still hoping to raise a lady, but already I had other ideas.

"I don't want to be a teacher any more," I told her one Saturday as I tried on glasses at the optometrist.

She looked at me in the mirror.

"Well, what else can a girl be, besides a secretary?" she asked.

"Anything she wants," I answered.

My mother returned to work, at a boys' high school, when I went to college. Today, I think she would tell a little girl that, certainly, she could be anything she wanted. I had to figure this out for myself, though, and somehow I did. The mysteries I read were all solved by women. An eighth-grade teacher included feminism in her lesson plan. I had no role models outside of school, but in 1971 I wrote:

> I'm becoming very strong on Women's Liberation. I don't see how any woman can be against it. After all, isn't it only fair that we should be able to do what we really want to do, even if it is playing football or keeping house? I either want to sing, be a baseball player, umpire, or lawyer. I also wouldn't mind being involved with football. Of all, umpiring is most appealing.

Give Mom some credit here — she knew I couldn't sing, any better than I could play the clarinet. I knew I couldn't play baseball as soon as my younger brothers began to throw hard enough to sting my hand through the padding on my mitt. And I didn't think I could be a successful umpire because no woman had ever done that.

So I elected a journalism major at the University of Maryland with every intention of enrolling in law school when I graduated. That ambition drove me to straight A's my freshman year, and I really began believing what I had told my mother: I could do anything I wanted!

"I always knew I could make it if I tried and now I'm proving I can survive without anyone pushing me but myself," I wrote in my journal the day my perfect 4.0 grades arrived. "My resolution for 1976 and always: Whatever I do, relax, take it easy, have fun, but be aggressive, competitive, and be the best I know in my heart and mind I can be."

But, at what? I still wasn't sure.

At 5:00 p.m. on April 25, 1977, a young woman named Valerie knocked on the open door to Room 437, Elkton Hall, with the answer.

I think of Valerie as some kind of spirit. She disappeared from my life before I even knew her last name, and she changed my future with the simple question, "Can you type?"

Valerie urgently needed to find someone who could go with her to that night's Oriole-Yankee game, 50 miles away in Baltimore, and type the sportswriters' stories into computer banks that would transmit to the newsrooms.

"But I have a film class tonight and we're watching the most important movie of the semester," Miss 4.0 told Valerie.

The pay would be $3 an hour, and Miss 4.0 reconsidered. Opportunity had knocked, and I would take a B in film class to answer the door.

I never did see *Citizen Kane*, but I went to dozens of Oriole games, an LPGA tournament, the Preakness, and even the World Series with Sports Comm that year.

The company eventually would fail, driven out of business by the personal laptop computers that replaced the tiny, noisy typewriters the sportswriters used to carry. Today the sportswriters say, "How did I ever work on those things?" At that time they were saying, "How can I work without my trusted typewriter? Press the wrong button on a computer and all of your hard work is zapped into air." They were scared enough to trust me to retype their hard copy into my computer and make their deadlines for them.

I am grateful for their fear of technology, for this was, to me, an all-star job. My first impression: "I get to sit in the press box, eat press food, watch the game, make money, and read everything the writers wrote, immediately after they finished. I love it."

I was fat and happy. And the writers I handled — Ken Nigro and Lou Hatter of the *Baltimore Morning Sun*, Dan Shaughnessy and Michael Janofsky of the *Evening Sun*, and assorted out-of-towners — took a kind interest in my journalism education.

I should say their interest *seemed* kind. It may also have been somewhat lecherous, me being a 19-year-old college sophomore in that shabby, open-air press box that was so seldom inhabited by women. The first woman sportswriter I remember seeing there was Lesley Visser of the *Boston Globe*. She was a friend of Shaughnessy, who had moved from Boston seven weeks earlier, and I remember Janofsky peering down at her on the field through his binoculars and saying, "Nice legs." I had been on the job only a month when I wrote:

> There are a hell of a lot of male chauvinists in the baseball press box. I have gotten undue attention because I am the only young female there. Maybe if I wasn't getting it I wouldn't say this, but I am tired of getting attention based on my physical characteristics and not on my emotional and intellectual qualities. When you begin to think that you're only getting attention because of your appearance, it can make you wonder if you HAVE any of those more important qualities.

Looking back, I think I was realistic in recognizing that I was neither a beauty queen nor a brilliant typist. I just happened to be the only young woman in a roomful of mostly middle-aged men late at night.

I know I was opportunistic. Recognizing the basis for the attention I was getting did not stop me from capitalizing on the opening it presented. One night I let Janofsky, who had developed the hots for me, drive me home. Jim Palmer had given up five home runs that night, and, after the game, he told the writers that he had been feeling tired and had asked Oriole manager Earl Weaver to take him out. Janofsky drove along and then suddenly blurted, "You know, I think he's finished."

I said, "What!"

"Palmer, I think he's finished. He is mentally defeated."

I was stunned. Palmer was only 31. But the "inside scoop," as told to me that night by Janofsky, was that Palmer hated Weaver, that when Palmer asked Weaver that night to take him out of the game, Weaver answered, "Well, I'd rather have you lose than the guys in the bullpen."

By now, I wanted to be a sportswriter. I wanted Jim Palmer to tell me the inside scoop, and I wanted to key in my own copy on my own computer. During every game, I'd think about what I'd be writing if I were Nigro or Shaughnessy. Usually I was right on track. After the games, I'd correct Shaughnessy's spelling and catch Merrill Whittlesey referring to the Seattle Islanders rather than the Seattle Mariners. I felt as if I'd spent my summer taking a nine-credit course in sportswriting. I didn't think I wanted to be a sportswriter for life, because I didn't know any women sportswriters of even middle age, but I thought that sportswriting at least would squeeze me into a profession where everyone else seemed to want to become the next Woodward/Bernstein.

Journalism school enrollments peaked in those post-Watergate years, because those two *Washington Post* snoopers temporarily curtailed the rising interest in radio and television and restored some glamour to the print media. I would be Betty Cuniberti now and Woodward/Bernstein later, I decided. Watergate II could wait.

"I'm sure, now, that I'm on the right track," I wrote in my journal in November.

By then, I was working at an intensive 15-credit program at Maryland called the J-Semester. My professors, intent on preparing us all for the real world of deadlines and newsprint, enthusiastically excused my absence for the better part of two weeks so that I could work for Sports Comm at baseball's playoffs and World Series.

I did not score a 4.0 that semester. I did not care. I was so thrilled to be at Yankee Stadium that October that I did whatever

I could to stay calm and help out. The night games made for so much deadline-induced tension among the writers that the most important parts of my job seemed to be kidding with them, handing out cups of coffee, or just winking here and there. I got to really examine how these guys — and yes, they were all guys except for harried Melissa Ludtke of *Sports Illustrated* and an unidentified woman radio reporter — make their livings. I liked it.

I liked the traveling and the work and the independence. And especially I liked the writers. I chatted with them in lobbies and bars until finally, in an idle moment, I sat down at an unused typewriter in the New York Sheraton press room and wrote my own story.

It was an essay on the sportswriter — as imagined by the public (Oscar Madison) and as he really is (a nervous wreck). I discounted Jack Klugman's portrayal of a sloppy, beer-drinking, cigar-smoking, balding, overweight, divorced bachelor with my own generalizations about sportswriters. They love to tell stories, I noted. They love to give advice. And while they are working the story takes precedence over all else. I concluded, "Our real-life Oscar Madison may have curly hair and wear a three-piece suit, but he is still ulcer material."

I showed "The Sportswriter" to my friend Steve Winter at rival Canfax. He giggled and guffawed, and then he said he loved it. Really loved it. So I got up the nerve to show the piece to Dan Shaughnessy, who had already become a good friend. He saw himself, and laughed. My Sports Comm employer showed it to some editors, and one of them asked me for a copy.

All of these compliments were fine, but I still hadn't shown "The Sportswriter" to the person whose judgment I most valued at that time, Bob Ryan, a passionate and colorful columnist with the *Boston Globe* who had inspired the piece.

"I've learned so much here, I should write a report for my class," I'd told him.

"Write one — then show it to me," Ryan had suggested.

At 3 a.m. on the last night of the Series, Ryan walked over to give me a farewell drink as I was working. Very shyly, I offered him my story. He snatched it up and rushed off to a corner to read it. I'd glance over now and then, trying to tell if he liked it, but I could get no feel for his reaction.

"Oh God," I thought, "please let him not hate it." But he didn't seem to be smiling. Finally, he brought it back, thrust it into my face, and shouted, "You can write! You can! Just keep it up!" With that, he kissed my hand and left.

This was validation. I needed no more A's, no more teachers' notes of approval. To me, it was as if Shakespeare had said I could write. A couple of weeks later, the *Baltimore Sun* published my story on the front of its sports section and sent me my first check.

It was just a few weeks after I posted that first byline that *Sports Illustrated* and Melissa Ludtke filed suit against the Yankees and major league baseball for denying her equal access in the clubhouses (baseball lingo for the locker room) at the playoffs and World Series. Bill Tanton, the sports editor of the *Evening Sun*, wrote a column in support of Ludtke's cause, and I — entrenched already in the cause of my future — dropped him an approving, preachy note:

> There must be a lot more competent female sportswriters than were visible at the Series, but their editors chose to send competent male sportswriters in their places . . . Who can fault them if locker room exclusion was one of their considerations? . . . Women athletes accommodate the press in postgame interview rooms, so why are women writers handicapped when men athletes are interviewed? Surprisingly, the answer may lie more in the press itself than in the major leagues. One of the gentlemen on your own staff once told me, when I suggested postgame interview rooms, "That's like saying we should build ramps everywhere just because there are a few paraplegics in the world."

I told Dan Shaughnessy—the sportswriter I had quoted—about the note I had sent to Tanton, his boss.

"I don't want it published," I told him, as if that would make him feel better.

"Don't worry — it won't be," he said, laughing. It was anyway.

I really didn't need the clipping for my files, because I had snagged a regular sportswriting job by now, my junior year. I was working for the *Diamondback*, the University of Maryland's prize-winning daily newspaper. During my J-Semester, I had con-

nected over deadlines and pizza with a group of earnest writers.
One of them, Rob Doherty, became a long-term friend. Rob was
a jock at heart who loved rehashing the weekend's football and
dabbling in pick-up basketball. He also happened to be sports
editor of the *Diamondback*, and he hired me to help with production and cover some swimming. I made my first roadtrip that
February, busing to Charlottesville, Virginia, all by myself for the
Atlantic Coast Conference swimming and diving championships.

I look back on that trip and realize that it foreshadowed
every roadtrip I would take in my career. It was only the Maryland swim team that kept me company, but it could have been the
San Francisco 49ers or the Oakland A's. As soon as the swimmers
and divers realized I was there on my own, they adopted me,
driving me to and from the pool and taking me out for pizza. Here
are a few of the highlights from the journal I was forced to keep
that semester for Mrs. Stevenson, the English professor who
taught me about writing even while wishing I'd write about
something besides sports:

> I sort of became one of the guys, and I liked it but I didn't.
> One reason I was really glad to get home last night was because
> every minute was spent with the same people...
> I got my story in on time...
> I learned what it's like to deal with someone who is
> unhappy. My diver-subject had a really rough time, and he was
> supposed to have a shot at first place on his board . . . I tried to
> talk to the diver in the car on the way back. I didn't know how
> to take him aside and speak with him alone. But I learned and
> I did it right the next day. Then we all went out and had a few
> beers and everything was better . . . I decided that I would not
> quote anyone unless they could easily understand that I was
> talking to them for that purpose. I would not quote anyone over
> beer. But I could talk to them and learn a lot for later questions.
> And I did that...
> I found out what it's like to be one of the guys. I found that
> one out in the car on the way home, when one of the coaches
> told the "true" (pornographic) story of Cinderella, and the
> three bears, and a bunch of other ones. Whew, I'm glad it was
> dark because I must have blushed at some point. But it was
> good for me and I have to say I enjoyed it. Even though I have
> three brothers, they are never as frank with me as those guys

were. That's amazing. Seeing how they all got along, or didn't, made me wish I was one of them. And for a while I was, but not quite. I know I learned a lot more and I will learn a lot more, but I think I will be able to deal with professional athletes on a professional level. At least I had this chance to make all of these mistakes with people who will still talk to me the next time. I doubt if Reggie would be so kind.

How did I know, even then, that Reggie Jackson would not be so kind? Soon, I would find out that even college baseball players might not be so kind.

Rob awarded me the baseball beat that spring — not such a plum, considering that Maryland usually was an also-ran in the Carolina-dominated ACC, but it was the assignment I wanted. I wrote in one of my early stories about a pitcher who had such a rough outing against George Washington University that he looked up at the Washington Monument and said, "Maybe I should take the elevator up to the top and throw myself off."

I felt quite good about that story and received a few compliments. Then I ran into the pitcher in the dining hall. Probably frustrated over his performance, he screamed at me, "Don't you ever come near me again. I'm not a professional athlete, I'm only a student. Can't you cut me any slack?" He didn't talk to me at all for about a week. I took it to heart enough to write to Janofsky and ask what he thought.

His reply to me began, "Of course it's okay to waste a kid if he blew the game... You're actually doing the guy a favor. Look at it this way. If he ever amounts to anything, he already knows how to deal with a hostile press — even female reporters." He added that I may have been a little hard on the kid but we all have our jobs to do.

This disturbed me, because I didn't like thinking that I was getting ahead at someone else's expense. So I reread my story a few times before I decided I had done the right thing, and then I wrote in my journal, "I know this will happen again many times in my career." Meanwhile, the coach, Elton "Jack" Jackson, convinced me the pitcher was an asshole.

Coach Jackson wasn't as convinced, however, that I should go on the road with his team when it visited North Carolina the following weekend. Later, I learned from some players that a female sportswriter had taken a trip with them in the previous season and practically — so they told me — undressed on the lap of that same alleged-asshole pitcher in the back of the bus. No wonder Jackson hesitated. But the *Diamondback* wasn't going to pay for my transportation unless I hitched a ride with the team, so I pressed on. The night before the three-game trip, I talked Jackson into giving me a chance. At the end of the weekend, we all had a beer in the parking lot, and some of the players asked me if I'd had a good time.

"I didn't really think I would," I told them. "But I did."

"Why did you think you wouldn't — because you're a girl?" they wondered.

"That, and also because I'm a reporter," I said. I had expected them to ostracize me because I had already shown them I wasn't afraid to write what they might not like.

They told me they hadn't thought I would have a good time either, but they said they were glad I did. So was I. My sportswriting experiences that spring were helping me make a decision I never would have faced if Valerie hadn't knocked on my door and if that unused typewriter at the New York Sheraton hadn't beckoned. The *Sun* offered me a paying summer internship in sports and at the same time the *Hagerstown Morning Herald* awarded me its prized general-reporting internship.

Sports vs. news — if I'd read much of Red Smith, the most famous sportswriter of all time, I'd probably have gone to Hagerstown to "learn what the newspaper business is all about before you become a specialist," as Smith advised would-be sports scribes. My mother gave me some good advice: Call your friends Ken Nigro and Dan Shaughnessy, who were in Miami for spring training with the Orioles. I listed pros and cons in the journals I was keeping for Mrs. Stevenson, who, by the way, thought I had no interest in anything but sports.

Dan, who had never heard of Hagerstown, told me he didn't think I had anything to decide if I knew I wanted to become a sportswriter. I said, "It's like you don't like Brussels sprouts, but they're good for you so you think you should eat them." I had always been fond of a "Leave It To Beaver" episode where the Beav hides his Brussels sprouts in his pocket to make it look as if he'd been a good boy and eaten them.

I was never one to eat Brussels sprouts, even if they were good for me. I went to the *Sun*.

I spent the summer working on the sports copy desk and writing a story a week. Mostly, I followed various writers around on their beats to get a feel for what I wanted to do. My editor there, Bob DuPont, must have asked them to treat me with courtesy, because I remember that all of them — even the department fossils who, I can't help thinking, must have wondered what on earth I was doing there — took the assignment seriously and went to great lengths to share enthusiasm about what they were doing.

The highlight of my summer was a feature I wrote on Mike Morgan, an 18-year-old pitcher who had been assigned to start for the Oakland A's with no minor-league experience.

What an interview — 20-year-old intern meets 18-year-old rookie over tuna salad sandwiches. I'm sure the matchup made him comfortable: He told me how scared he had been when he pitched in his first game one week earlier, even though he didn't look scared, going the full nine innings for a 3-0 loss to the Orioles. And he told me, "I wish I was 20 or 21. I'll be there one of these days . . . I don't want to get too old too fast." We exchanged big-league oohs and aahs over lunch, then I drove him around town looking for a post office so that he could send his girlfriend in Las Vegas a stuffed animal.

When I finally got to the ballpark that evening, I met the Orioles at the batting cage and learned to eat sunflower seeds. The players seemed exceptionally nice to me. I felt like an outsider, and I guess they knew that. They said more than just "Hi," while I could hardly say even, "Hi," I was in such awe. That was in 1978, before money had spoiled the players and persuaded them that they didn't need to be nice to anyone anymore. I wouldn't want to be a 20-year-old intern in the Oriole clubhouse today. I didn't go into the clubhouse that night, though — women still weren't admitted. I guess I really was an outsider.

But by the time my senior year in college began, I was already a sportswriter. That fall, Rob had started working in news, so I became sports editor of the Diamondback and began to confront some of the issues that would recur for the next 14 years.

I found many of them amusing. There was, for instance, the night I had a date with a fellow aspiring journalist. I thought our date would begin after the basketball game I was scheduled to cover that night. He thought our date *was* the basketball game, and that we were to sit at the press table together. Here's how I dealt with the situation in my journal:

> It didn't take me long to realize that women sportswriters have enough trouble being taken seriously without dragging their dates along to work. I suppose I could have sat in the stands with him, but I refused. He went home and watched the game on TV. I guess that showed where my devotions lie — more in being a sportswriter than in being a woman.
>
> Some writers from the old school say it's not good to be both anyway. Shaughnessy says he thinks the *Boston Globe's* Lesley Visser has been hurt by her looks. She's very attractive, and, unless she is on TV, apparently that means the editors think she is just another pretty face.
>
> I guess that means we should get up in the morning, put on a purple wig, green makeup, cutoffs, flipflops and a T-shirt. Then we'd be taken seriously?

I took myself so seriously in those days — it's funny today. More interested in being a sportswriter than in being a woman, huh? No good to be both, huh? I guess when you're 20 you worry about these things. My mother had tried to raise me to be a lady, and I couldn't dispense with the feeling that that's what I should be — even as I pursued a career that required, cultivated, and rewarded such unfeminine traits as aggressiveness, competition, and sports knowledge.

But instead of approaching the apparent conflict with anger or defiance, I automatically tended to laugh. Sure, I was serious — but funny things kept happening. While drinking one night at the Vous, the Maryland hot spot, I was pinched on the behind. I whirled around, disgusted, to face the culprit, who just stood there and grinned at me. I glared back and walked away. On my next trip around the bar, I pinched him back. A few weeks later, I was interviewing a goalie after a lacrosse game when another player interrupted. It was the pincher! I lifted off my sunglasses so he could get a good look at me. "Do you remember me?" I asked the fellow. "I sure do," he said. "I guess you're not going to give me any pub (publicity)." And we both laughed.

At least he didn't pinch me while I was interviewing his teammate on deadline — as Giants first baseman Will Clark did one night in the San Francisco clubhouse in 1991. Clark's pinch — a retaliation pinch, I confess, for one I had playfully put on him in a Cincinnati bar a full year earlier — crossed the imaginary line I was drawing back in college: You can pinch in the bar if you can get away with it, but no pinching on the job.

College also established my "honey do, honey don't" policy. Invariably — and this happens to women in every profession — a writer or a source would address me as "honey" or "sweetheart" or "dear." Robin Carr-Locke, communications director for the San Francisco Giants, was so excited the day she met the team's many new owners and, she said, "Not one of them called me honey!"

If one had called me honey, I'd look for gray hairs and bifocals before I responded: If the terms of endearment came from a man who was probably older than 50, I smiled sweetly and responded as if he'd never used the terms. If the words came out of the mouth of a man younger than 50, I tended to tell him, "I'm not your honey (or sweetheart or dear)" before continuing the conversation. And in my more confident later years, I was sure to address him in turn as "studmuffin" or some other comparable and dubious compliment.

This was one of those areas that demanded tolerance. When Philadelphia's Terry Mulholland pitched his no-hitter against the Giants in 1990, I volunteered to get a quote from the official scorer, who had assigned third baseman Charlie Hayes the lone error in Mulholland's otherwise perfect game, and share his words with the rest of the San Francisco area media contingent. The official scorer was past 50. When I returned to my seat, I read them the full quote: "It was a wide throw that pulled (the first baseman) off the bag. No doubt about it, honey." We all laughed.

I respect laughter, and I have had my biggest problems with people who can't laugh at themselves or situations. There were lots of those people, even in the entertaining business of sports — and even back in college!

Maryland had a rough-around-the-edges basketball player named Ernest Graham. Graham was, like me, from Baltimore. One night he'd score 41 points and flash his gold-toothed grin, the next night he'd score 11 and stick his tongue out at the visiting team. Once, he told me he never wanted to talk to me again. Another time, he told me he wanted to roll up my story and strangle me with it. So I stopped dead in my tracks when I spotted him at the private dock of a Holiday Inn where we were all staying on a roadtrip one weekend.

"Come on down," Graham said.

"No, you'll drown me," I hollered back.

He answered, "No, I won't. I want to thank you for the story you wrote the other day." I decided I needed no thanks, and I was taking no chances.

The atmosphere was no sunnier in the offices of the *Diamondback*. These were the purposeful post-Watergate years, when newspapers seemed driven to expose all of the evils of society/the corner grocery store/your mail carrier/etc. at the expense of fairness and balance. All too often, story assignments began with, "See what dirt you can dig up on . . ."

The *Diamondback's* student editors carried this approach to an extreme, and I declined to cultivate a nose for news of that odor. It is one thing to pursue an angle based on a tip or tidbit; it is another thing to contrive a story based on self-promotion.

The editors — antisports ersatz intellectuals in the first place — stuck their noses up, in turn, at any cheerful or humorous column I would write about the university's mostly outstanding sports teams. Once, I received a hand-written note from the football coach, Jerry Claiborne, thanking me for the preseason football section we had produced. I thought that was classy; the editors thought it was revolting. When Claiborne sent me another note a couple of months later about a column I'd written, I just smiled and put it away.

The antisports editors especially had it in for one coach, Lefty Driesell. Driesell coached the men's basketball team into the Top 20 almost every year and into the Top 10 throughout the 1970s, but he finally took his fall in the 1980s after star player Len Bias died of a cocaine-induced heart attack. Bias's death led to more revelations that reflected poorly on the team's coach. At that time, as a concerned alumnus, I wrote a letter to the university's president advocating that Lefty be fired, because Lefty either knew of the drug problem or — being a college coach of that particular decade — he should have.

I always liked Lefty, though. I thought he was fair and I thought he was honest. He'd yell and scream at you for something you wrote, and an hour later he'd be answering your questions again in his curiously hick (for all of his education) manner of speech. He got upset enough to call me at the offices a couple of times, and usually I'd just yell back at him. But on one occasion I thought he was justified in his outrage, and I told him so in a tone of voice loud enough to be heard by the antisports editors.

I had written a story about the exceptional efforts that are applied so that student athletes can play sports and pass. It was a long piece that included a juicy tidbit about the baseball coach warning Driesell not to send "any more of his (basketball-playing) dodos" into the baseball coach's classes. Driesell's response: "If Coach Jackson told you that, he is a liar..." This was a tiny part of the big story, but the antisports editors put this line in big type and boxed it with an unflattering photo of an angry-looking Driesell.

It was, I thought, an out-of-context cheap shot. I hadn't played up the incident very much in my story because there existed the slightest possibility that Driesell might have been telling the truth and Jackson not. The quote box, which was assembled by another editor, did not reflect the essence of my story. It did, I believed, ventilate the anti-Driesell, antisports persuasions of the *Diamondback* staff. My thought, so stated in a letter, got me fired by the editors.

The timing was perfect. By then, I was ready to start earning my living doing something other people would pay to do: watching sports.

**3**

# I Never Peeked!
# (I swear it)

In a 1982 B.C. Hart comic strip, a woman asks another woman, "How can you possibly concentrate on an interview in the men's locker room?" The woman wearing the press hat replies, "Easy . . . I wear the horse blinders UNDER my eyes."

Real-life women sportswriters laugh about that, because we reply, "I carry a big notebook!"

I have only heard sportswriters of the male gender admit to having looked below the belt in the locker room. All of the women are either too professional, too embarrassed, or too polite to look, or else they lie. At a talk I gave for the Sacramento 20-30 club one winter, one of the 300 in the audience of men in their twenties and thirties stood up and asked, "Who is the most well-endowed player in baseball?" As if I knew!

I gave him an answer, though: "Reggie Jackson thinks he is."

And I said so because Reggie seemed to be the exception to the unarticulated clubhouse rule: put your towel on when you see a woman sportswriter approaching. Reggie didn't merely refrain from putting on his towel — if he'd already put one on, he'd take it off. Just for us.

Sorry, Reggie. I never looked.

I always thought that I would, just once, just for the book, take a peek around the Oakland A's clubhouse before I left the baseball beat. But I never did. Sometimes the men writers would talk about how well-endowed so-and-so was ("especially for a white guy," they'd say) and how poorly endowed so-and-so was ("especially for a big guy," they'd say).

I listened; I just didn't look.   It wasn't for lack of interest, though. When I worked at *USA Today* and wasn't regularly covering one particular team, I saw nothing wrong with dating athletes whose paths I crossed. I never, ever saw anything wrong with saying, "That's a good-looking man."

I spent 13 years working around handsome young men, and I noticed their looks. I always eagerly anticipated the Major Indoor Soccer League's annual 10 1/2 award (translation: Eat your heart out, Bo Derek!) to the player the fans had voted best looking. He was usually goalie Zoltan Toth, a tall black-haired Hungarian I considered to be so gorgeous that I never wanted to talk to him and, so I thought, spoil the illusion. That male misconception of women having either brains or beauty but not both must have rubbed off on me. I figured Zoltan was so beautiful that he had to be stupid, or unpleasant, or both.

One night I felt I had no choice but to interview Toth, because he had performed so heroically for the New York Arrows that they won a playoff game in Baltimore. How I dreaded the moment when Zoltan would open his mouth, and (so I thought) my prince would turn into a frog.

Of course, he turned out to be absolutely charming. When I introduced myself to him, he said, "Oh, I know who you are," and gave me a hug and a kiss. Fortunately we were not in the locker room — but, even if we had been, in this case I'm not sure I would have been mortified. The soccer players never did create a hostile environment, like the ones of professional baseball or football, that said, "We don't want you here." Their sport was young and on the fringe, so they needed any and all press. The hospitable atmosphere they created made it easy for a woman sportswriter to be herself and not worry about appearances.

This has never been true of baseball. I consistently ranked Oakland pitcher Dennis Eckersley and Kansas City pitcher Mark Gubicza as the best-looking players in their game. I told them so, too, because they're both down-to-earth guys. Eckersley seemed flattered; Gubicza seemed embarrassed. The Kansas City players always made a big deal to Gubicza when I'd come in their clubhouse — usually to talk to him because he'd pitched another great game against the A's. "Hey, Mark, here she comes," they'd holler. It got worse when pitcher Storm Davis was traded from the A's to the Royals and blabbed to all of his new teammates.

I couldn't understand what was the big deal. My male friends say this is because when a man sees a beautiful woman he automatically wants to "jump her bones." One man says, "She's gorgeous," and other men interpret this to mean, "I'd like to get her into the sack." So the Royals equated my comment about Gubicza's looks with ulterior motives.

Women seem to know better. Once, Kim Boatman of the *San Jose Mercury News* was leaving the Minnesota Twins clubhouse when she crossed the path of Kirby Puckett's wife, Tonya. Kim said Tonya asked, "Do you see my husband naked?" Kim explained that Mr. Puckett might have his clothes off in the clubhouse, but that he probably had on a towel and she definitely had more important things to do than look at him. Tonya accepted Kim's explanation with a nod. I'm sure if I told Nancy Eckersley and Lisa Gubicza, "Your husbands are gorgeous," they'd probably accept the compliment with the understanding that I didn't want to marry Eck or Gubby or sleep with them, I simply admired their looks. I hope they would say, "Thank you."

In any case, though, I'd have died if either Eckersley or Gubicza gave me a hug and a kiss, especially in the locker room. Claire Smith, the quiet baseball writer for the *New York Times* who oozes warmth, cringed in 1988 when Oriole manager Frank Robinson gave her a hug at the end of his team's 21-game losing streak. The male writers asked Frank and — to her embarrassment — Claire why they didn't get hugs, too.

The locker room is an unusual kind of place. It's not the holy chamber the general public seems to envision, yet I always felt I needed to be on my best behavior when I entered the baseball clubhouse. Maybe I knew that people were scrutinizing my every move. Many years later, Carlos Deza, a friend and San Francisco Giants video specialist, told me of noticing a credentialed woman sportswriter in Houston standing in the Giants' clubhouse in a position to gaze into the shower.

"I watched her for a long time, and she was just standing there, looking around," he said. "She didn't seem to be waiting for anyone or taking any notes. She just looked. Finally, I pointed her out to Matt Fischer (the Giants' media relations director). He watched her for a while, then went over to her and asked her if he could help her. She got out of there right away."

"Carlos," I asked, "did you ever watch the men writers to see if they were scoping around?"

"Nope," he said. "I know they were." We laughed. It was OK for the men to look—and they weren't being watched like we were.

I thought it was important to disappoint those who wanted to catch us in some unprofessional act. The biggest reason was my respect for the efforts of my predecessors to gain equal access for women sportswriters. It had taken them so many years to get us in there, I certainly did not want to give anyone a reason to say, "See, she doesn't belong."

The struggle for women's access to the locker room took lots of time and toil. Mary Garber became sports editor of the Twin City (N.C.) *Sentinel* in 1944, when women were doing men's jobs everywhere during World War II. Demoted at the war's end, she then spent 40 years covering sports for the *Winston-Salem Journal Sentinel*. I met Mary at a convention of sports editors in 1984, and she said that her biggest problem back then was just getting into the press box. There was never any question that she would not be allowed into the "dressing" room, as Mary called it. She wasted many hours of her career standing outside those doors, waiting for stars and coaches to come out and talk to her.

Then in the early 1970s, Betty Cuniberti's "Gang of Four" came along. The three other women covering men's sports she included in her "gang" were Robin Herman of the *New York Times*, Jane Gross of *Newsday*, and Lesley Visser of the *Boston Globe*. But there were others in that decade — Lawrie Mifflin covering hockey, and Stephanie Salter and Melissa Ludtke covering baseball.

During the 70s, access battles broke out all over the place. By 1976, the National Basketball Association and National Hockey League allowed women complete access, and rarely did either league encounter a problem. The National Football League, on the other hand, did not mandate equal access until 1985, when it finally began to hear the word "lawsuit" from some sports editors.

The threat was a bit tardy, considering that the precedent had been set when the New York Yankees and major-league baseball lost to *Sports Illustrated* and Melissa Ludtke in court just after the 1978 baseball season. *SI* had sued on Ludtke's behalf because she had been denied equal access at Yankee Stadium in the 1977 postseason. Oh, she was allowed to watch Reggie Jackson hit all of those home runs. She just wasn't allowed to go into the clubhouse to talk to him about them.

Baseball's commissioner, Bowie Kuhn, defended the closed-door policy in an affidavit claiming "sexual privacy" for the players. Kuhn also called up the integrity of his holy sport, adding: "To permit members of the opposite sex into this place of privacy, where players, who are, of course, men, are in a state of undress, would be to undermine the dignity of the game."

Kuhn's side lost. U.S. District Judge Constance Baker Motley agreed with *Sports Illustrated* that the equality guarantees of the 14th Amendment prevented the league's discrimination against Ludtke and ruled that keeping Ludtke in the hallway would place her at a "severe competitive disadvantage." Judge Motley ordered the Yankees to install curtains or swinging doors for the players if they felt it necessary "to shield them from the roving eyes of female reporters."

Although the court ruling applied only to the Yankees, the rest of the American League complied. National League teams were allowed to set their own policies as late as 1984, when the Padres booted Claire Smith out of their Wrigley Field locker room in the National League playoffs with the Cubs. Smith had been assured that playoff access would be handled by the league, not the Padres, yet she was literally pushed out of the door on the first day. Padres general manager Jack McKeon told her, outside, "It's Dick Williams's clubhouse." And Williams, the Padres' manager said, "That's right — we'll bring out whoever you want to talk to." She asked for pitcher Eric Show and was told he did not want to talk to her. Other reporters told Claire that she missed the worst of it — Show and other players were saying vile things about her.

Baseball commissioner Peter Ueberroth intervened, and Claire went back in — uncomfortably — the next day. Ueberroth dispatched orders in both leagues the following spring that women would have full and equal access in all clubhouses.

Legally, Ludtke's victory did not apply across the country or run the professional sports gamut beyond baseball. Sports editors, some not caring and others not wanting to expend money and effort, never united to bring the kind of massive class-action suit that would have been required to equalize access in an entire pro sports league, much less a huge national body like the NCAA. So the battle usually was fought on the local level. It took the launching of a national newspaper, *USA Today*, to force the issue in the NFL, and probably only a publication with as wide a scope would ever dare to call the NCAA on the carpet.

But the Ludtke ruling did send out a cheerful postcard. The ruling spotlighted the access issue and — most importantly to short-sighted yours truly — may even have gotten me a job. Suddenly, newspapers seemed to be feeling pressure to hire "a" woman in the sports department. So Russ Brown, the nutty professorial sports editor much hated by the old geezers on the all-male staff of my hometown *Baltimore News American*, interviewed three women for a general assignment opening in 1979. Fortunately for me, the first two candidates declined Brown's offers, and I started by default on May 7 — 11 days before I even graduated from the University of Maryland — at $250 a week. They didn't tell me for three years that I had ranked third on their list of three. But when I left the *News American* in 1982, sports editor Ralph Vigoda took me to lunch and told me I'd worked out much better than they'd expected.

Of course, they hadn't expected much.

My first assignment was to sit next to baseball writer Peter Pascarelli and write a sidebar to go with his story on the Oriole game that night. But, first, I had to bring a permission slip from my father so that I could get into the clubhouse. OK, maybe I really didn't HAVE to bring a note. But that's what the Orioles' chain-smoking, sassy manager, Earl Weaver, had announced when the Orioles decided to open their clubhouse to all in response to a Kuhn memo in March.

"I think they should have to bring a note from their fathers," Weaver said cutely. Sandy McKee of the *Evening Sun* and some other women showed up on Opening Day with their notes. But, once they had made their news, some of them not even asking a question about the game, they left the locker room all to the men again.

There were exceptions. There was Susan Reimer of the *Sun*, who needed to talk to Jim Palmer one day and had to first endure a grilling from Weaver about why women wanted to get into the locker room. And then there was me.

I handed Earl my note. Dad had written, "With quivering pen, I hereby give my daughter Susan permission to enter the Oriole locker room, mainly because I know that even if I don't, she'll find a way to get in there anyway ... Yours in gentlemanly spirit, Bill Fornoff."

Earl read the note silently, then said it was the best he'd gotten. But he was worried. When, he wondered, would I want to go into his office to interview him after the game? The manager's private office, reached only by a walk the length of the Orioles' long main clubhouse room, contained its own shower, and Earl didn't want to be surprised by me. Finally, we agreed that he'd talk to me immediately after the game if I wanted. If not, he'd close his door, take his shower, and then talk to me. I just sighed.

The Orioles lost the game my first night, and Pascarelli suggested I write about what happened to their heretofore hot hitters. As I entered the locker room to investigate the Orioles' missing hitters, the doorman announced, "Lady in the locker room," to dead silence. These introductions always irked me — I understood that the intent was to protect the privacy of players who wanted to cover up, but I couldn't understand why the doorman couldn't just say, "Media in the locker room," when the doors opened after the game. In some locker rooms — the Detroit Tigers, I remember, and Helene Elliott of the *Los Angeles Times* tells me they're still at it in Motown — the doorman's "Lady in the locker room" proclamation amounted to a call for hoots and hollers from the players. Believe me, a woman sportswriter feels conspicuous enough without the accompaniment of a public address announcer.

I was a rookie that night in Baltimore, so I didn't complain. I just shyly whispered my questions to selected players, who answered between bites of fried chicken. None of them said a rude word to me. Then I went to talk to Weaver, who was holding court already with a handful of men writers.

Casually, lightly, I asked him what happened to his hitters. Weaver offered me a beer — I can't remember whether I accepted — and then ranted on and on about how what happened that night was just baseball. On and on. What a dumb idea that was for a story, he told me, at great length.

I probably blushed. I know I took notes furiously the whole time. And my little sidebar — on the miracle of baseball being that you can hit the lights out one night and swing as if blind the next — came out just fine. A few days later I had another assignment at the ballpark. And when I arrived, Earl said, "Susan, I have to give you credit. That was a horseshit idea, but you made a pretty decent story out of it."

Could I have made that horseshit idea into a decent story if I hadn't had access to the clubhouse? Maybe. But maybe the players I really wanted to talk to would not have been willing to leave the clubhouse — especially after a loss — to stand in the hallway and talk to me, a 21-year-old reporter they did not know. And maybe Weaver — without the male reportorial audience in attendance — would have been boring rather than rambunctious out in that hallway. I don't know. I don't want to know. I had a story to write, just as the men had stories to write, and I deserved the same access they enjoyed.

That wasn't the first time I had been in a locker room. Yes, I remember the first time — we all remember the first time. It made all of us nervous.

Lesley Visser was 22 when she first went into a locker room. The World Team Tennis's Boston Lobsters welcomed *anyone* wearing a media badge, so in went Lesley — staring straight into every player's eyes, she wrote 15 years later, "with the maniacal intensity of a Charles Manson."

"The team, desperate for coverage and blessed with a progressive owner, didn't care who went in the locker room after a match," she writes. "The coach was a crazy Romanian, Ion Tiriac, and he was all for being on the cutting edge. Even so, I remember having a near anxiety attack my first time in. I held the notepad so close to my nose that I looked like Rosannerosannadanna, and I blurted out the questions I'd memorized in machine-gun fashion. Tiriac merely pulled a towel around his waist and shrugged his shoulders. In Romania, apparently, it was no big deal."

There was such a buildup, we had to wonder, "What exactly are we going to find in there?" I guess I found what Mary Garber found when, after 31 years in sportswriting, she was admitted to a locker room. Mary said, "All these years I've been trying to get into this room. Heck with it."

My first time, I was covering a University of Maryland men's basketball game for the school paper, and the conference's new policy was to open the winner's locker room to all media for the first 15 minutes after each game and the loser's locker room to all media for the next 15 minutes. As the *Washington Post's* Betty Cuniberti and the *Evening Sun's* Sandy McKee lined up with me for entry on this first night of the new policy, the school's sports information director, Jack Zane, suggested to the players that they keep their pants on a little longer than usual. They did, and we got our interviews without incident.

When we finished, I asked a few of the players if they minded the new policy. One of them said he wasn't too crazy about it.

"I just want to get my shower," John Bilney said. "I don't want to be all sweaty and pimply."

And Albert King, the team's star, kept tugging at his shorts as if he couldn't wait for us to leave.

I felt angry on my way home that night. I thought, "It hadn't been that big a deal, and I would not have cared if Albert did take his pants off if he couldn't wait to do so. Everyone in there had a job to do, and they did it very quietly and very pleasantly. There were not any corners or cubbyholes for anything immoral to occur. It's all open. All that fuss, and several lawsuits, just for that."

Lesley Visser remembers covering a Boston Celtics playoff game against the Lakers at Boston Garden on a hot June day in the 1980s.

"About 20 reporters were pressed against each other trying to get a quote from soft-spoken James Worthy," Visser recalls. "Diane K. Shah, then a columnist with the *Los Angeles Herald Examiner*, turned to me, sweat dripping down her face, and said, 'We fought for the right to get in here?'"

That experience illustrates another reason why I never looked. There is nothing sexy about the locker room. It is not a place where anybody — even a man, who we women are taught think generally of nothing BUT sex — would entertain sexual fantasies. It's certainly not a place where a woman would go looking for naked men. It smells bad, until the postshower colognes start splashing. Dirty laundry flies around, sometimes all too close. The lighting is usually not what you'd call romantic. No, not even those slow Luther Vandross tunes playing on the boom box could turn this grown-up version of a tree-house into a love shack.

So why do we want to get in there, anyway?

We HAVE to get in there to do our jobs. And, please believe me, that's what we do in there. We don't go into the showers or whirlpools. The doors open a few minutes after the game, reporters pour in and usually head straight for the coach or manager for about 10 minutes before they return to the main locker room to interview players. Small groups usually surround the game's stars so that they don't have to repeat their comments on their heroics a dozen times. Some reporters make the rounds, stopping to ask a question here, a question there. The players often do interviews before they head for the shower, while they eat, and after they shower, as they dress.

Any player who really felt very shy could change his clothes in the privacy of the trainers' room and then return to his locker for interviews. But lots of teams provide robes or towel wraps that allow the players to put on their underwear under the coverup, without any sportswriter, male or female, spotting the goods. It's really not a case of a fully clothed woman walking into a roomful of stark naked men. At least, it doesn't have to be — that's up to the men involved, and I would feel sexually harassed if I walked into a locker room where all of the men stood naked and untowelled in front of me.

The entire process takes no more than 30 minutes, because the writers must usually hurry to make their deadlines — or because that's all the time it takes to glean the intelligent quotes from a locker room. This time constraint renders impractical the alternative of a separate interview room, to which players are brought to talk to the male and female media while the locker room itself is off-limits, except in individual sports like tennis and golf.

Impracticality doesn't stop the players from lobbying in favor of the interview room alternative. They tend to resent any media intrusion anywhere.

"(The players) spend so much time (in the clubhouse)," said New York manager Buck Showalter, "that it's a haven for them, a home. Some of them detest even having to talk. They see it as such an invasion."

But if formal interview rooms replaced clubhouse access, we'd all be stuck listening to Joe Theismann drone on and on when we really needed one quick quote from Tony McGee.

Even worse, imagine the scenario where women can't go into the locker rooms but the men writers do. The men are inside interviewing the players. The women are outside waiting. I covered a Washington Redskins game this way in 1984 for *USA Today*.

Theismann was nice enough — or, as everyone knows, so loved to talk — to come out, wearing nothing but a small towel, into a cold hallway where he could talk to me while fans surrounded him asking for autographs. Another star of that game, Tony McGee, came out, too, but he was clearly tired of answering questions about one particular play, and I knew I wasn't getting the good stuff the guys inside had heard. I was getting a syllable at a time. Meanwhile, I had spent so much time waiting for these two guys that I did not have time to go to the opponents' locker room and get the losers' side of the game.

What's wrong with this picture? I could not possibly have written as complete, balanced, and colorful a story as the men did and still make my early deadline. I didn't get the fresh quotes because I couldn't get in. I didn't get the opponents' quotes because I had to wait for two players on the other side. I didn't see any spontaneous event that might have occurred inside the locker rooms while I was waiting outside in the hallway. I didn't have time to talk to any fringe players who might have been accessible and quotable inside the locker room. And I certainly could not establish any new contacts that might tip me off to the kinds of stories that gain sportswriters promotions.

Worst of all, I probably felt too frustrated to do a really good job on my little football story — especially when I didn't know, from week to week and city to city, what kind of access I might encounter. Sometimes we couldn't get into the locker room because the 79-year-old security guard wouldn't believe that our "Locker Room Pass" cards applied to women too.

"Honey, girls can't go in there," he'd say.

Sometimes we got in and then were kicked out. Lesley Visser remembers the pride she felt when she received an armband allowing her locker room entry at the Cotton Bowl on New Year's Day 1980. "Isn't this terrific?" thought Visser, a sportswriter since 1975. "It's a new decade." She was inside interviewing the Houston quarterback when head coach Bill Yeoman saw her. He should have been in a good mood — Houston had just beaten Nebraska, 17-14. But he was not happy to see Lesley.

"I don't give a damn about the Equal Rights Amendment. I'm not having her in my locker room," Yeoman hollered, pushing Visser out the door. Humiliated and storyless, she sat alone in the top seat of the empty Cotton Bowl thinking it wasn't such a new decade after all.

Even equal access policies could change without notice from week to week with a single team. One season I had full access at Baltimore Colts games; the next season my hand was on the doorknob when one of the team flaks put his arm across the door and said, "You can't go in there." Without a leaguewide policy until 1985, NFL teams could do whatever they wanted.

Michele Himmelberg and the *Sacramento Bee* cramped the NFL's style in 1981, when they took the Ludtke precedent into a San Francisco court — the *Bee* and Himmelberg vs. the City of San Francisco and the San Francisco 49ers.

Himmelberg had been covering pro football since she started working in Fort Myers, Florida, after graduating from the University of Southern California in 1979.

"At (USC), John Robinson was the coach, and he made it clear that as long as I was covering the team I should have the same rights as anyone else," Himmelberg said. "So there I am in college, covering John Robinson's team, thinking, 'This is how the world is now.' I went to Fort Myers for my job interview, and they asked me, 'How can you cover the (Tampa Bay) Buccaneers if you can't get into the locker room? Aren't you concerned about this?' And I completely shrugged off their concern, saying, 'No, no, Melissa Ludtke . . . John Robinson . . . That's not a problem anymore.'"

It quickly became a problem, when the Bucs asked her to settle for separate access — interviewing players outside the locker room — rather than equal access. After a few games, Himmelberg and her editors said, "This isn't working," and cited the Ludtke case. So, Tampa Bay officials created a foyer of sorts, a cramped area at the front of the locker room where everyone would go for postgame interviews.

"They'd crowd everybody into this place, behind a partition, which came to be known among the media as 'The Himmelberg Wall.' It wasn't my idea — I wanted to go inside the locker room! But I had to take the brunt of it. Lots of people had the nerve to tell me that I had staged this thing just so that I could make a name for myself, which was the last thing I wanted to do.

"My worst horror story occurred during that season. I was traveling with the Bucs, and I decided to call every team's public relations guy ahead of time and ask what their policy was. They'd usually say the locker room was closed to women, and I'd tell them that I'd be covering the game and would you please provide equal access.

"When we went to Minnesota and sat down in the press box, we found little sheets of paper at our seats that said, 'Because of a woman reporter from Florida who is covering the game today, the locker room will be closed.' Again, it's my fault! I was besieged by other writers. Then the teams played this incredible game — Tommy Kramer for the Vikings and Doug Williams for Tampa Bay must have thrown for a total of about 850 yards (and six touchdown passes, including four for Williams), taking the game down to the wire. And after the game (a 38-30 Vikings victory), Minnesota officials can't get the players to come out of the locker room to talk to the media.

"Two radio guys — former Vikings, I think — then cornered me and said, 'Why did you do this? You're just a voyeur and a pervert,' and I started to cry. It was like an attack — and I was on deadline. The saving grace of the whole thing was that one of the local writers followed me all day because he thought the whole thing was dumb, and he wrote a column that won an APSE award." Associated Press Sports Editors' awards are sports journalism's miniature replicas of Pulitzer Prizes.

Two years later, Himmelberg was backing up on the San Francisco 49er beat, doing her sidebar-feature work outside the locker room while the men went in. Then, in a game against Atlanta, the 49ers' hard-hitting defensive back, Ronnie Lott, hit somebody too hard or too late and picked up an unsportsmanlike conduct foul at a critical juncture. He also got injured. Michele was assigned to write both incidents as her sidebar, so, of course, she needed to talk to Lott, one of the most cooperative and least sexist 49ers. But 49er officials told her Lott was in the trainers' room and would not be emerging for interviews — with anyone.

The next day, every newspaper except the *Sacramento Bee* included quotes from Ronnie Lott in its game package.

"It was the perfect example of why we need to be in there," Himmelberg said. By the following Sunday, the *Bee* had obtained an injunction requiring the 49ers to provide equal access to Himmelberg. And the locker room, at least the 49ers' locker room, opened to women.

These cases clearly were going to be won by those newspapers that chose to press the issue with their local teams. But NFL president Pete Rozelle continued to claim, however, that he had no jurisdiction over NFL teams during the regular season — as if they could all play football by their own rules in their own stadiums!

That's the way it is on the college level today, with no blanket NCAA policy regulating the sexism of stodgy schools, like Notre Dame, who choose to ignore the implications of the Ludtke ruling; and no teams of lawyers are preparing class-action suits against them. Michelle Kaufman of the *Detroit Free Press* was caught unprepared for Notre Dame's no-women policy when she was assigned to cover a football game between the Irish and Penn State several years ago. Notre Dame Heisman Trophy candidate Tim Brown had a great game that day, and Michelle decided to write her game story around him — except that when she went to the locker room, she learned that she would not be able to talk to him.

"I was on deadline, so I thought, 'OK, I'll just run over to the Penn State locker room and talk to their players *about* Tim Brown,'" said Kaufman.

So she ran to the Penn State locker room, only to discover that the Nittany Lions weren't going to let her in either. She wrote a story, but it was not one she'd use for future job applications.

The Associated Press Sports Editors got so disgusted about a similar incident last fall—when women, not men, were barred from the San Diego State locker room after its game against Southern California—that it conducted a survey. It found that many conferences, including the football-happy Southwest and Big Ten, do not have written policies requiring schools to provide equal access. Big Ten schools, especially, tend to change the rules from week to week, depending on whether any women are covering their games. And more and more schools, the survey concluded, use the presence of women as an excuse to curtail general media access to athletes.

But most universities who expect big-time media coverage have established equal access standards. And access no longer is a discrimination issue at the professional level, except in isolated instances where some coach (for example, Sam Wyche) goes bonkers over a loss, or in cases where an athlete (for example, Zeke Mowatt) harasses a female reporter and the response is to argue about whether the woman should have been there in the first place. It's so exasperating to see this debate resuscitated time and again. Whether that woman "should have been in there" should no longer be an issue, especially since Melissa Ludtke's visit to the judge 15 years ago.

Today it is decorum — how women should behave in there and how the men ought to conduct themselves — that continues to present all sorts of perplexities.

# Keep Those Pants On

In an old (1979!) Tank McNamara comic strip, the heroine is ruminating about women's fight to get into the locker room. She thinks, "I'm a professional and all I want is to do my job. I've been laughed at, ignored, condescended to . . . But here I've made it." In the final panel, she stands inside the locker room thinking, "Now, if I could just stop feeling like I'm 12 years old and I've walked into the wrong restroom."

That strip reminds me of Cleveland Municipal Stadium, where the visitors' locker room is so tiny and cramped that it is impossible to respect privacy — *and* the press has to walk right by the wide-open shower and toilet area (yes, urinals) to get to the manager's office. They don't teach us how to handle these situations in Journalism 101.

I would hold up my notebook, shielding my peripheral vision as I walked by the sensitive area, as if it was my own personal stenographic shower curtain. And I never, ever, grew accustomed to this layout. I don't think the players did, either. It seemed to create a lot of tension. San Francisco Giants players responded to a similarly uncomfortable situation in their Candlestick Park clubhouse by posting a sign over the shower area. "No dick watching," it said.

Classy.

Fortunately, one of the Giants' top executives, Al Rosen, had been working for the Yankees in 1978. He remembered the judge's advice in the Melissa Ludtke suit, so he spent a couple of grand on a heavy partition for the shower area and thick terry-cloth wraps for the San Francisco players. "(Discomfort) will always be a problem," Rosen said, "even in the year 2100, too." Maybe so. But at least Rosen accepted some responsibility for solving the problem instead of making the standard male chauvinist protest statement, "But, honey, you don't belong in there."

I say, why couldn't they build better ballparks? My old buddy Dan Shaughnessy was the sportswriter who once said of women getting into the locker room, "That's like saying you should build ramps everywhere because there are a few paraplegics," but now that he's become a more enlightened sports columnist, husband, and father, even he notes that today they do indeed build ramps in ballparks!

I remember the blank looks I got at a meeting of the Baseball Writers Association of America when I said, "Hey, you guys (almost everything I said to them began this way), there are new ballparks going up in Chicago and Baltimore — why don't we take some interest in the clubhouse design and make sure that privacy is not a problem?"

They looked at me airily, perhaps thinking that the players' association would be better solicited to protect the players' privacy. What I couldn't quite say to my fellow writers was, "I hate having to walk by urinals and bump into naked men, and that's unavoidable in some of these antiquated facilities." But that's what I really felt.

Joan Ryan of the *San Francisco Examiner*, an afternoon paper with luxuriously late deadlines, felt so strongly about the privacy issue that for a long time after becoming a columnist she conducted her interviews outside the clubhouse. She had suffered one of the worst improprieties in open locker room history in 1985, when she covered a United States Football League game between the Orlando Renegades and Birmingham Stallions. The USFL had installed an equal access policy at its formation, and Joan was inside the Birmingham locker room trying to interview running back Joe Cribbs. She heard a lot of four-letter words tossed her way, and then she felt something crawling up her leg. It was one of the long-handled razors the players use to cut off tape!

Ryan started screaming at the player brandishing the razor, then saw a man in a team sweater grinning at her across the room.

"I went upstairs and wrote my sidebar, then I started flipping through the team's media guide to find out who that guy in the sweater was," Ryan said. "It was the team's president, Jerry Sklar!" She called him the next day and was told — shades of Victor Kiam! — that her incursion of the team's locker room justified such treatment. Joan retaliated with the backing of her newspaper and wrote a column — "And they wonder why we call them animals" — about what had happened.

Birmingham did not apologize, but Joan resumed her locker room duties the following week without incident.

"There was a time when my stomach turned every time I had to go into the locker room," she said. "But you have to get used to it if you're going to succeed."

"Getting used to it" is most difficult early in your career when you have no self-confidence and you're not sure your boss has much confidence in you either. Kristin Huckshorn was just a junior at Indiana University when she covered Bobby Knight's basketball team for a local paper. She waited outside the locker room, as she'd been told to do, for nearly an hour — so long that she worried that no one would ever come out. Finally, she went in, walking past Isiah Thomas's warning of, "Better not go in there. You'll be sorry."

Of course, by then everyone had dressed and most players had disappeared out another door. But when Knight — as famous for losing his temper as he is for winning championships — saw Kristin, he completely trashed her with a verbal tirade that left her knees shaking and her tongue tied.

"I was so scared," she said, "I couldn't move. Finally, I think somebody guided me out into the hall, where I found a corner and cried." Her sports editor, by the way, was inside sitting near Knight, silently watching the entire episode.

Kristin got used to the locker room, though, and covered sports for 10 years at the *San Jose Mercury News* before moving out of sports and into the metro department. When she still covered sports, she stood up for Annette John-Hall in a similar locker room situation early in the 1980s, when Annette was a reporter with the *Oakland Tribune*.

"We were both covering an Oakland Invaders (USFL) exhibition game in Fresno," said John-Hall, "at a high school or college facility that was inappropriate for a professional football team. The locker room was very, very small, and, as soon as I went in after the game, I knew it would be a problem. You had to say, 'Excuse me, excuse me,' to get through all of the naked guys. And Bobby Hebert, who we wanted to talk to, was on the other side of the room.

"On the way, I hear this voice yelling, 'What's that bitch doing in here?' It was Ruben Vaughn, a big defensive end who was imposing and mean-spirited, not to mention didn't have any clothes on. And Kristin, who is tiny, walked over and stuck her face out at him and said, 'She belongs in here ROOben!' "

Annette laughs thinking of Kristin's intimidating tone. "She told him, 'She's a reporter for the *Oakland Tribune*, and if you don't like it I suggest you take it up with Mr. Lombardi, ROOben!' (Vince Lombardi, Jr., was the Invaders' general manager.) Kristin taught me how to treat people who disrespect you. If you stand up to people, more than likely they will back down. He clearly backed down and everyone noticed. After that, it was no big thing.

"That was really a learning experience for me," Annette recalled. "Until that point, I thought I had no business being in the locker room. And I do. We do. Still, when I push open that door, I feel squeamish about what might happen and what might be said."

Annette got used to the locker room, as Kristin Huckshorn got used to it, as Joan Ryan got used to it, and as — with the exception of that awful Cleveland setup — did I. You learn to establish certain policies and to respect certain boundaries.

The Association for Women in Sports Media (AWSM) has recommended guidelines for reporters in the locker room:

1. Allowing a player the 10 seconds or so it takes to slip on his pants before you begin asking questions.
2. No lingering near or in the shower area.
3. Verify with the team PR director that all his players know women reporters have access and probably will be in the locker room, and don't be offended if, "Woman reporter coming in," precludes your admittance.
4. Be courteous. Use common sense and discretion.

These are not necessarily the policies I refer to, because I happen to think that No. 4 is the only one that matters. No. 1 is really up to the players to follow, and No. 2 is silly, and it's covered by No. 4. No. 3 I do not care to follow. I prefer that athletes and team officials be responsible for themselves. By the time they reach the big leagues, they should already have been schooled to accept women as sportswriters and to expect their presence in the locker room area whenever other media may be present.

I think it's up to the athletes to protect their privacy, to ask for 10 seconds if they want to put their pants on and to take a quick look around the room for women. These suggestions are made in AWSM's locker room code of behavior for athletes and team management. Their code also includes No. 4: Be courteous. Use common sense and discretion.

AWSM president Michele Himmelberg of the *Orange County Register* compiled that code in the fall of 1990, in the aftermath of the "Zeke Mowatt incident" in Massachusetts. (This is an inside joke for AWSM. The incident is widely referred to as the "Lisa Olson incident," but we figure that Mowatt was the culprit and so it's his incident. Olson was just the victim.) Mowatt was charged — and fined by the NFL — for exposing himself directly in front of the *Boston Herald's* Olson and daring her to touch his manly tool. She was more interested in continuing her interview with Mowatt's New England Patriots teammate Maurice Hurst. Other players joined Mowatt in harassing Olson, who halted her interview and left the premises.

Mega-publicity ensued, resulting in a 60-page report by the NFL and $72,500 in fines for the Patriots and Victor Kiam, the team's owner, whose response to the *Herald* was, "Your paper is asking for trouble sending a female reporter to cover a team. Why not stand in front of her if she's an intruder?" With this attitude, it was all too predictable when Kiam called Olson a bitch.

Olson fled her job and country, heading for Australia to write news features and recollect her sanity. She brought suit against the Patriots and won an out-of-court settlement a week before her 1992 trial date.

Meanwhile, the rest of us were stuck on the mainland trying once again to counteract the public's feeling that, "Honey, she didn't belong in there." One of the Chicago White Sox coaches told Claire Smith, "This is good. Maybe it will get all of the women out of the locker rooms. I really like you, I really respect you, but you don't belong in there."

Betty Cuniberti, by now living in South Carolina, emerged from the newslands to write an answer for the short-lived sports daily called *The National*, "The locker room is a no-win proposition for women: Stay out and you'll get beaten in stories and fail in your profession. Go in and you're forever assigned the Scarlet Letter."

The Mowatt incident turned out to be a Clarence Thomas hearing of sorts for women sportswriters. It resuscitated the old debate, of course, about a woman's place in the locker room. But it also opened a dialogue about the way men and women should conduct themselves in such an environment, and the way these inevitable instances ought to be handled by the participants and their superiors.

I remember being bothered by Olson's willingness to do interviews and appear on television programs during the height of the debate and dialogue, because I felt she ought to have continued doing her own stories — the way I had when Dave Kingman sent me a rat and the way Joan Ryan had when a razor crept up her leg. But perhaps if Joan and I had pursued our tyrants and raised a stink, Mowatt might have steered a different course that day in the New England locker room.

That Olson effectively ruined her career by appearing on "Entertainment Tonight" might have saved another woman sportswriter from a similar case of harassment, but acknowledging this was uncomfortable for many of us. As Huckshorn wrote: "I wish Lisa Olson would shut up. She makes me wish I hadn't."

You see the dilemma: We were always trying to decide when to laugh off something, when to tell someone to fuck off, and when to take off for the nearest editor or lawyer. The *Boston Globe* reported, a year after the Mowatt incident, that one of Olson's editors had told her to go back into the locker room and "act like a man." Maybe the guy was an idiot, like Kiam. If we give him the benefit of the doubt, maybe that editor meant, "Forget you're a woman sportswriter and just be a sportswriter."

But this was so hard for us and so hard, too, for the players. Bret Saberhagen, a pitcher for the Kansas City Royals and New York Mets, used to carry magic tricks on the road with him. I always enjoyed talking with Bret. He was like a regular guy. I still owe him a bottle of wine because he pitched a quick game once in Oakland — I was always trying to bribe players and even A's manager Tony La Russa into speeding up the game times so I could make my deadlines with plenty of their quotes. On one trip into Oakland, Bret brought a pet snake in his bag of tricks. At least, it sure looked like a real snake. I was waiting to talk to somebody, and he tried to scare me with the snake. I held up well. But, on the way out of the clubhouse, another writer asked, "Should I make a big deal out of that?"

He was wondering if Saberhagen was harassing me, the way Kingman had with the rat. I told him it was nice of him to ask, but I knew Saberhagen and he was just being friendly. There was a difference, I thought, between a mean trick and a harmless joke. When Kingman sent me the rat, Joan Ryan wrote that if Jose Rijo — a sweet, friendly, young pitcher — had done such a thing, I would have been puzzled, but not upset. With Kingman, the message was quite clear.

It was a similar story with the pinch from Will Clark. He pinched me in the locker room, on my behind, hard, when I was standing among a group of writers interviewing Trevor Wilson. I gave Clark an outraged look, but he looked so pleased with himself that I couldn't help but laugh. Another writer saw this and asked if he should make a big deal of it, and I had to explain that Clark was getting me back for a pinch I'd given him a year earlier. I reamed out Clark the next time I saw him. He had crossed the line I'd drawn in college.

"Why is it OK for you to do and not OK for me to do?" he asked.

I told him, really loudly, "Mine was in a BAR, not in the clubhouse. We were not working. There's a distinction there."

So, what happened to my sense of humor? I felt that I had to make a serious point to Clark that night. But I tried to always take a light approach into the clubhouse. I thought that as long as you knew your stuff, you could be friendly and professional at the same time. And if you showed you could laugh at yourself and the kooky situation of being a woman in a men's dressing room, it would relax the men and make them more accessible for the job at hand.

The classic locker room legend involves a naked football player who sees a woman in the crowd around his locker stall and asks her, "See this? Do you know what this is?" Of course, he is holding his penis. Of course, she tries to mind her own business. But he keeps asking.

Finally, she looks up from her notebook and says, "Well, it looks like a penis. But it's smaller."

Michelle Kaufman of the *Detroit Free Press* has a similar tale that might become a classic, too, for the way she handled herself. She was covering the Tampa Bay Buccaneers in 1989 and had befriended an offensive lineman there. "You must look," the player would kid Michelle. "How can you not look?"

One Sunday, the offensive line decided to play a trick to catch Michelle looking. She was doing her locker room interviews after the game, and her friend, stark naked, followed her from locker to locker. Meanwhile, the rest of the linemen watched Kaufman. It was their assignment to confirm that she had indeed seen him.

"I pretended I didn't see him," she said. "I just ignored him and went about my business. He must have followed me to five different interviews. The next day, he said, 'You know what, Michelle, you really don't look!' I played dumb and asked him what he meant. He said, 'I followed you around in the locker room yesterday to see if you would look at me and you never did.' I said, 'Oh, I must have been so busy getting my work done that I didn't even notice.' "

And to think the joke was supposed to be on her!

My most embarrassing locker-room moment could have been absolutely humiliating with a humorless person. During the 1989 postseason, I had to write a special section story on the "unsung heroes" of the World Series-bound A's. All day, I was circulating through the clubhouse and around the field, talking to people about "Unsung heroes. Unsung heroes." Well, just try saying that a bunch of times and see what comes out.

I walked over to the cubicle of Gene Nelson, which happened to be next to that of Dennis Eckersley in the Oakland A's clubhouse. Eckersley was a star, but Geno, as he was known, was a mere middle reliever who set up the saves for Eckersley. So I told Nelson about the "unsung heroes" story I was working on.

He said, "Why do you want to talk to me?"

I replied, "Well, you're not very hung, are you?"

Nelson's eyes widened. Eckersley's eyes widened. My eyes widened and my mouth dropped open. I turned red and started laughing uncontrollably in between apologies. It wasn't a Freudian slip at all — I have no idea whether Gene Nelson was very hung or very unhung! It was just a twist of the tongue. I couldn't do the interview, I was laughing so hard — and I never collected myself enough to go back and try it again. I could not even look at Nelson or Eckersley again that day without bursting into laughter.

Fortunately, Nelson and Eckersley thought it was funny, too. Later in the day, pitching coach Dave Duncan told me he had to go to a staff meeting.

"Have to go talk to my unhung heroes," he said.

Another of my embarrassing (at my expense) locker room moments occurred when the Baltimore Blast won the Major Indoor Soccer League championship in 1984. It was my first experience at champagne celebrations, and I remember thinking in advance that I should wear something washable. Unfortunately, the dress I chose — a very nice Italian design of yellow and black — turned clingy when wet, and it was as if I was wearing a wet T-shirt. The players I interviewed seemed to have a hard time maintaining the eye contact I'd always strived for when *they* were inappropriately or insufficiently dressed.

I was much more careful in the future, dressing in layers and even going so far as to wear a rain poncho for one of the A's pennant victories because a woman in the clubhouse — more than any of the men — was always an automatic target for the bubbly. This was, to me, a form of harassment. Yes, it was all in fun. But these players had finished doing their jobs — we sportswriters were, as we tried to take notes in their wet clubhouse, just getting started. I remember sitting cold and wet in the press box one night after the A's had clinched a pennant, trying to write great copy about the A's season as my teeth chattered and my hands shook.

I think I did talk to a few players about it later, nicely. They smiled back sweetly at me and then dumped cheap champagne on me again when they swept the playoffs a week later.

It was also embarrassing to me when the clubhouse attendant in Tiger Stadium's visiting clubhouse asked me, on one visit, if he could take my picture, frame it and hang it on the wall of the clubhouse! I declined, but I told my friend Mickey Morabito, the A's travel director, about the request. Mickey laughed and said, "Imagine visiting teams who have seen you in their clubhouses coming in here and seeing your picture hanging on the wall. Then they'd *know* you're a bimbo." I laughed, too. I much preferred having them merely speculate that I *might* be a bimbo.

I know that women sportswriters had to get serious about some of the flack and take some incidents to superiors — but which incidents? I always thought that if someone did something that hindered your ability to do your job or insulted your professional integrity in front of others, then you ought to try to do something about it.

This is why I'd like to put Sam Wyche in the stocks at a future AWSM convention. What a jerk! The NFL had installed a clear equal-access regulation (specifically, "equal, prompt, and courteous") by the time he made a seemingly impromptu decision, a few days after the Zeke Mowatt news broke in 1990, to bar *USA Today's* Denise Tom from his team's locker room in Seattle.

Wyche was the head coach of the Cincinnati Bengals that day, but he had been quarterback coach with the 49ers when Michele Himmelberg had made her inroads in 1981. Now Himmelberg was president of AWSM, and it was part of her duties to call Wyche in protest of his treatment of Denise Tom.

"What's the deal?" she asked him the next day. "You know this can work."

Wyche embarked on a moralistic tirade with Michele, who didn't get anywhere. Then, he went on "Good Morning America" and inaccurately quoted her as agreeing that a 20-minute time limit on postgame interviews would work! He mugged for every camera crew he could find that week, while camera-shy Denise — we called her "the mouse" when I worked at *USA Today* — hid behind her editors, her answering machine, and AWSM.

Fortunately, the NFL joined Himmelberg in protest. It fined Wyche a week's salary — $27,000, which was paid mostly by donations from fans who agreed with Wyche's oh-so-moral stance against women in the locker rooms. Everybody knew this for what it was, though: an attention-getting ploy by one of sport's big egomaniacs. The very players Wyche claimed to be protecting were telling women reporters, "You guys don't deserve to be treated this way. You shouldn't have to wait outside."

"It doesn't take a very intelligent person to put on a towel or a bathrobe after a game," Wyche's quarterback, Boomer Esiason, told the press.

It wasn't a matter of intelligence, it was a matter of ego — Wyche's ego. One NFL coach told Michele, "If Sam can steal headlines from Saddam Hussein, he'll do it."

Wyche was so clearly wrong, Denise Tom knew she had grounds to complain. But there were other instances where women didn't understand what was wrong but *knew* something wasn't right. Melody Simmons of the *Baltimore Evening Sun* headed for the Oriole locker room one July afternoon in 1989 to interview the Ripken brothers for a free-lance piece for another publication and was greeted with the chant, "Wool, wool."

She asked a player she knew, "What?" and the player screamed "Wool," back at her. Simmons got the feeling that there was "something lewd" going on, but she finished her work without further incident. Then, she lodged a complaint with the Orioles, received an apology, and Manager Frank Robinson held a 70-minute forum two months later with media and players. What was this episode all about, anyway? Nobody ever really knew — it just didn't feel right, and Melody thought she should stop it. So, apparently, did the Orioles management, backing up their apology with a discrimination awareness seminar.

Detroit Tigers management should have been paying attention. Their team president, former University of Michigan football coach Bo Schembechler, sounded too much like Victor Kiam when, in the summer of 1990, the *Detroit Free Press* complained to him about the treatment received by sports intern Jennifer Frey.

Frey, a Harvard graduate who would eventually become a full-time sportswriter for the *New York Times*, had scheduled a pregame interview with Tigers catcher Mike Heath on July 18. Heath didn't show before the game, so Frey had to remain and try to talk to him afterward. She waited and waited — uncomfortably, I have no doubt — at his cubicle for him to emerge from the shower or the trainers' room, or one of the locker room nooks and crannies where players can hide when they really want to. Meanwhile, she decided to approach pitcher Jack Morris for some quotes on baseball's latest collusion settlement. Morris barked at Frey, "I don't talk to people when I'm naked, especially women, unless they're on top of me or I'm on top of them."

What should Frey say? What should she do? Another woman might have confronted Morris right there. Johnette

Howard was covering the Detroit Pistons for the *Free Press* when burly forward Mark Aguirre greeted her arrival in the locker room with screams of, "Damn, damn, damn." The soft-voiced Howard admonished Aguirre, saying, "I've been around here for the month you've been here. Don't act like this is the first time you saw me. Put a towel on, and don't scream at me. I don't like it." Johnette always thought that if someone misbehaved, you ought to call him on it. Other veterans, like Tracy Dodds and Michele Himmelberg, preferred to ignore taunts. After my dozen years in the business, I'd have probably snapped at Morris, "I'm not here to mud-wrestle, I need to know..." and asked him my questions.

Frey smartly chose none of these options and instead gave the Tigers another opportunity to embarrass themselves. She found no humor in Morris's remark and left the clubhouse to report the comment to her editors. Their complaint to Schembechler was answered with this inexcusable defense: "Your intern watched men from 20 to 65 years of age undress for more than half an hour without asking questions." Therefore, wrote Schembechler, Morris's comment could be deemed "out of line but predictable."

This pathetic defense brought a public response, on sports talk shows and in letters to the editors, solidly on Frey's side.

I must point out here that Jack Morris wasn't even naked that evening. He was wearing shorts, and he was being an asshole. Too many men in the sports business use the presence of women sportswriters in the locker room as an excuse to be assholes. They pretend to be gentlemen protecting their modesty, when in fact they are endlessly trying to prove their virility and toughness at the expense of someone smaller and less well-paid than they are.

The men who are truly morally offended by the sight of women in their dressing quarters have found gentlemanly ways to cope. Bruce Hurst, a pitcher for the Boston Red Sox and then the San Diego Padres, always objected, on the basis of his Mormon denomination, to women in the clubhouse. Hurst never embarrassed me, though.

I heard that he'd say things when I was interviewing another player out of earshot. But he would ask, as I left the clubhouse, if I had finished my work in there, so that he would know he was free to undress. He told *USA Today* that if he were commissioner of baseball for a day, "I would work out a feasible way for women reporters to be competitive and still have the dressing room all-male. I respect women who make that their chosen profession, but I don't want to lose my right to dress. I dress in the trainer's room so much, I might as well change lockers with him."

One night I had to wait so long to talk to Hurst's hotshot teammate, Roger Clemens, that I actually apologized to Hurst for having to dawdle for so long in there. Funny, after all of the years and all of the fights, there I was *apologizing* for being in the clubhouse!

It was that old comic strip feeling again, that feeling that I'd just walked into the wrong bathroom. It was hard to shake. I'm ashamed to say that as I grew experienced on the baseball beat, I got so tired of fighting it that I tended to avoid entering unfamiliar territory. If I didn't know a visiting team well, I swapped quotes with a visiting writer rather than put myself through the hassle of dealing with the inevitable comments until I proved myself.

Claire Smith, who is black, said that being a woman in those locker rooms is like being black in America: "It's difficult for me, even today, to go into strange clubhouses, because you have to prove what you're not. Being black, you have to show that you're not going to pick that pocket and you're not going to steal that car before you can be accepted and respected. So many times, (as a woman in the locker room), you'd get this wary look from someone until you asked an intelligent question. Then you'd see this look of relief cross his face as you knew he was thinking, 'Oh. She's OK.' That gets tiring."

I too got tired of feeling like a suspect for a crime, and I grew less and less tolerant of adult men using my presence as an excuse to show off their short-word (four letters, no more, no less) vocabulary. Instead of telling myself, "Ignore it," I found myself thinking, "Who needs this?" If I could, I stayed away.

However, this is not the solution. IT IS THE PROBLEM!

After I'd covered the Oakland A's for a few years, other women sportswriters I didn't know would remark, "I've never been in a locker room before where the players were so polite." A's players had grown up, just as most of the other players around the major leagues had, playing in small minor-league towns where they rarely interacted with professional women.

But the A's expected to see a woman — me — in their clubhouse every day for five years. When Kim Boatman took over the A's beat for the *San Jose Mercury News* in 1989, they expected to see two women in their clubhouse every day.

If it is really a problem for women to be in men's clubhouses, then it would follow that more problems would occur with more and more women bursting through the doors. This was absolutely not the case, nor was it the case with the other team in baseball that was most used to seeing women in the locker room, the New York Yankees. In reality, familiarity did not breed contempt — it bred comfort and accommodation on both sides. How I used to hate hearing, "She's just one of the guys." I didn't want to be one of them. But I did want to be accepted by them.

That would never have happened if I had shied away from the pregame clubhouse scene or rushed my interviews after games. That would never have happened if I had made myself scarce. As long as sportswriters are allowed in locker rooms (and they are!) it is essential for women sportswriters to make themselves at home there, too, to come and go as freely as their male counterparts.

By staying out of visiting locker rooms, I was not merely avoiding indecent exposure. I was impeding decent exposure, the exposure of athletes to women professionals. If I had handled their hostility or catcalls and gone about my business, maybe I might have shown more of them that women can be competent baseball writers. And maybe I could have lightened the load of life for the next woman who came through those doors to talk to those same players.

It can work, this business of being a woman sportswriter in a men's locker room. It's not an ideal working condition, but I know it can work. The Oakland A's know it can work. And every time it works, the chances increase that it will work again. Players get traded and sportswriters change papers. Suddenly, now there is somebody managing the Colorado Rockies (Don Baylor) or the San Francisco Giants (Dusty Baker) who knows it can work.

And, once more, it does. Now I think we need to share this little secret with the men in charge of the newspapers. They've got a locker room of their own.

# 5

# The Locker Room in the Newsroom

"You're in my seat," I growled at the columnist.

He jumped.

I laughed. "I've always wanted to say that to a columnist," I told him.

This particular columnist was my friend and co-worker, Tom Jackson of the *Sacramento Bee*. As he moved cheerfully from "my" metal chair in the Oakland Coliseum press box to another just like it, and I unpacked my computer and scorebook to cover that afternoon's baseball game, I told Tom about Richard Kucner, the stern and cold columnist at my first newspaper, the *Baltimore News American*.

Kucner was a wonderful writer, but I don't know how he ever coaxed anyone into telling him anything. He was tall and bespectacled, and his slow-moving demeanor gave him a pious, preacherlike aura—except that he had such a mean and sarcastic sense of humor, you'd be more inclined to pray for him rather than with him.

In one of my early assignments at the *News American*, I was to cover a Washington Bullets' championship series game on deadline. Kucner drove the two of us down the interstate to the Capital Centre and agreed to feed me some quotes because I would not have time to cover the locker rooms adequately and he did not have to make an early deadline.

He covered the locker rooms, all right. He just never shared any quotes with me.

A week or so later, I was assigned to write a sidebar at an Oriole game for beat writer Peter Pascarelli. So I sat down next to Peter in the front row of Memorial Stadium's open-air press box, as I had the last time I was there, hoping to glean an idea or two in the course of watching the game with him.

Just before game time, in walked Kucner. He slammed his bag onto the tabletop in front of me and said, "You're in my seat."

It was not a pretty scene. He insisted on sitting in that particular seat, even though there were others, empty, around us. Peter shrugged at me. No one said a word. So, I moved. A few days later, assistant sports editor Ralph Vigoda called me into the office. "I heard about what happened at the ballpark the other night," he said. "It's stupid, I know, but just let him have his way."

Over the years, I would encounter many Richard Kucners. One of them, Nick Peters, covered the San Francisco Giants for the *Oakland Tribune* and then the *Sacramento Bee*. He never got to know me, yet wasted no opportunity to snipe at me behind my back. Of course, I heard about every attack, but would just say, "That's too bad. I have no problem with Nick." I saw Peters as the typical cigar-smoking, sexist, white guy high on boosterism and low on talent who gets his kicks by kicking anybody who threatens his security in any way.

Guys like that are all over the sports journalism business. At an editing seminar she conducted, *New York Times* deputy sports editor Sandy Bailey was asked by one young woman how to handle a writer who constantly argued with her about story changes.

"Are you getting this because you're a woman?" Sandy asked her.

"No, I think it's age-ism," the young woman replied naively. "I think it's because I'm younger than they are."

"I used to think that," Sandy said. "I used to think people were harder on me because I was young and new to the business. But I don't think that's why anymore." Today, Sandy can recognize sexist treatment. She knows a Richard Kucner or a Nick Peters when she sees one — and she sees all too many of them.

But, at 21 years of age, it took me many months to understand the dynamics behind what became known as the "seat incident." First of all, Kucner was my preview for Dave Kingman. He did not think women belonged in sportswriting, sports departments, or sports locker rooms.

Secondly, I was a 21-year-old college senior, fully prepared to "pay my dues" at some tiny, rural paper for a job, when my hometown *News American* hired me — and, naturally, I was thrilled. I had been smiling for no apparent reason since I was a baby: now, I really had something worth smiling about, so I kept on smiling — at editors, co-workers, athletes, coaches. This did not go over so well in the sports department, where the preferred posture is a slump and the common countenance a frown. Long ago, Red Smith had described sports as "the toy department" of newsrooms, and why not? It was the one place people seemed to be having fun. Somewhere along the way, though, Smith's metaphor came to signify a lack of integrity, professionalism, and purpose in the sports department. And the people in sports responded defensively.

Instead of thumbing their noses at the rest of the newsroom and gaily going about their business, the people in sports said, "We work harder than anyone: Look at our posture, see how exhausted we are?" and, "Covering sports is horrible work — everyone is so mean to us, it makes us miserable." It was fashionable to whine — and it seemed to me that the very best writers (I remember among these Peter Pascarelli at the *News American*, and Dan Shaughnessy and Michael Janofsky at the *Evening Sun*) constructed the most elaborate and convincing complaints. They must have been among those who believed that you had to starve to succeed as an artist, so they tried to look hungry.

The people in sports departments also appeared to dislike most of the people they covered, to such an extent that they would have preferred not to do any interviews at all in conjunction with game coverage. They had to do these, though, because television already had informed the fans on the "What" of the games and the writers were left to tell readers the "Why." How wonderful, I thought in those early days, to be able to talk to Jim Palmer right after he'd pitched a one-hit shutout. But the more experienced writers seemed to rev their engines higher if Palmer got shelled.

I think this was because they took too literally the concept of the "adversarial relationship" between reporter and story subject. One of the roles of the press in the United States is to serve as a watchdog over government or, in our case, sports. As a result, some in sports journalism believed that this meant you could not play tennis with Jim Palmer or even like him without forever soiling your professionalism. Perhaps the media and the sports world were adversaries and should be, but I did not interpret this to mean that Susan Fornoff and Jim Palmer ought to view each other as mortal enemies. Instead, as a 21-year-old rookie writer for the *News American*, I smiled at everyone and made friends. Guys like Richard Kucner, who smiled only at mean jokes, didn't like that.

But the biggest reason for the Kucner-seat powerplay was Russ Brown's decision to make me a full-time general-assignment sportswriter. Most rookies start their careers covering the high school beat — preps, we call it — and work their way up. But I had been covering college sports as a part-timer when I was still at Maryland. I never covered preps for the *News American* — Jack Gibbons did, as he had for years. Instead, I backed up on the Orioles and Colts, and covered the University of Maryland football team too. That must have been humiliating to Jack. But he didn't seem to blame me for that humiliation, and he never, ever, took his frustrations out on me. So Kucner did it for him.

Gibbons had become the sports editor of the *Baltimore Evening Sun* — with several women, including assistant sports editor Molly Dunham, on his staff — by 1989, when AWSM held its annual meeting in Baltimore. There, he talked with me about those *News American* years. "You had to put up with a lot, and you didn't deserve that," he said. "You did a good job. I'm sorry you had to go through that."

Why did I have to go through that? Here's one explanation, excerpted from an unsigned memo written for Henry Freeman by a woman on his *USA Today* sports staff in 1984:

> There are more women in the business than there should be who do not have a solid sports background. This is, in part, I think, due to some poor hiring practices. In the late 1970s, when it became fashionable to have a woman on the sports staff, many editors, in their desire to "get one," hired hastily and not

very well. Once they had their woman reporter, they tended to want to put them in visible roles — the first in this locker room or that press box — instead of giving them a chance to gain experience slowly. This created a difficult situation for the reporter tossed in over her head, (the way I had been) and for the male writer, (Jack Gibbons, for example) who rightfully resented not getting the opportunity.

It was, in the 1970s, "fashionable" among sports editors to have "a" woman sportswriter on staff. Maybe some of the sports editors had heard of this newfangled legal maneuver called a sex discrimination suit. Or maybe they were just looking for somebody to cover the area disdained by the men on their staffs, women's sports. Whatever the reasons, Blackie Sherrod of the *Dallas Times-Herald* told *Time* magazine in 1976: "I wish I had one. Everybody's looking for one. What I'd give for a good one!"

But "good" women sportswriters do not come out of college — not even one with a top-notch athletic program and award-winning daily newspaper — directly onto a top beat at a major metropolitan daily newspaper. This is like taking a pitcher out of high school and starting him in a critical game against the Toronto Blue Jays: It can be done, and the pitcher may even succeed a time or two, but, all the while, he will be missing out on essential basic training.

Tokenism ran rampant in the 1970s and early 1980s, and I was both beneficiary and victim. Beneficiary, because I got a good job. Victim, because I was not experienced enough to be covering major-league sports and interviewing major-league athletes.

If a woman was smart and could write, she could learn these other things, just as the 18-year-old pitcher could be tutored to harness his erratic fastball. Some exceptional sports editors recognized this and coached young women along. The late Dick Sandler at *Newsday*, and Michael Davis, now with the *Sun*, wrote me long, encouraging letters when I was job-hunting. Paul Anger of the *Miami Herald*, the *Boston Globe's* Vince Doria, John Rawlings of the *San Jose Mercury News*, and George Solomon of the *Washington Post* had reputations for inspiring progress among the women they hired. I would love to have worked for any of them.

More often, it was as this anonymous letter writer told AWSM: "I feel like (my editors) want me to succeed, but only so they can brag about it at their annual meetings. No one ever tells me when I do something right, but I get phone calls from editors in off-hours to tell me about something I did wrong. Praise is non-existent."

Most of us quickly found that sports editors were not interested in schooling us or supporting us — just in hiring us so as to stay in fashion with their fellow sports editors. Perhaps women executives like sports editors Cathy Henkel of the *Seattle Times* and Tracy Dodds of the *Austin American Statesman* can make a difference in the '90s — if they can ever feel like they actually belong to that mostly white-male group known as APSE, the Associated Press Sports Editors.

"I don't go to the annual summer meeting (of APSE)," said Henkel, "because I find it to be a very social event where everybody brings his spouse. I don't find much meaning there. The first time I went, about five years ago, nobody would speak to me. I went into the hospitality suite and I didn't know anybody, and they didn't know me. I think nobody talked to me because they thought I was a spouse."

Sandy Bailey certainly has been doing some talking. A former copy editor at the *Washington Post*, now deputy sports editor at the *New York Times*, she was APSE's president for 1992-93. But, instead of trying to be "one of the guys" and work on her golf index, she used her platform to enlighten her fellow — and I do mean "fellow" — editors on the issues of harassment and gender equity.

"My point is that harassment is not just pinching people, it's creating a hostile environment where women feel uncomfortable because they are women," she said. "(Looking at this has) been eye-opening for everyone. I don't know if it's just a one-year issue — if they see it as, 'That's Sandy's thing, she can make a stink and then we can go back to discussing about whether we should vote in the college football poll.' But I don't want to be one of the guys anymore. It doesn't work. We're not just like them — we are different people. We can put out sports sections that are just as good as the ones they put out, but we are different.

"A lot of them are genuinely puzzled by this. They have worked in departments staffed by white men, and they don't really know what is expected of them when it comes to women and minorities."

In 1989, though, those same white men voted a woman into the ranks that lead to APSE's top office. That could never have happened fifteen years earlier, when these editors — who had risen through sports departments staffed exclusively by white men had no idea how to manage, much less work alongside, women.

In 1981, my sports editors were put to the test when the Baltimore Colts refused to let me in the locker room for their home opener against the Buffalo Bills. I had regularly entered the postgame locker room during the 1980 season. Now, a club official told me as I began to push the door open, there was a "new policy." Women, he said, could no longer go into the locker room.

The editors at the *News American* didn't want to ruin the paper's relationship with the Colts. So they agreed to have Ken Murray, the beat writer I backed up, survey the players to decide whether I should be allowed in or not. From what the players were saying to me, I naively thought they'd say, "Yes." Colts players weren't telling me what they really thought, though, and they voted, "No," by a 2-to-1 ratio, despite my lobbying efforts. It took another week for my editors to reach the logical conclusion that Melissa Ludtke's editor at *Sports Illustrated*, Pete Carry, had carried into a courtroom on her behalf three years earlier: Whatever the players thought, however they voted, the club had a legal obligation to provide fair and equal access to any credentialed media member.

This was the argument — which I believe included slipping in the word "lawsuit" — that ultimately convinced Colts officials to admit women to the locker room, because they were unwilling to alienate the male reporters by closing the dressing room and setting up a separate interview room. All they asked was that the women take a longer, hallway route from the coach's interview room to the dressing room, rather than walking through the shower area as the men did. That was my pleasure. I ought to have thanked them!

I had two editors at the *News American*, first, Russ Brown, who hired me, and later Ralph Vigoda, the assistant sports editor to Russ who worked with me more than anyone. They had no inkling about coaching me in matters of deportment or defending me in cases of harassment. One of the Colts' players, a big defensive lineman named Herb Orvis, used to stop what he was doing on the field and stare at me when I'd arrive in training camp. It upset me, because I did not even know the man, who declined to be interviewed by any reporters. It upset me, but it was a big joke to everyone else, including the men in my office.

The problem was eventually solved, but not by my bosses or colleagues. I ran into Orvis outside the dining room and was preparing to run the other way immediately, when he told me he'd heard I was uncomfortable. I stopped in my tracks. "You bet I am," I answered.

Then he told me he hadn't meant to intimidate me, he just thought I was pretty. I explained that that was fine for him to tell me that when it was just the two of us standing there, but I did not enjoy being subjected to his admiring gaze in the workplace. From talking to him, I decided that he wasn't the lunatic he seemed to be on the practice field — he seemed intelligent and well-traveled. He was, in other words, a human being. I hope he found out I was the same. At least from that day on he said "Hello" instead of staring, although he never did let me interview him.

Another incident made me the butt of more jokes with my co-workers. One day I sat in the interview room at Colts camp, minding my own business, when Bert Jones came in to visit. Jones was the team's star quarterback, but he acted so goofy that I think he'd lost a screw in one of the many sacks he had taken. That day, he sat down next to me on the sofa, and we blew big pink bubbles on the gum we'd procured from the locker room downstairs. Then, Jones reached for the neckline of the dress I was wearing. I pushed him away, pointing at him as if to say, "You'd better not do that," and then we both laughed. The entire sequence was captured by a *News American* photographer who was having some fun with us. He gave me copies a few days later, and I showed them around.

This wasn't one of my brainier moves, of course. For one thing, they showed me having fun. Sportswriters are supposed to complain constantly and pretend they've got the worst jobs in the world. For another thing, they showed me having fun with somebody I covered. And sportswriters, especially women sportswriters, are not supposed to even appear to have fun with a source.

Neither of my bosses said a word about the photographs, until I went in to talk to Ralph because I was disappointed that I was not even interviewed to fill the Colts' beat job when it opened up — for the third straight year —after the 1981 season.

Ralph explained that he didn't think I was ready to cover the Colts full time. I asked why. I had been covering the Baltimore Blast indoor soccer team better than anyone in town, which showed that I could build contacts and handle competition — two of the prime components in covering a major beat. I had backed up on the Colts for two years running. I had some shortcomings, I was sure, but — "Please tell me," I implored Ralph — what exactly did I need to do to qualify myself for the more prestigious and, I hoped, better-paying Colts beat?

"I can't explain it," he said, squirming uncomfortably.

I waited.

Then he said: "The pictures."

He couldn't pick up my clips and say, "This could be better, that needs work." He could not find much to say about my writing or my reporting. He could only say, "The pictures."

Could it be that my style was too fun-loving, too — dare we say — flirtatious, for my supervisors? This style seemed acceptable when it came to enlisting somebody to chase down the owner, Robert Irsay, for an exclusive interview, or for assigning someone to track down player nicknames for a feature story. In those cases, my approach was an asset to my newspaper. At those times, it was OK for me to be what I was, a 23-year-old woman Herb Orvis thought was pretty. When it came to a promotion and a raise, though, forget it.

My sports editor was not alone in his application of this double standard. Cathy Harasta, an outstanding feature writer and columnist for the *Dallas Morning News*, was assigned by her paper to do some time in spring training with the Texas Rangers baseball team. A spring training trip to sunny Florida is considered an all-star assignment, especially for a one- or two-week stint. But problems developed. Cathy planned to stay at the newspaper's spacious Florida condo — until the wife of one of the men who was also staying at the condo balked. Cathy said her supervisors responded by withdrawing her from the spring training team. She accepted their decision, but shared remorse with her women sportswriter friends at the next AWSM convention.

Another woman was hired to cover an NBA team for a large newspaper in a highly competitive market. Her boss, she said, called her into the office before she took to the road with the team.

"He tried to give me this subtle warning that there are dogs who are NBA players," she said. "He said, 'Now, you know how they can be. It's going to be very, very difficult covering these guys. Be leery. Be careful. Everyone's going to be watching you.' I didn't need to hear that. I was 29 years old and had been married for five years. Was he threatening me? It was very, very insulting — and I knew he wouldn't say that to the guys, some of whom needed to hear it, who wanted to be the 13th guy, who wanted to be all chummy with the players, who were betting on the games. They think because you're a woman and (the players) are men, there's going to be something sexual going on."

I cannot, under any circumstances, imagine a male sports editor lecturing a male sportswriter about acceptable sexual conduct. It is irrelevent for them. Why does it have to be an issue for us?

I dealt quickly with the double standard issue at the *News American* that prevented me from moving up to the Colts beat. I picked up my clips and my photos and accepted an offer to work at *USA Today*, just one month before it was launched in September 1982.

What a change! The *News American* was a newspaper dying of declining readership, increasing budget cuts, and periodic layoffs. *USA Today* was a twinkle in the eyes of publisher Al Neuharth. He practically doubled my little $17,000 salary.

The opulence was overwhelming. TV monitors surrounded the sports copy desk. The building glittered on the D.C. skyline, towering over the Northern Virginia city of Rosslyn, just across the Potomac River from Georgetown.

Loaners — staff writers and editors imported on trial from other Gannett papers — came from all over the country and were housed next door at a condominium called River Place at the paper's expense until they became permanent hires. Many of them left their families at home during the trial period, and a dorm mentality permeated the condos.

The sports staff seemed to lead the company in parties, but nobody could throw one the way Neuharth did — for the launch, for Christmas, for anniversaries. A lot of gigantic prawns and tender oysters found their way off the ice sculptures onto my plates.

Neuharth also made a pointed effort to hire women, lots of them, in all departments. Henry Freeman's original sports staff included at least six women and usually numbered around 10. So at *USA Today* I was no longer a token. That meant only that I wasn't standing outside all by myself anymore.

Inside, though, the sports department at *USA Today* was just another locker room. Those TV monitors clustered around the sports desk? They were often tuned to porno movies at night. And male staffers — including Henry — used the vantage point of the 14th floor to peer down through those glittering windows at the couple that regularly made love in their condo next door. Once some of the men went into Henry's office and turned out the lights so that they could see better.

Yes, there were lots of women — I believe the male terminology, coined by editor John Bannon and copy editor Ed Christine, was "hags" — in the department. But we had our places. We covered tennis. We covered women's sports. We covered amateur sports. We covered the Ladies' Professional Golfers Association tour. The men ate the surf and turf — major-league baseball, football, basketball, and top collegiate men's basketball and football. The quiche and the spinach salad went to the women.

It was like going to a bar with a man and ordering a beer while he orders white wine: The server — the same one who took the orders — invariably returns with the drinks and invariably puts the white wine in front of you, the quiche-and-spinach salad eater. And when an editor did put the beer in front of us, it was always with some twist: You were to go to the Super Bowl, but only to do a sidebar or a profile . . . something, well, soft!

Men did the hard stuff, women did the soft stuff. This was so evident at *USA Today* because enough women worked there that the pattern surfaced. But it was true elsewhere — sometimes even when women had gained prestige and position. Sportscaster Karie Ross was working for the *Sports News Network* in the fall of 1990 when a promoter offered her a job hosting a show with Pittsburgh Steelers quarterback Bubby Brister. Ross, who was 30, considered the possibility a tribute to the progress she'd made — until she learned that the promoter's press release on the program promised plenty of "sexual innuendo."

Ross said no such thing had ever been discussed. "No credible sportscaster would take that kind of job," she said. "If they really want a woman for this, they need to get Miss July."

They certainly weren't going to ask a *man* to do that. There were certain stories sports editors could assign to women that they would never ask a man to do. Joan Ryan of the *San Francisco Examiner* is still embarrassed, six years later, about a column she wrote entitled, "The cutest 49ers." She had just moved from Orlando, hired away as a protegee of *Examiner* editor Dave Burgin, when she wrote this column listing — and describing in detail — the 10 cutest 49ers. She gave Dwight Hicks a nine for leading the "All-Buns team" with his "great tush." I won't embarrass Joan any further now.

I did, then. I wrote her a letter that absolutely lashed at her for tearing down what little credibility women sportswriters had managed to assemble in the last 15 years. I didn't know her. I thought she was an utter bimbo, and it was about a year before I began speaking to her. I gradually learned that Joan is as much bimbo as Madonna is virgin. She writes with conscience and compassion, with so much color that she has won several awards and set a high standard for columnists of the essayist genre. But it wasn't until 1992 that I raised the subject of "The cutest 49ers" in a luncheon conversation.

"That column set my career back three years," she said. "I still don't feel comfortable talking about it." She told me, then, that Burgin had urged her to write the column as a spoof of what a man would write in judgment of, say, the 49er cheerleaders. A more confident writer —a man, perhaps, or a more experienced woman — would have declined the assignment. Joan's is not a spoofing style, yet she followed the boss's orders and received, for her off-the-mark efforts, a ton of letters just like mine, which she handed over to her editor.

Burgin did not, of course, answer my letter. But Joan said she asked him not to. She just wanted to forget the whole episode and return to writing her usual colorful and compassionate columns on main-course subjects like Joe Montana.

It's not necessarily *bad* to swallow the quiche and spinach salad. Women writers like Betty Cuniberti infused life and a fresh perspective into statistic-laden sports pages during the 1970s and 1980s. Maybe they came into their jobs knowing less about the sports and more about the writing than did their male co-workers. Maybe they simply asked different questions. And

maybe they liked the more sane working conditions, the struc-
tured schedule, of the quiche feature writer.

Some women — and, more and more in the 1980s, men —
preferred even the lower profile beats and assignments because
these made it easier to guarantee some presence at home with a
spouse and children. These also made it easier to deal with
editors, who tend to be less demanding about sports they know
nothing about. They aren't spending their Sundays concocting
all sorts of obscure story possibilities as they watch women's
basketball on television, the way I think they do when they watch
those NFL games. And former athletes who become women
sportswriters may like the idea of covering women's golf or
women's tennis because these venues feel comfortable to them.
Here's a locker room where they feel they belong.

A guilt factor exists for most women in the media when
it comes to covering women's issues, and that translates to
women sportswriters and women's sports. Women sportswriters I've spoken with do seem to feel a sense of responsibility to
propel stories on women athletes into the newspaper, so we write
them.

But we just don't want to make our livings that way,
because it is only by covering the big revenue-producing sports
that we can become big breadwinners. Many of us want to cover
a surf-and-turf beat, want to qualify someday for our own sports
page columns.

Clearly, I was not going to advance far or fast by covering
soccer for *USA Today*. I liked having a beat, even soccer — it kept
me out of the line of the editors who were bound to throw me fluff
about a 100-year-old bowler to keep me busy otherwise. I did not,
however, like my chances at rising through the male ranks to the
pro football beat.

Not that women weren't covering pro football games for
*USA Today*. We were — and doing so led us into an attorney's
office in 1983 to contemplate bringing a suit against our own
employer.

Each week, the *USA Today* sports department would
dispatch writers to cover every NFL game. It was a grueling
assignment: Usually, we flew into a city Sunday morning, found
our way to the stadium, covered the game, filed a story and notes,
and then found our way back to the airport for a flight home. If
you got home 14 hours after you left, you were lucky.

In those days, Pete Rozelle's NFL had not established an equal access policy for women sportswriters. Sometimes the locker rooms were allegedly open, until we arrived at the doors. Once I couldn't get into a supposedly open locker room simply because the guard had not been told women were allowed in.

The New York Giants were the worst offenders of all: They provided no access and no assistance for women assigned to their game. I remember waiting for their quarterback, Phil Simms, outside the locker room, but the Giants hadn't yet won the Super Bowl and I could not have recognized Phil Simms in street clothes unless he happened to be wearing his number on them. He walked right by me, while I kept waiting, and waiting, and waiting, until I realized that practically the entire team already had boarded the bus.

It was so frustrating that I occasionally inserted a sentence in my story telling the reader, "Phil Simms was unavailable for comment to women sportswriters." Of course, it was really my editors — primarily Henry Freeman — I was trying to talk to.

Henry's intentions seemed right-placed. He talked to Rozelle every year about our plight. But I don't think he realized how much the NFL's bias was hurting his readers, his section, and his staff until we women had our meeting with a Washington media attorney. We went to see him, secretly, because we felt our newspaper was putting us in an impossible competitive position. We could not do our jobs well under the circumstances. And women were under such a microscope at that time that we could not afford to be placed in situations where we were destined to do a bad job.

Sportscaster Gayle Gardner still refers to this as "The Black Quarterback Syndrome." We were the black quarterback for the last-place team who got to play only against the top defense in the league: We could not win by ourselves, and, when we lost, it reflected on all of the would-be first-string quarterbacks who looked like us. If our stories weren't good because we couldn't interview the game's heroes or gain entry into both locker rooms, then editors could compare the bylines and say, "The men's stories are all better than all of the women's stories. So men can cover sports and women can't."

The attorney told our group of six or seven that we would be wasting time and jeopardizing our careers — not to mention spending a lot of money — if we sued *USA Today* for putting us in such an impossible position. He advised us to meet with Henry and tell him that we had consulted an attorney out of our frustration with the working conditions. We should, he said, urge Henry to take up our cause with the NFL.

We did that, and somehow I — perhaps because I was the radical one with the big mouth — got stuck doing the talking. We sat down around a huge table in one of the building's glass-walled conference rooms, and, my voice shaking, I told Henry, "If the NFL were discriminating against blacks or Jews, *USA Today* would not stand for such policies for one minute."

Of course, any time the word "attorney" makes even a cameo appearance in conversation, people put the popcorn down and lean forward to follow the plot. Henry listened supportively that day, and said that he hadn't realized how frustrated we were. He promised to consult with the paper's legal advisors and pursue the matter with the NFL. By 1985, Henry had forced the issue to such an extent that the NFL mandated equal access arrangements — either in the locker rooms or in separate interview rooms — for all media.

Henry Freeman was not a man who had had much experience managing women sportswriters and copy editors before *USA Today*, but I think the effort he made at learning to understand their issues and adjust his agenda — once there were so many of us surrounding him — was exemplary. Henry sent at least two $1,000 checks from *USA Today* to AWSM, and he attended our convention in Baltimore. He requested memos from his women staffers when they reported incidents of harassment or encountered sexism. I remember telling him once that I hated to sound like a whiner and come to him about every little thing, and he firmly replied that this was the only way those "little things" were going to stop turning into big problems.

I wasn't the only woman who felt that way, although others hesitated to tell sports editors their war stories for different reasons. Sometimes, they simply didn't want to become the epicenter of an earthquake. Michelle Kaufman was a University of Miami student selling stories to the *St. Petersburg Times* in 1986 when sports editor Duke Maas asked her to interview Mark Duper, the Miami Dolphins receiver. Kaufman arranged the interview, a one-on-one in a comfortable spot outside the Dolphins' locker room quarters, and began questioning Duper about the season.

"You know, your blouse is buttoned too high," Kaufman says Duper answered. "You need to open your top button." Kaufman tried her question again, and was told, "Oh, you must not have heard me. I said you need to undo your top button on your blouse."

"Finally, I said, 'I'm here to do an interview with you,'" Kaufman said. "But he kept carrying on, and finally I just gave up. But that meant I wasn't going to be able to do this story, so I had to call my editor and tell him what happened. He was even more outraged than I was."

Kaufman and Maas argued about how they ought to react. She convinced him she should handle the matter herself — essentially, do nothing — rather than confront the Dolphins or the NFL. "I'm still not sure I was right to do that," she said in 1992.

In May 1984, Henry took me to a small meeting of sports editors in Philadelphia to talk about the plight of women sportswriters. They decided to present a seven-woman panel in front of the full APSE that June, and I spoke again. I told them that our problems were their problems, too. Our problems forced them to choose between failing to land the complete story because they had assigned a woman reporter or risking violating employment discrimination laws by not assigning a woman reporter.

My own employer finally decided to assign me to a surf-and-turf beat: men's college basketball. It sounded too much like meat and potatoes to me, though — not my taste. Henry and Curtis Riddle presented me with their idea of a promotion (no raise, though — not my idea of a promotion) on February 1, 1985, and it occurred to me that I would now be confronted with an entirely new set of closed doors.

The NCAA has always been a run in the nylons of women sportswriters. The association itself does not discriminate against women sportswriters, and equal access policies are enforced in all post-season tournaments that are run by NCAA officials. Legally, this may be a safe anti-lawsuit stance.

But the NCAA does not police its members' media relations during the regularly scheduled seasons. Individual conferences and teams set access policies, and, as Henry Freeman himself told AWSM, "In many instances, it continues to be a situation where the coach is God in his town." The sports information director, who assigned media credentials and arranged interviews, might favor opening the locker rooms, but if his coach said, "I'm not exposing my boys to the evils of women," the locker room doors stayed shut or opened only to men. So Natalie Meisler of the *Denver Post* was allowed to vote for college football's biggest award, the Heisman Trophy, but not to interview winner Barry Sanders at the Holiday Bowl because, OSU coach Pat Jones told her, "We're a little backward in the Midwest, and we can't have any women in there."

Often, women are expected to call the schools in advance of their scheduled assignment so that the sports information directors can make special arrangements. Debbie Becker of *USA Today* told me she always refused to do that.

"I never ask," she said, "because I assume that I'm going to get in everywhere. I don't want to ask and be told no and have to make a scene. I'd rather go assuming I can go in (to the locker room) and make a scene *there* if I can't. I assume I can get in where the men can get in, and so I purposely do not ask. I don't want to say, 'Fine, bring players out,' because it isn't fine."

By 1985, I had been a sportswriter for six years, and I didn't want to ever again say, "Fine, bring players out." Battling the NFL had taken such a toll that I would decline a so-called promotion if it meant more of the same with the NCAA.

But I wasn't being *asked* if I wanted to cover men's college basketball, I was being *assigned* to it. I thanked my editors uncomfortably. I was not uncomfortable merely with the probability of encountering more closed doors; I was also uncomfortable because I was pursuing a new job. I had boarded a plane to Sacramento on January 24 to interview with the *Bee*, and I had been led to expect a job offer any day now. I wanted to work for a local newspaper again, covering one team at a time with more than six inches of copy at a time.

The offer — covering either the Oakland A's or the San Francisco Giants — came from *Bee* assistant managing editor Jim Dawson on my 27th birthday, February 4. While baseball had been my first love since I was eight years old, the luster of a full-time baseball beat had worn off ever since I realized the grueling travel schedule it entailed. Yet this beat sounded appealing. Dawson and *Bee* editor Gregory Favre assured me that the *Bee* would never undertake a full travel schedule with either team, that the baseball writers would make, at most, three-quarters of the teams' trips each season.

Furthermore, these same editors had already forced the San Francisco 49ers to liberate their locker room in support of Michele Himmelberg, whom Dawson had hired a dozen years earlier as a 17-year-old intern. They would never hesitate, they pledged, to summon their attorneys on my behalf. They even seemed to like the idea — I believe I saw their eyes flickering at the prospect of a good fight.

I had been inside the 49er locker room, interviewing players without incident or comment, while encountering closed doors elsewhere in the NFL. "Wow, things are different on the West Coast," I had thought. Now, I was being offered a job with a paper that had helped make that difference.

The boyfriend I had met on a Club Med vacation at Magic Isle, Haiti, that May was from the San Francisco area, and I had fallen in love with the city on first sight, September 1984. My new editors told me I could live anywhere in the Bay Area — 100 miles from their offices in Sacramento — that I wanted. Everything conveniently fell into place, and there was no reason for me to decline their offer.

I had quite a birthday party that February 4. Henry Freeman seemed sad and disappointed when I gave him the news, but I was ready to go. The card from my friends at *USA Today* said, "Congratulations on your new job. May you have more Thrill of Victory than Agony of Defeat."

# 6

# Kong the Rat

I decided not to title this chapter "The Rat Lady," even though some friends still introduce me this way at parties. They will say, "Remember when Dave Kingman sent a rat to a sportswriter?" Then they point at me and I blink innocently as I repeat my line, "Can you believe it? ME?" I don't mind being referred to as "the rat lady" as long as everybody recognizes who was the real rat. I plead not guilty. I plead, in fact, utter innocence.

This little tale — and perhaps even the little tail of Kong the actual, living rat — begins in the spring of 1985 under the bluest skies and on the greenest grass in the world. It begins in Phoenix, Arizona, with my first spring training. My eyes widened with interest and pleasure at my first look at the desert, my first encounter with the saguaro cactus, and my first meeting with the Oakland A's.

While all of it seemed new, none of it appeared to be terribly intimidating, although I felt far more prepared to survive in the desert with the alien cacti than I was to cope with the A's. And probably I was.

I had been assigned to cover the A's just a few weeks earlier, when the *Sacramento Bee's* senior baseball writer, Bob Padecky, decided he would prefer to cover the San Francisco Giants. A lifelong American League fan, I was pleased to draw the A's by default. The franchise had declined for the better part of 10 years and played backup in the baseball-snobbish Bay Area to the Giants. But the team played its home games in a beautiful, usually warm, coliseum not at all like sterile, chilly Candlestick Park, and the A's visited my hometown of Baltimore at least twice a year. I could stand that.

Besides, my baseball writing friend at *USA Today*, Ken Picking, had told me that the other A's beat writers were a lot of fun and would probably do their best to make me feel comfortable. I soon learned that Picking's recommendation translated to, "They like to drink, and they'll be crazy about you because you're blond and female."

They certainly did seem to be awaiting my arrival with some curiosity — I wonder what advance notice Pick had given *them* about *me*, since I had been quite the party girl in my days at *USA Today*. (It's my book, so I don't need to elaborate.)

There was Kit Stier of the *Oakland Tribune*, a tall, handsome silver-haired man who probably was the best reporter among us and the worst writer. The man he called Roomie was his former roommate, Glenn Schwarz of the *San Francisco Examiner*. Schwarz, a large man with a friendly, bespectacled face, seemed more mature and professional than the rest of us; it's no wonder he would become, in just three years, the sports editor at his paper.

Bruce Jenkins and Bud Geracie I think of as a team, even though Bruce wrote for the people's choice, the *San Francisco Chronicle*, and Bud was in his rookie season with the South Bay's *San Jose Mercury News*. They both tried to be hip and funny, succeeding easily in comparison with the rest of us. I think they both shopped at ACA Joe. And they seemed to have an awfully good time after hours, judging from the Dean Martin eyes and Don Johnson shadows of their mornings after.

Me, I was above that sort of thing that spring — the Miss Goody Two Shoes of the sports department. Appearances meant everything. It didn't matter to me who I was or even, unfortunately, what I knew; it mattered how I presented myself to all of these men I'd be working with nearly every day for the next eight months. I did not so much as want my toes to show through a pair of sandals. If I thought I looked a little too "butch," I was sure to put on some lipstick, just as I was certain to replace a skirt with pants if "party girl" might appear to be the message. I wanted to be seen as a sportswriter, yet I didn't want to make a "guy wannabe" impression. I remember carefully picking out a conservative (dull) trouser-blouse outfit for my first day at Phoenix Municipal Stadium, so that I would seem professional yet feminine — not, of course, too pretty to be a sportswriter.

(This dress-for-sportswriting-success drill would be a daily challenge for the next year or two. Not until I became confident in my ability to do the job and in the players' perception of my professionalism did I become comfortable in my own style of clothes. I knew I'd finally gotten there when, years later in a cramped Comiskey Park clubhouse, Jose Canseco looked at me and loudly announced, "Susan's wearing new lipstick," and I could laugh unselfconsciously. He was, by the way, correct. Estee Lauder Perfect Tulip, purchased daringly that afternoon on Michigan Avenue.)

All of the A's writers greeted me pleasantly. So did Jay Alves, the team's friendly public relations director, and Mickey Morabito, the team's shy travel director.

I had taken Mickey out to lunch when I went house-hunting in the Bay Area a few weeks earlier. He was nervous about having a woman (then one of only three in the major leagues) on the traveling beat, but proved to be a wonderful friend and an invaluable business associate. I don't know how I could have survived five years on the beat without his cooperation. Mickey was a generous man who would offer to let the writers send their luggage on his flights, even when the team traveled commercially, or set up our loved ones with complimentary tickets without hesitation. The players appreciated him so much that they voted to include him in their shares of postseason earnings beginning in 1988.

I had no understanding, though, of his huge role with the club — it was just dumb luck that he was the person I took to lunch. At that time, he later told me, he suspected that I had no clue about what I was getting into. He was right. My years at the *News American* and *USA Today* had cultivated my expertise in other sports, and I was probably well qualified for a full-time professional football beat. But I knew nearly as much about planting and raising cacti as I knew of covering and living the baseball life.

Fortunately, the players were friendly, too, and they tolerated my ignorance generously that spring. An outfielder, Michael Davis, survived an interview with me even though he was plainly irritated that I was pursuing the obvious angle of why a lousy 1984 season had followed a fine 1983 season for him. He had tired of being reminded that he had just plain sucked inexcusably, and I'm surprised he didn't just smash my tape recorder. But that's part of what spring training is all about, though — patience, tolerance, generosity, and all of those other good things that get put away on Opening Day.

On one March afternoon, I talked at length to the team's manager, Jackie Moore, who can only be described as a Nice Man. He made me feel welcome and comfortable — he just didn't have a lot of answers when I began asking him questions about his managerial and strategic philosophies. I think Jackie, who had ascended from third-base coaching to managing, really didn't have any of those philosophies at the time, and he wasn't any more ready to manage a baseball team than I was ready to cover one.

I managed to please my new editors, however, by writing to length and making deadline — two talents I had honed at *USA Today*. And I stretched my writing to fit the new parameters. Ken Picking had dismissed the writing style of *USA Today* thusly: "It's the only place I've ever worked where I'm writing stories that are shorter than my dick."

I usually tried to plan my stories so that the *Bee* copy desk would have time to find photos or compile charts to illustrate what I was writing. About once a week, I'd tell the editors what I had in mind for the next five or six days, and they'd occasionally ask for a specific feature or story.

One of my first lengthier assignments that spring was to do a Sunday story on Dave Kingman. Kingman was a much-traveled slugger who, conventional wisdom now had it, had finally found a home in Oakland. The New York Mets, the seventh team to acquire him in his 12-year career, had released him in the spring of 1984. He was a troublemaker, it was said, who struck out a lot and didn't want to know how to use a glove, and his reputed attitude explained his failure to remain with any one team for longer than three consecutive seasons.

He could hit home runs, however, and, as slender short-stop Ozzie Smith once told me, "There's no substitute for power in this game." Kingman had hit just 13 homers for the Mets in 1983, but merely the longshot possibility of him hitting 25 or 30 led the A's to sign him for the following season. He hit 35 homers for them in 1984 and won an assortment of awards, including comeback player of the year and designated hitter of the year. He had had one controversy during the season, but it was Kingman who was the victim: He had been inexplicably omitted from the American League All-Star team.

By then, he had charmed the local media into reporting that Kingman had either changed or he wasn't the same guy who had dumped a bucket of ice water over the head of Arlington Heights (Illinois) *Herald* sportswriter Don Friske just a couple of seasons earlier. Readers seem to like stories of reformed bad guys in their sports pages; they never like to hear that so-and-so is really a prick, because they're supposed to cough up 10 bucks to sit on a hard seat and cheer the guy for three hours. Jenkins, however, caught a clue in the off-season, when Kingman became embroiled in a contract dispute with the A's and called on the cool *Chronicle* writer to be his mouthpiece.

"He had me pick him up at the airport, because he had to go somewhere to do something about his boat," Jenkins said. "When I picked him up, he said, 'Let me drive so you can write.' And he got behind the wheel of my car and just went off, chewing his nails the whole time until he actually had blood on his hands."

Kingman was indeed a strange man, sort of Paul Bunyan-like. I pictured him as much more comfortable in the woods chopping trees than in the big leagues taking cuts. Kit Stier even christened him "The Woodsman," some time after Kingman had fallen out of favor.

That hadn't yet happened when I met Kingman in my first spring training. The A's signed him to come back again for the 1985 season, and I regularly encountered him in the dugout, where Kingman, all bat and no glove, spent most of his "work-out" time on the rare days when he bothered to venture out of the clubhouse. We had been small-talking pleasantly enough out-doors, so I comfortably told him about my assignment to write a Sunday feature on him. We agreed vaguely to meet later in the week.

Silly me — I actually believed he was going to initiate the interview at any moment.

"Later in the week" came and went, and finally it was just plain late. It was Friday morning, and I had a Friday afternoon deadline. So I went searching for him in the clubhouse, where he was talking to another reporter — a man. Kingman irritably told me to wait for him outside. I waited a long time and went in again. "I'll be right out," he said, glaring at me. Oh great, I thought miserably: This was going to be one terrific interview.

Finally, he did venture outside, onto the planks that serve as a red carpet to the clubhouse. And for the first 10 minutes, we talked exclusively about women in the locker room. He didn't like it, never had. He didn't think women belonged in the clubhouse. "A lady," he said, "should be a lady." And he said, over and over again, "Just don't come near me in the clubhouse."

I acknowledged his feelings and agreeably asked where he would like to do interviews, how we should manage the logistics in light of his discomfort. He merely repeated his mantra, "Just don't come near me in the clubhouse." I had that strange and disconcerting feeling of trying to communicate on a rational level with someone who is completely irrational. It was worse than maneuvering through Europe speaking only English: Kingman wasn't even trying to grasp my point. There was no common language here, no basis for understanding.

Finally, I surrendered and changed the subject to his boat and then to baseball. The conversation produced enough of Kingman to write my story. It was the last "conversation" we would ever have. Morabito and Moore, consulted by me and by my fellow beat writers who had heard of the problem, assured me that Kingman would be available when I needed to talk to him. But that never happened.

Oh, Kingman talked to me, all right — just not when I needed him to talk to me. One day in Anaheim, I got onto the team bus too late to take an empty seat. Kingman was sitting in front, where the writers usually sit, so I moved to sit next to him. "No way," he said. "You're not sitting here. Thunder thighs."

Another day in Seattle, I was walking down the street. He walked toward me. I opened my mouth to say, "Good morning," and he looked the other way before the words came out. I shut my mouth. I know he had plenty to say about me. I'd hear things from whichever writer served as his mouthpiece of the month. He'd choose someone — first Bruce Jenkins, then Glenn, later

Bud — to whom he could be chummy and tell his side of the story, but that was never me. I was the enemy.

It was in Seattle, on August 10 of that summer, that Kingman hit the 400th home run of his career. It was a newsworthy milestone. Every player who had hit 400 runs before him had been voted into the Hall of Fame after his retirement. His home run was the story of the night, and we all headed for the clubhouse to hear what he had to say about it. I may not have been happy for him, but I intended to conduct myself in a courteous, professional manner, and to write with enthusiasm of his accomplishment and career.

A group of perhaps 10 of us stood there in the entryway to the Seattle visitors' clubhouse. Kingman looked at me and said, "If she's here, I'm not talking."

"Can't we just be professionals for once?" I asked him.

"You stay and I'm leaving," he told me. "Don't ruin this for me."

I looked at the other reporters. I think one of them said, "Come on, Dave." The rest of them just looked at me, waiting for me to leave. Jay Alves, the team's public relations guy, stood by silently, looking at me apologetically but saying nothing.

Then I did a really stupid thing. I threw up my hands and left. Why? Basically because I already knew that Kingman couldn't stand me, but I didn't want the writers who sat beside me nightly to hate my guts as well. So I went back upstairs and wrote my story without any Kingman quotes. I think my paper pulled some off the newswires. My editors knew what had happened and didn't blame me for my failure. Another writer, Rick LaPlante of the *Peninsula Times Tribune*, offered me his quotes. He was the only sportswriter who was not an object of my wrath the next morning in the Seattle Kingdome, as I slammed my books around and let them know I thought they were a bunch of selfish pigs. Schwarz looked sympathetic, but I didn't care.

Stier said, "I thought you should have talked to him sooner to work all of this out." I replied that I had cooperated with Kingman and left him alone in the hope that, when it was really important, he would cooperate with me in return. Kit seemed more sympathetic then, but they all still seemed like assholes to me that morning and for some time after that. I like to think that if we did it all over again, I would have stayed in that group of writers and Kingman would have left, then we all would have written quoteless stories and gone out for a beer and a trash-Kingman session. I blew that one.

"That one, I don't know if I would have done any differently," Bud recently told me. "We all could have walked away, but I don't think that would have done anybody any good. We were squirming, but if you had stayed and he had refused to give any of us quotes, that would have been OK. I just don't think we realized it at the time. But then all of our stories would have said, 'Kingman refused to comment.' "

It would have spoiled Kingman's party. But I didn't let Kingman spoil my party. My editor, Stan Johnston, wasn't about to let that happen. He couldn't do anything to make Kingman talk to me the night of the 400th homer, and that was that. Jay did not succeed, either, in establishing any lines of communication with Kingman. So, after the season ended, Stan initiated meetings with the A's to try to reach some agreement on how Kingman would treat me in the future. For once, I had real support — not lip service — from my newspaper. In July of that first season on the baseball beat, I had endured an incident with the Boston Red Sox when I was right up against deadline.

I had to talk to Dwight Evans, the team's classy right fielder, and fast. He cooperated, but, behind me, players were screaming and throwing things at me. The screaming was so profane that the radio reporters next to me weren't able to use their tapes of Evans's comments about his victory-saving throw to home plate. "Knock it off, you guys," I finally said. I wanted to kick ass and take names, but I just didn't have the time to look behind me and see who was who.

Later, I saw the team's general manager, Lou Gorman, and I told him what happened. He seemed sincerely polite and kind, looking a bit like a beardless Santa Claus, but he said he didn't think there was much he could do about such behavior. That pissed Stan off more than anything. He wrote to Gorman:

> I do not and will not accept the boys-will-be-boys thinking . . . The action of your ballplayers was unprofessional at best . . . The *Bee* considers this a very serious matter. And if Susan is harassed by the Red Sox players again, we will take any steps necessary — beginning with a formal protest to the commissioner's office — to insure that she can do her job. I

think you *can* affect the behavior of these players. Thank you in advance for doing so . . .

Stan sent copies of the letter to the owner of the Red Sox and the commissioner of baseball. The Red Sox baseball writers got wind of the whole thing and — accomplished adversaries that they were — trashed the players in the Boston newspapers. Later that summer, at Fenway Park, several Red Sox players made a point of searching me out and apologizing. I, in turn, made a point of telling their writers what had transpired, so that they could make the players concerned look good. I never felt uncomfortable in that team's clubhouse again.

Buoyed by his success with the Red Sox, in the off-season after the 400th homer snub Stan made contact with A's officials regarding Kingman. We pretty much accepted that this one player in 25 would not be talking to me, and decided that I could do just fine without Dave Kingman's weird words. We did request that he not bother me any further.

The team's young president, Roy Eisenhardt, talked to me about the situation. He had married into the Haas family, which owned Levi's, and performed his team president stint in between dabbling in the computer world and becoming the director of San Francisco's Academy of Sciences museum. Roy was one of the fairest men I encountered in sports, and I believe he cared not only about discrimination but also about the appearance of discrimination. He said he had talked to Kingman about me, but, he said, he honestly did not think that anything had been resolved. I see in retrospect that this was a warning.

Roy asked me if I would please do him the favor of telephoning him if (or did he say "when") I had any more problems with Kingman. He wanted the chance to try to resolve the situation peacefully before my combative editors became involved. His concern impressed me so much that I said I would give him that chance.

Keeping that promise to Roy Eisenhardt ended Kingman's career, but not in the way you might think. I never managed to connect with Eisenhardt when I next had serious problems with Kingman, early in June of 1986.

Kingman had been an asshole that year to just about everyone, letting off sulphur stinkbombs in the clubhouse as the team slipped to 25-35 with its eighth straight loss on the night of

June 11. I had no intention of talking to him ever again: I was interviewing infielder Tony Phillips at the locker next to Kingman's. This was Cleveland, though, home of the most cramped and worst designed visitors' clubhouse in baseball, so Kingman's locker was practically on top of that of Phillips. I'm sure the poor working conditions and lack of privacy provoked the ensuing confrontation.

I don't remember what I asked Phillips, but Kingman interjected, "That's a stupid question." He might have been right, because it's not easy to invent a really good question to ask of a really bad team. But that wasn't the point I wanted to make.

"Notice I'm not asking *you*," I told him, turning back to Phillips.

"What kind of a question is that?" Kingman said, louder now.

"Just bug off, will you?" I said.

Phillips laughed about the incident later, with me and not at me, I thought. "You know what comes next after *bug* off," he said, eyes full of mischief.

I knew, but I was still trying to behave like a lady, sort of. I stormed into the manager's office and said to Jackie, "Get him off my back, will you? Just get him off my back." Jackie looked up at me wearily from behind his desk. He had problems, I knew. He thought he was about to be fired. I left.

Later, I learned from Bud Geracie that Kingman had approached him during that same visit to Cleveland (Bud had replaced Bruce Jenkins as Kingman's rotating media mouthpiece these days) to find out if he had "some dirt" on me, "something I can have fun with."

Said Bud, "I was incredulous. I had no idea where he was coming from, yet he persisted until I understood just what he was talking about. Then I went from incredulous to another level of incredulousness. I think I told him he was sick. And he laughed."

So, as I had promised, I tried to call Roy before enlisting the help of my editors. But the team's president was vacationing in Hawaii, far from any telephone. I explained to his secretary why I needed to talk to him, and he did return my call with a message on my answering machine, but we did not connect. Meanwhile, two days later in Oakland, I tried to talk to Sandy

Alderson, the team's general manager and Eisenhardt's second in command, about Kingman.

Alderson, a bespectacled, jean-clad attorney educated at Dartmouth College and Harvard Law School, is widely considered to be intelligent and fair. When Fay Vincent resigned his commissionership in 1992, some owners suggested that Sandy ought to be a candidate to replace him. But every time I hear someone talk about what a great guy Sandy Alderson is, I cannot help but remember our conversation that day. Sandy screamed at me in the hallway outside the team's clubhouse, "I don't give a shit about you and Dave Kingman!"

That, I decided, would be the last battle I would wage alone. The next time, my editors would get first call.

And that's where things stood two weeks later in Kansas City, on June 23, as the A's entered the second inning of their 15th consecutive road loss and a package arrived at the press box addressed to, "Sue Fornoff, Sac Bee."

It looked like a corsage box, and I quickly ran through my mental rolodex. I had good friends in Kansas City, but they were not likely to send me a corsage. I certainly had not met any romantic prospects the night before, and my boyfriend at the time was not the corsage-sending type. He once gave me a birdhouse for Christmas.

So I looked suspiciously at the other writers — among them on this night, my old *USA Today* buddy Ken Picking, plus our regulars, now including King Thompson of the *San Francisco Examiner* — and joked, "OK, what are you guys up to?" but they blinked back at me as innocently as a gang of sportswriters could look. That's not very innocent, though, and, naturally, I was still suspicious. So I opened the box slowly, then closed it quickly when I saw the tissue paper inside move.

"It's alive," I said to them.

Bud Geracie today swears I looked at him and said, "Did you send me this?"

I don't remember that. I was stunned, I think. I looked at Morabito, and we both knew, instantly, the identity of the sender. "It's his writing," Mickey said, recognizing the awkward printing on top of the lid and not even bothering to identify the name behind "his."

The Royals Stadium employee who had handed me the box — his name was Danny Goldsmith, and he was feeling guilty about his small role in this caper — quickly ascertained that the box had indeed come from Kingman, via a clubhouse kid, and that it contained a live rat, with a tag attached to its foot bearing more of that familiar printing.

The tag said, "My name is Sue."

And do you know what I said, once I realized what had happened and that it had happened in front of all of my colleagues in the middle of a baseball game? I said, "I've got him now. I've finally got him."

Of course, my stomach was churning and my heart pounding. But, even as I absorbed the nastiness of Kingman's message, I thought, "Finally, people will realize that this is wrong."

The words "I've got him now" were never reported, however, because my friendly colleagues were just beginning to realize that a gift-wrapped story had been delivered to them. Bruce Jenkins told the others, "I'm writing this." Because he wrote for the *Chronicle*, the most-read paper that traveled with the A's, the others began to agree that they, too, were going to have to write about me and the big guy that night. It would be fun for them, after covering all of those boring losses, but it would be touchy, too, because they had moved over to my side over the course of a long and depressing summer. Now they would have to move again, this time into the middle, and the transition from colleagues to interviewers-and-interviewee was not going to be an easy one.

They hashed this out among themselves and decided not to quote me until it was clear to me that that's what they intended to do. Meanwhile, I immediately called Stan. "You're not going to believe this one," I said. "You'd better sit down."

Stan was outraged. He instructed me on how to answer the questions of the other writers and refer them to him for official comment.

So I told them, "From day one, he asked me to stay away from him, and I've tried to do that. He's been so unbearable this year, I just want him to stay away from me." Then I gave them Stan's number and turned back to my scorebook to catch up on the inning or two I'd missed. Meanwhile, Stan told them the paper was prepared to file a sexual harassment suit against the A's if it did not get satisfaction from the team.

I was the only writer who actually covered the game — another loss — that night. The others were covering me and Kingman. Directly after the game, I went into the manager's office, where poor Jackie Moore tried weakly to defend his player. "He said it was supposed to be a joke," Jackie told the reporters, with me standing there awkwardly. "It was something that was let loose around the clubhouse and from there I don't know what happened." Jackie obviously did not think it was funny, though, and promised to look into the matter further.

I wasn't in the clubhouse very long that night — just long enough for Kingman to throw a tissue box in my direction while I was interviewing another player (on the other side of one of the largest visiting clubhouses in baseball), then holler, "Kleenex? Kleenex anyone? Anybody crying?" I was trying to interview the pitcher, Curt Young, but I heard Kingman saying, "Don't cry now. This is a men's clubhouse."

I didn't hear the rest of what he had to say to the other writers, but I read about it in the papers the next day.

Kingman told them: "I can see you're all coming at me with daggers in your eyes. I've always been a practical jokester. If you can't handle it as a practical joke, then you should not be in a major league clubhouse. If you can't take it, move out."

And he said about the rat, "I did have a lot of fun with it in the clubhouse. I just furthered the joke by sending it to a dear friend... I make a lot of jokes on other guys and I don't apologize. I do some bizarre things. She's a bizarre person."

Some of the other players were quoted, too. They seemed puzzled by the whole thing — apparently Kingman, who had let the rat run around in the clubhouse before the game, hadn't let them in on the "joke" before it was played. I'd like to think that's because somebody would have said, "Hey, Dave . . ."

Catcher Mickey Tettleton told Jenkins, "She's just doing her job, as far as I can tell. I don't think she's bugged anybody." And Carney Lansford said that although he and many other players do not care to deal with women in the clubhouse, "I've never paid her much attention, to tell you the truth." And one player who would not be named — I'm going to go out on a big, fat, solid limb and guess that he was Dusty Baker — told Bruce, "I don't know what the hell Dave Kingman is thinking about."

It was nice to hear that there was some support for me among the players, but the issue quickly became a matter of Us (the writers) against Them (the players). In the bar that night at the Adams Mark hotel, all of the writers and media people sat me down at a table and rehashed the whole thing. King Thompson, the writer at the *Examiner* who had recently replaced Bud as Kingman's designated media mouthpiece, said he felt guilty just listening to the guy. I had their support, which really touched me, considering that a year earlier I had felt like an alien.

The only time I got upset to the point of tears was when I realized that one player who had been a pretty good friend of mine (he, too, was from Baltimore) stood on the other side of the bar with Kingman and glared at me. It was as if the man had undergone a personality transplant — I think he'd even, coincidentally, gotten a haircut that day, which made the transformation appear even more extreme. His name was Moose Haas, and he was promptly renamed "Mooselini" by our media crew.

I also saw Jackie in the bar talking to Kingman; later he came across the room to visit with me so as not to appear to take sides. It was a weird setting that night, so warm on one side and so cold on the other at Quincy's, the bar, which fortunately stayed open until 3 a.m. I don't think we adjourned even then, congregating in somebody's room for another hour. When I finally went to my room, my phone rang.

It was Rick Langford, a veteran pitcher on the team and a chum of Kingman's. He was calling to tell me, "Baseball is a fraternity, a fraternity of men. And you will never understand that or be a part of that because you are a woman." Then he told me that Kingman knew he'd made a mistake, and more or less asked me not to punish him. To think they actually feared that I could! I told Langford it was all out of my hands now; it was between my bosses and Kingman's bosses.

I knew exactly where my bosses stood; I had yet to learn the official position of the A's. And Sandy Alderson, of all people, was on his way to Kansas City to present that position.

I awakened that morning at about 6 a.m., to a phone call from some radio guy who couldn't tell time but called me to be on his show. I told him I was sleeping and hung up. The calls kept coming, to a point where I asked the front desk to hold all of them and put a Do Not Disturb on my phone. Sometime that afternoon, the bellman dropped off a stack of messages. There must have been 30 of them. Suddenly, I wasn't writing the story anymore — I had become the story.

I didn't want to talk to anybody but my editors that day. They showed a lot of compassion for me, even suggesting that I might like to take the evening off. I thought that would be a copout. A letter immediately went out from our assistant managing editor in charge of sports, Jim Dawson, to A's president Roy Eisenhardt. He charged Kingman with sexual harassment and demanded that the A's take action immediately. And he hinted at a lawsuit in the event of another incident. Gregory Favre, the editor of the *Bee*, even went on television from the newsroom in Sacramento to take up for me.

I went to visit my friends in Kansas City, the ones I had known wouldn't send me a corsage in the press box, for the afternoon. When I arrived at the park near game time, Kingman was not in the lineup and everyone wanted to interview me. But Sandy was there, and he wanted to meet with me first in the dining room. I looked at him, thinking, "If only you had done something two weeks ago."

He knew. He said, somewhat begrudgingly it seemed to me, "I'm sorry about all of this." Then he told me the organization was not going to tolerate Kingman's behavior, and he outlined his proposal. It was this: Kingman would be fined $2,500 and he would apologize to me or else he would be suspended for the remainder of the season. I accepted the proposal immediately, knowing that Kingman would not apologize to me and therefore I would be rid of him and his pranks, probably for good.

When I returned to my seat in the press box, the other writers were dying — in their typical cool, sweatless manners, of course — to know what had transpired. I had agreed to keep the agreement off the record for the time being, so I sort of crossed my fingers and said, "It sounds good. Let's see if it really works out that way."

How naive of me to think that it might, to think that Kingman actually would be gone. Of course, it didn't work out that way and he wasn't going anywhere. During the game — a victory without Kingman, by God! — Alderson met with the prankster for 45 minutes. Kingman refused to apologize, and the terms were revised without any input from me. He'd be fined $3,500 — pennies from his $600,000 salary that year — and *released* "immediately without compensation if an incident of a similar nature occurred again," said the statement Alderson had ordered rewritten, retyped, and released that night to the scribes.

The A's statement included an apology and condemned Kingman's conduct as "not only a serious affront to Ms. Fornoff, but also to the dignity of baseball." I think I managed to react graciously, even though I didn't feel satisfied. The others, not knowing all of the details of the earlier agreement, thought I was disappointed because Kingman would not issue an apology like the statement distributed by the team. But I didn't want an apology from Kingman. I wanted nothing to do with him at all.

In truth, I was only disappointed because he was still going to be hanging around, calculating the chances that the team actually would let him go (while he was hitting a team-high 35 homers that season) if he played any more tricks on me. What constituted a "similar incident," after all? And how many witnesses would I need to have to make my case?

I was a little scared; on the road, there would be many opportunities for him to make me miserable, if he so wished, without a single person to see.

Of course I didn't say any of those things when the writers consulted me on the record. I had talked to Stan, and we agreed that the fine was just a slap on the wrist, but that if the organization really meant what it said then we could accept the terms. "If this discipline is to be taken at face value, he'll be without a team before we have to file (a lawsuit)," he said.

I told the writers, "Nothing they give me on paper could satisfy me. All I want is for the harassment to stop... I don't want him to talk to me, acknowledge me, or see me. I just want him to leave me alone."

That hadn't happened yet. Before the game, Kingman had asked Goldsmith if he could have the rat back in exchange for some cash. But Danny had taken the creature home to a five-year-old science nut in his neighborhood — it was mine to give, I figured, and I requested only that the boy, Matt Marble, name the rat Kong. Matt had become so attached to Kong in only one day that he wasn't going to sell his pet at any price. Besides, Danny still felt so badly about giving me the box in the first place. (He probably planned to personally inspect every future delivery to the Royals' Stadium.) His terse reply to Kingman's offer: "No way." This gave me some perverse pleasure.

And I was curious about what Kingman would tell the writers that night after the game. I was in the press box, having written a game story already, when the others, who had to write the Kingman story, came in from the elevator laughing loudly. They were making fun of Kit Stier.

It seems that Kingman had made them wait 45 minutes before he came out of the trainer's room, and then he didn't say a word as they asked their questions. Kit's face had turned Cincinnati red, and finally he said to Kingman, "You're not going to talk, are you, you big prick?"

I loved that moment, because Kit had given me such a hard time in spring training that I had walked out on a writers' dinner at the Pink Pony. He had been telling me I had to work harder if I wanted to be successful, and I had told him that I did not have to break every story in order to be successful. I had finally tired of listening to him pontificate over his Jack Daniels, so I had gotten up from the table and left — an unceremonious habit of mine that came to be known as "Houdini-ing." Later that night, Kit had phoned my room, and we came to the respectful understanding that his way of serving the readers of the *Oakland Tribune* was to try to break every single Oakland A's story and my way of serving the readers of the *Sacramento Bee* was to try to write lively, interesting stories. Now, I took it as a real sign of his affection and respect for me that he was calling Kingman a big prick.

Finally, we writers were beginning to laugh about the incident and do some bonding of our own. Maybe the rest of our media crew finally realized it wasn't so easy to be a woman baseball writer. There were more cocktails that night, more jokes. Again, the players stayed on their side of the bar. Again, my phone rang at all hours. But I felt supported by my peers — competitors though we were — for the first time in my sportswriting career. Or maybe it was the first time in my career that I welcomed such support, I don't know.

The us/them chasm with the players expanded, though. The air conditioned clubhouse felt like an icebox, and most players were not talking to the press at all. Kingman told me, "Stick with me, I'll make you a star." I said nothing.

I had, however, begun saying a thing or two publicly. And, ironically, I learned a lot that I think has helped me empathize with the athletes. I found out what it's like to have to answer the same questions over and over and over (aggravating!) and what it's like to have a stack of phone messages all of which you can't possibly return (you call the bigwigs and your friends and feel sorry for the rest). I found out what it's like to be portrayed in cartoons (yes, Tank McNamara and others forced me to laugh). I found out what it's like to read what people think of you (thank you, Bruce Jenkins, for writing that I "managed to balance femininity with a 'one of the guys' approach from the day she arrived" and you, Dave Newhouse, for describing me as "a nice person, rather on the quiet side, and a good writer"). And I discovered that reporters often make mistakes (no, the rat was not dead, and, no, I did not break down and cry when it arrived) that are never corrected.

I also learned that people wanted to believe that I somehow deserved what happened. One of the Kansas City writers, Randy Covitz, told people at his paper, "Well, what do you expect — she's always talking and laughing with the players," as if this were cause for such malicious behavior. It seemed that the public did not want to believe that Kingman had no gripe with me other than the simple fact that I am a woman.

In fact, I probably was charitable to him to an unprofessional extreme in my stories. With my editors and his employers knowing about our situation, I never wanted to write anything that would seem to be a cheap shot. He was an easy target due to the laziness and selfishness of his two-dimensional — home run or strikeout — game, but I did not pull my trigger. I remember an interviewer from National Public Radio asked me, "Was it something you wrote, something you did, that angered him this much?" and I replied, quietly, shaking my head into the phone, "No. Nothing." The man seemed amazed. He didn't speak for a moment — and that's rare in radio. He wasn't quite sure where to go from there.

I turned down other requests for interviews, though. Years later, I watched Lisa Olson on "Entertainment Tonight" and just about every other tabloid talk program, discussing the "Zeke Mowatt" incident, and I wondered if I had made a mistake. I guess I could have become better known through the exposure, maybe even made a few bucks. But I was compensated in other ways that saved me from having to leave the country as Olson did. I gained respect among my peers for shunning the spotlight and for just trying to do my job. I turned down "This Week in Baseball," which offered to go anywhere at any time to interview me. I couldn't accommodate any more requests, I told them: I was covering a manager who was about to get fired, and I would be busy reporting that story.

Yes, Jackie Moore got the ax while we were still in Kansas City. If this wasn't the longest four-game series in history, Dave Kingman wears negligees. (Maybe he does; maybe it *wasn't* really the longest four-game series in history.) It was Thursday, the last day of the trip, and I had gone shoe shopping. When I returned (empty handed for once), I learned that the other writers had been summoned to Jackie's suite for the announcement, made by Alderson with Moore present. This firer-firee co-conference was unusual in sports, but not surprising when it came to Jackie. That Nice-Man quality that hindered him as manager shined upon him as a fired manager.

I reported to his suite immediately to do my work, and he welcomed me warmly, walking across the empty room toward me as if to give me a hug before we both stopped awkwardly. Sportswriters and managers don't usually hug.

Jackie was all class. He refused to blame the team's long list of injuries for its failures, and he didn't mention Kingman or Ricky Peters. Peters was the pinch-runner who had forgotten the situation in the ninth inning the night before. The score was tied, 4-4, and Peters was on third and another runner on second with two out when Jose Canseco was walked. Peters, thinking the bases were loaded, started jogging home and was thrown out easily. Afterward, Moore paced that manager's office angrily. "A player does something like that and we look like idiots," he said. "Like a bunch of fucking idiots." Then he looked at me and apologized for his language. Always a gentleman.

On the day he was fired, Jackie even put on a suit and tie and went to the ballpark to say good-bye to the players before the game that night. Then he met with us in his office for one last interview session, and now I finally was crying, pulling toilet tissue out of the manager's bathroom. I thought perhaps I felt such profound heartbreak because of some sense of responsibility for his termination. Perhaps, I thought, if I'd handled Kingman in some other way, Jackie would not have seemed so lacking in control of his players and would instead have remained as manager. I felt better when I learned I wasn't alone in my tears — Bud said he'd broken down when he left Jackie earlier in the day.

Kingman wasn't talking, and neither were many of the other players. Even on the occasion of the dismissal of a manager they all liked (if not entirely respected), they were boycotting the media for its coverage of the rat incident. They felt that published reports had made it sound as if A's players did not support Kingman, which made it seem as if the A's were not a cohesive team. So what if all this was true — the leaders among the A's decided that it simply wouldn't do to allow the public this insight. Steve Ontiveros, Alfredo Griffin, Dusty Baker — today himself a manager with the San Francisco Giants — and Peters were among the few players to bust the boycott and voice their regret at Jackie's dismissal.

It was a sad night that ended with a flight home. The team was scheduled to play Chicago with postgame fireworks in the Oakland Coliseum the next evening.

I didn't cover that game. I went to lunch and to a museum with a woman sportswriter friend of mine, who had picked me up at the airport and offered me her ear. Meanwhile, at the ballpark that evening, Kingman had financed the distribution of "Rat Patrol" T-shirts among his teammates. Many of the players put them on, others stashed them in their lockers. And local reporters were canvassing the fans to hear what they thought — not of the firing of the team's manager but about the delivery of the rat.

Rob Knies of the *Oakland Tribune* included these quotes in his account:

"I think it's rude, crude, and socially unacceptable."

"He was just being a macho man. I thought it was a repulsive thing."

"I think it was funny myself. I think she made a big deal about it, but maybe she's bugged him."

"I think he should have some privacy in the locker room."

"Grow up. Realize that women are in the locker room these days."

But the one overriding sentiment of the fans was this: Keep the big guy around as long as he's still hitting home runs. I still believe that Kingman's ability to do this — remember those words of Ozzie Smith, that there's no substitute in this game for power — kept Kingman in uniform all that summer. He had hit 17 home runs before that June night when he sent me a gift. If he had hit just four or five, I think the club — perhaps hoping that, at 37, he'd outlived his baseball life — would have sent him packing. But, as Jenkins wrote so dryly, "Just hit those home runs, baby, and everything's fine."

I did spend some time, on that off day, skimming the pile of Bay Area clippings and newspapers that my boyfriend had collected for me. I was again amazed at the outraged reactions Kingman's gift produced among my colleagues. And I was surprised to see that all of the area columnists called for Kingman's dismissal, even at the team's expense of swallowing his substantial salary. One of them wrote that I should send Kingman a lawsuit as a thank-you note.

I had something else in mind, however. As I told Tony Kornheiser of the *Washington Post*, I didn't want to sue Kingman or punish him or hurt him in any way. I just wanted to outlast him. I had become enamored with the job of covering baseball, in spite of the last-place team and its designated hitter. I loved the cities we visited and the games we watched. I wanted to know what it would feel like to cover a team that wasn't so horrible. And I especially wanted to know what it would feel like to cover a team that didn't have a sportswriter stalker in its midst.

"Give me one year without Kingman," I thought. I promised myself to stick with it until he'd left for at least one season.

I thought the wait would be a lot longer than six months, though. Former Chicago White Sox manager Tony La Russa took over the team on July 7, and I worried about having to prove myself all over again to a new skipper who brought with him a reputation as a "players' manager." I also fretted on his views about Kingman.

At La Russa's first press conference, Sam Skinner, a veteran radio reporter, asked, "What will you do if one of your players sends a rat to a sportswriter?" I squirmed, La Russa hemmed and hawed, and Sam persevered, repeating the question verbatim. I squirmed some more. Finally, La Russa said he didn't know enough about the situation between me and Kingman to make a call like that one. This made me nervous. I felt that La Russa was among those who assumed I must have done something to deserve the presentation of a rat.

I didn't feel much better when, during my first hotel-bar conversation with the new manager, La Russa started talking about his family and asked me if I was an animal lover! I know now why he talked so much about animals — he and his wife are involved in all sorts of animal rights and rescue causes, and he probably was just making conversation about a favorite subject with a person that he didn't feel comfortable with . . . me. I did not feel so comfortable, though, when he told me about his daughter's new pet rat. For a moment I thought I was really in trouble with the new manager.

La Russa took charge, however. Unlike during Jackie's regime, there was no question of who had the authority. Tony threw some tantrums and dumped the food table, inspiring a healthy element of fear (not to mention hunger) among his employees. That's what the players now had become: employees.

We reporters were a little bit in awe, too. Tony noticed which of us showed up for workouts and when, and he rewarded a good question with an elaborate answer. We began showing up earlier, to be sure to touch base with La Russa daily. He loved to talk baseball, and I learned to love to listen to him. Many managers do not like to answer questions about strategy and decisions, because they interpret questions as criticism. Not Tony. He'd share the baseball part of his mind with such generosity that, if you bothered to pay attention to his answers for a few years, there weren't too many "Why did you . . ." questions that needed to be asked anymore.

I did not speak to him about Kingman, who was still playing every day, until August 24. We were in New York that weekend, and I had begun to feel that Kingman was up to something again. I could tell by now: He'd kind of sit in his corner of the clubhouse and brood, staring at me all the while as if he were Norman Bates plotting his next move in the shower. The other writers noticed this, too. No one seemed to know exactly what it was I should do — he hadn't, after all, *done* anything yet — but I was not going to ignore the signs this time. Besides, I liked the new manager and I did not want to see him put in the position that had led to Jackie Moore's dismissal. So, that morning at Yankee Stadium, I very nervously approached La Russa behind the batting cage.

I told La Russa that I was doing my best to stay away from Kingman, but that I could tell from the way he was looking at me that he was up to something. Tony looked at me curiously and directly. He asked me about what had happened before, and why it had happened. So I told him that there was absolutely nothing between me and Kingman except his dislike for women sportswriters. Tony said he'd been meaning to have a talk with Kingman about the rat incident, and now he certainly would.

Kingman never bothered me again. I asked Tony later what it was he'd said, and he told me he does not remember even having a conversation with Kingman. I think he must have, because Kingman would not have listened to anyone else.

Tony wanted Kingman on his roster again for the 1987 season, however. The A's had a young slugger in the lineup, Jose Canseco, who had won the 1986 Rookie of the Year award with 33 homers and 117 runs batted in, and Tony felt he needed another slugger in the lineup to protect Canseco. (This is baseball jargon: it would not be Kingman's role to act as bodyguard for Canseco, but to provide another big bat in the lineup so that opponents would not try to pitch around or walk Canseco.) I guess Kingman had been on his best behavior under the new manager: There was no discussion about what sort of poor example his work habits would set for an impressionable (albeit all-knowing) 22-year-old like Canseco.

At least, there was no such discussion publicly. But the Oakland A's organization did not back La Russa on this particular personnel decision. The club made no announcement on Kingman, merely letting his contract expire without making another offer by the December 6 deadline. There was no great public outcry or celebration.

OK, so I celebrated, but I waited until midnight in the hotel bar at the Fort Lauderdale winter meetings, when I was having a drink with my friend Ken Picking from *USA Today*. I ordered a glass of champagne and toasted the A's. I had outlasted my nemesis.

And I would have three years on the beat without him. OK, so we got stuck with Reggie Jackson in his designated-hitter spot for the 1987 season—another set of problems, to be sure, but problems for everyone and not just me. We survived.

The following winter, I ran into Jackie Moore at the winter meetings in Dallas. He was now coaching for Buck Rodgers in Montreal.

"Tell me something," Jackie asked, taking me aside. "How was it covering the team without Kingman around?"

I told him that it was wonderful not to have to look over my shoulder, and that I felt I'd done a better job than ever with Kingman gone. He just nodded and smiled at me. "I thought so," he said. What a gentleman.

This was not the case, of course, with everyone. Several A's players told me their team would have been much better in 1987 with Kingman in the lineup; they not only had Canseco now, they had discovered the subsequent rookie of the year, Mark McGwire, who was hitting 49 homers that season. Pitching coach Dave Duncan went so far as to tell me, "This team would have won the pennant with Dave Kingman in the lineup." We talked baseball all of the time, yet that was the only conversation I can recall that ended with Dunc saying, "I know baseball more than you do." No kidding. He could have shortened every one of our discussions with that truism.

Besides the fact that it hurt me to hear the hidden blame that accompanied these comments, I had a hard time believing Kingman would ever have helped the A's win a pennant — he had played for just one division champion in all of his 15 years. And it continued to amaze me that a player's ability to hit home runs would supersede all issues of character and sportsmanship. But I don't think this will ever change, particularly as winning becomes more and more valuable, financially, to baseball franchises.

Nevertheless, I do think some things have changed because of Dave Kingman's little present. As a result of USA Today's coverage of the incident, there was a lot of dialogue among athletes and sports insiders about the issue of women sportswriters covering male-dominated sports. I think this is healthy. Guys, not just women, were saying, "What a jerk!" And even if they didn't believe it, at least it had become the politically correct thing to say.

Mary Garber, who with 40 years of service is the dean of women sportswriters (Mary and I prefer the gender-neutral cliche "dean " to the more feminine one of "old bag"), wrote in one AWSM newsletter, "The best thing that has happened to women sportswriters in the last few years is Dave Kingman's present to Susan Fornoff... When that happened, the men on the beat reacted against Kingman and the ball club. They were angry because a fellow sportswriter had been put upon. They weren't upset because Kingman had done something mean to a girl. He had done something mean to a sportswriter. Susan had earned their respect."

The sportswriters and media people who traveled with the A's perhaps went off the deep end in my favor. Professional objectivity does not shine through the scrapbook of clippings I have kept from those days. But I think these men felt they had some dues to pay: When it became publicly known that I had been putting up with a whole lot of shit from Kingman for a year and a half and they knew it, readers wanted to know, "Why didn't any of this come out sooner?" Their rush to my defense served as their apology. Best of all, for my next birthday — February 4, 1987 — I received a Dave Kingman bat, compliments of Bud Geracie via A's visiting clubhouse man Steve Vucinich. I've kept it unmounted and unencased, just in case I cross paths with another sinister slugger.

My peers nationwide had gained insight about these idiotic manhood tests we women sportswriters must endure, and they seemed to feel it necessary to officially acknowledge their new enlightenment. In 1987, I was asked to serve on the Board of Directors of the Baseball Writers' Association of America. It was the first time a woman had served in this role, and, to the other writers, this was an honor. It wasn't a big deal to me, because it was strictly an advisory position, but I realized they were trying to say, "Women are welcome here." The sentiment, I appreciated. And they didn't even put me in charge of coffee and donut service at our national meetings.

But the Kingman incident had raised the locker room question again, and I didn't appreciate that so much. It was, to me, a dead issue. Teams were providing equal access to sportswriters of both genders and all races. Now they simply had to learn to live with this.

Every time an incident occurs with a woman sportswriter, people say, "Well, she doesn't belong there." Well, yes, she does. I grew very tired of talking about the Kingman rat incident with total strangers who, upon hearing my name, said, "Oh, so you're the one . . ." But I grew much less tolerant of discussing the locker room all over again.

I guess that makes me appear to be as closed-minded as Kingman, who also was intolerant of discussing the locker room. But the difference is clear to me. Kingman sent me a rat, and I did not, as Don Baylor suggested later I should have done, "punch him in the nose." I did not mutilate the rat and return it to him, as I suspected Kingman would have done in my situation. I went through the proper channels to obtain a satisfactory resolution. If he didn't think I belonged in the clubhouse, he ought to have discussed the matter with his employers and his players' union and his teammates to try to find an equitable solution to the question of access.

He never did that. He sent me a rat instead.

But his higher-ups would not have gone through proper channels, either, had Kingman not sent me a rat during a game in front of a rowful of sportswriters. I thought the incidents in Cleveland and Seattle were much more serious than the incident in Kansas City, because they directly interfered — on deadline — with my ability to do a good job. Yet it didn't matter so much to the A's organization that he refused to talk to me or interrupted my interviews, because these were private insults that the team did not feel compelled to punish. Kingman could have called me names every day all year, yet I believe if I had complained I would have been considered to be whining. The A's took the "proper" stance on the rat incident because they had to. I will never forget Sandy Alderson's words, just 10 days earlier, in the Coliseum hallway: "I don't give a shit about you and Dave Kingman!" That I believed, more than any little fine or lengthy apology that came later.

The A's did give a shit about their public image, though, and that's why they did not offer Dave Kingman a contract for the 1987 season.

No one else signed him, either. Hard to believe there was no team desperate for a man, however troubled he was, capable of hitting 30-some homers and producing 90-some runs batted in. But I'm glad our paths have never crossed again.

Once, at spring training, I had a drink in the hotel bar before dinner and returned after dinner, only to hear that he'd been there while I was gone. Nice timing.

And a friend of mine who works for the San Francisco Giants played blonde bimbo at their annual alumni golf tournament (that was another of Kingman's former teams) just so that she could have her picture taken with Kingman and present it to me, her friend "The Rat Lady." He had no clue of her true mission, not even when she asked for an autograph made out to Susan.

"Who's Susan?" Kingman asked her.

"Uh, me," Robin Carr answered cheerfully.

"But your nametag says, 'Robin,'" Kingman observed.

"No, Susan," she said.

He signed. But I've heard he still turns down interview requests — these days at alumni appearances with his many former teams.

I'd like to gloat just a little bit more, except that I keep thinking of one Scott Sanderson, most recently of the New York Yankees. He's a pitcher, a good one, who maintains a public posture of not talking to women reporters in the clubhouse.

"It's nothing personal," he will say.

"He's very nice about it," his club's officials will say.

They just don't get it. There is everything personal and nothing nice about hindering the job of a professional because she happens to be a woman.

Kong the rat died of natural causes (old age) in January 1988. He was laid to rest in an oatmeal box in Matthew Marble's backyard. But the spirit of Dave Kingman's gift to me survives.

# 7

# Lady and Gentlemen

"Lady and gentlemen." That's how one flight attendant began her plea for attention on another of those wee-hour Oakland A's team charters. I was the lady she was talking to. Sometimes the TV crew might include a woman graphics expert. Often, though, I was the only woman on the plane besides the flight crew.

Of course, the usually pretty, always perky flight attendants acted envious. They'd say, "Wow, it must be really great to be the only woman traveling with all of these men." Sometimes, they'd add the obvious adjectives. Gorgeous . . . young . . . rich . . . athletic . . . men.

Yeah. Great.

NOT! The baseball life, half of which is lived on the road, is a lonely one.

And, for a woman, traveling with a major-league baseball team is like taking a field trip with an all-boys' high school that has been furnished with three kegs of beer and an unlimited supply of liquor miniatures. It's another locker room — only, now, alcohol and vulgarity are flowing freely.

"Why do guys act that way?" Claire Smith of the *New York Times* once asked me. "Women never act that way. These guys are saying something about every woman they see out of the bus window. They will say the most hideous things . . . about anybody!"

But you're not a real baseball writer until you've traveled with a team. Often, players who have come to accept women in their clubhouses cringe when they see women board their planes. Hazing is inevitable, as Claire remembers from her first trip in spring training with Billy Martin's Yankees.

"We were going (from Fort Lauderdale) to Tampa, and I asked the other writers, 'How do you get there?'" Claire recalls. "They said, 'Well, usually we take the bus.' So I got to the yard to get on the team bus and found out that the other writers had found other ways to go, flying or driving, and I was the only one on the bus. This obviously made the PR guy very nervous.

"I get on the first bus, and six coaches and Billy jump up, en masse, and say, 'Oh, no, no, you're not on this bus. You can't be on this bus. You're on the other bus.' So I slither off the bus, and I see Billy airing out the PR guy in the parking lot. I'm sitting on the other bus contemplating whether I really want to do this anymore — and I'm only three weeks into spring training! — when I get a tap on my shoulder.

"It was (bullpen coach) Jeff Torborg, asking me if I wanted something to eat. I told him no, I didn't want anything, and I sulked, looking out the window. Then he handed me this sandwich tray and said, 'Here, you have to eat. It's really OK.' And it was OK."

It was a long bus ride, though, which was unusual for any major league team. I had traveled that way with the Baltimore Blast soccer team in the early '80s, but the Oakland A's took me on the road in style. During the season, we stayed at the newest in-town hotels, usually near the swankiest shopping. Our luggage might have been carried from city to city by hotel bellmen, for all we knew. The team buses — players could choose between Mickey Morabito's lead bus or the quieter media bus that trailed — took us from hotel to ballpark, ballpark to airport. There, they drove onto the tarmac up to the steps of the team charter, where we would be served food and drink in spacious quarters until we arrived at the next bus and the next hotel. Onto the doorknobs went the "Do not disturb" signs, usually until noon that day.

Because the team usually departed one hour after the final game in a city, most of the time we writers had to do our own flying, commercially, on mornings after or days of games. Then we'd be cramped into coach and running late. The team paid travel director Morabito well to ensure that the delays that plague most business travelers simply did not exist for the ballplayers. However, this did not stop them from whining about such details as slow elevators or crowded lobbies — they had so few big reasons to complain.

The only times I really felt fortunate about traveling with the A's followed the annual AWSM events that often left me muttering, "Ugh, women!" Three days with 70 women often made me feel grateful to resume my eight months with 40 men. Much of the time, though, I wished I could have taken AWSM on the road with me. It was such a lonely life, so lonely that I could not have been adequately warned.

And I had been given clues. Jane Gross once wrote of covering the New York Yankees in the early 1980s, "I can remember a trip, when I first started out, when I called room service for my meals 19 days straight." Eventually, she grew used to dining in restaurants alone. Dan Shaughnessy wrote an article about his first season on the baseball beat. "Running on empty," he described the final days.

But I could have found the greatest clues of all if only I had read between the lines of the letters from the first baseball player I befriended. I should have paid closer attention to what Larry Sheets was telling me back in 1980 about the lifestyle that is baseball, when he tried to explain why he kept leaving.

Sheets was a 6-foot-4-inch, left-handed pile of muscle who could hit a baseball a long way in Bluefield, West Virginia, nature's air-conditioned city that was home to the lowest level (Rookie League) minor-league team of the Baltimore Orioles. Sheets had led the league in homers and runs batted in in 1978, then "retired" for a year. A parade of Oriole officials visited his home in Staunton, Virginia, to try to lure him back to ball. Nobody seemed to fathom why a talented teenager wouldn't want to hop the next bus for stardom. They even sent him to a psychiatrist, knowing there simply had to be something wrong with him.

But there was nothing wrong with him.

I witnessed some of Sheets's 1980 comeback when I went to Bluefield to do a story for the *News American*. One night while I was there, I went to a nightclub with a group of players. I found Larry to be an intelligent and sensitive person, who walked me to my room and promised to write.

The letters he sent testified to his enthusiasm for the game and his desire to play it well. They gave me my first encounter with an excuse I would hear so often, it became a cliche: "I am hitting the ball hard right at people." They also spoke of a lifestyle he disdained, mainly because he did not drink alcohol.

"I really did have a hard time adjusting to the atmosphere of drinking, everyone cursing all the time and so forth," he wrote. "But probably the main thing was being separated from my parents all the time. I just had to do some growing up. In Florida (instructional league), every night people went out to get bombed to escape from their problems. I had no real way to escape from them, so they just ate at me for two months, and it really hurt me."

That summer, again, Larry led the league in homers. Again, though, he "retired" for the next year to study at Eastern Mennonite College. This time, *Sports Illustrated* came calling for elaboration.

"You're supposed to be an adult so soon," he told them. "In college, people go home on weekends, but you don't do that playing baseball. Always being on the go, being gone six to nine months of the year, that bothers me more than anything. You're 18 years old, but you're supposed to be 23 or something."

Sheets was 21 that summer, 1981. The next year, joking "I only play in even years," he reported to Hagerstown to begin an uninterrupted professional career that would lead to six full seasons in the major leagues. It was a good career, one that provided well for his wife and daughter, though not a great career that etched his name into any record books. And Larry will always wonder how much better he might have been, had he stuck with the program.

But sticking with the program meant learning to live with such loneliness, whether for six weeks in spring training, every 10-day trip of the season or three weeks in the post-season. There was little choice, whether you were 18 or 28 or 38, whether you were male or female, whether you were married or single.

If you had friends in a city, they probably were working during the day, when you were usually free. If you brought along your own friend — "imports," we of the A's called these opposite-sex companions who jetted in from some other town — then you had to worry about yet another person's loneliness. In 1988, a wonderful man I was dating came to Cleveland, our most boring destination on the circuit, to see me one weekend. As much as I liked him, I could never forget about work and enjoy his company. And I was ashamed to realize that I actually missed hanging out in the bar with my fellow road warriors.

After he'd gone home, Jim Lefebvre, the energetic and effervescent third-base coach of the A's, noticed my glum face. "What's wrong?" Frenchy asked.

I told him I'd failed in the import business, that I felt I hadn't been attentive enough to my guest. "Oh, imports are overrated," Frenchy said. "We've all got our little routines on the road, and most of the guys don't really like the interruptions, either."

"I feel the same way when my wife comes to town," said one of the TV guys nearby. "And I love my wife."

Most families have conversations like these in their living rooms. Not the baseball family. There were the late nights of work — hours longer for the writers than for the players — when the only place remotely safe enough for a woman to walk into alone at 1 a.m., and probably the only place still open when we finished working, was the hotel bar. So the bar became our version of the family living room. It was at its most crowded whenever the team found itself on an especially hot tear and felt closer than ever — the 14-game winning streak that moved the A's to the division championship in 1988 comes to mind — or was mired in a horrible slump and was trying to manufacture togetherness.

Many of us drank more than we should have, just because there was nothing else to do. Sheets was one of the lucky ones, because he never got started. Two of the A's, Bob Welch and Dennis Eckersley, spoke openly about their drinking problems. Neither man became an alcoholic simply because of baseball, but the lifestyle seemed to conspire with the tendencies they brought to it.

"There's a lot of free time, but there's free time in anything," Eckersley said. "It's the late nights and the boredom. It's like the swing shift — if there's anything about baseball (that encourages alcoholism), it's the time."

Combine those late-night hours with constant travel, and it's no wonder that fidelity seemed to be an exception rather than a rule. Allison Gordon, who covered the Toronto Blue Jays for five seasons beginning in 1979, wrote in her book, *Foul Ball*, of being propositioned by a player who told her he'd been offered $500 by his teammates to bed Allison — with witnesses. The guy was not only sleazy, he was stingy: He offered Gordon $200 — not even half! — if she would cooperate.

Nothing that obnoxious ever happened to me. It was more likely that somebody was fined for his contact with me. The A's would hold kangaroo courts where they'd dish out stupid fines for stupid offenses. I could see them all nodding judgmentally when I danced with Dave Stewart one night. I think it cost him 25 or 50 bucks. That was OK, Stew was making a million and could pay the price. And he's a good dancer.

Pitching coach Dave Duncan had to be more careful. He got fined in spring training just for talking to me. It was 1 a.m. and we were sitting by the hotel pool. Just talking. Oops. He couldn't afford to pay the price on a coach's salary. I guess it was free to talk to me as long as we stayed in the bar.

I remember the first time I visited the hotel bar when I began covering the A's in 1986. I had filed my story and called my boyfriend; now I wanted a glass of wine. There were so many team faces in that Hyatt bar, I almost turned around and walked out — I was still feeling awkward on the team bus, where I already had made the mistake of sitting in the front row of seats. If I couldn't do the bus thing right, how could I handle the bar?

But a pitcher spotted me and bought me a drink. I mingled, but it was not comfortable — especially when I went to my room after last call and the phone began ringing. I made a momentous decision: I did not answer the phone. I simply watched it until it stopped ringing.

The message light never blinked on, so I figured that some poor fellow's luck had run out at last call and he'd decided to try my number. If I didn't take a late-night phone call that I didn't want, no one had to be embarrassed to look me in the eye the next day. If the caller was on the up-and-up, he would leave a message.

It was a good policy, I thought. Sometimes one of the writers would call me late at night, get no answer, and ask, "Where WERE you?" the next morning. Then, I had to explain. And sometimes I'd be expecting a call, pick up the phone, and hear the wrong voice on the other end. Mostly, though, I avoided the invitations to trouble. One scary experience was enough for me.

We were staying at the Pontchartrain Hotel in Detroit for a 1985 series against the Tigers. The Pontchartrain was remodelling its public areas, so it had cloaked some long metal tables in a penthouse banquet room to accommodate its would-be bar patrons . . . us. It was such a sterile setup that I almost took my glass of wine to my room, but some players invited me to join them.

One of them was a backup catcher, Mickey Tettleton, who was frustrated with the A's organization and catered to my eager ear. The bar closed, and Mickey suggested we move the conversation to his room. He just wanted to talk, he said. "Yeah, right," I replied, laughing. But he convinced me that he was happily married and wouldn't bother me. He hinted he had more to tell me about his teammates and coaching staff.

I bit. I invited him to MY room.

Mickey was shy and polite, with a wry, self-deprecating sense of humor. I didn't know, then, that his teammates had nicknamed him "Drac" for the transformation his personality underwent when he drank. And he put away several more beers there in my room.

Soon, I felt uneasy. It began to dawn on me that the man was bigger and stronger than I was, and here I had placed myself in what can only be described as a compromising position — hotel room, early morning hours, man, woman, alcohol. After he offered to "crack my back," I finally pushed him gently out the door, and the next day he apologized for making me uncomfortable.

I never told his superiors or mine what had or hadn't happened that night in Detroit, and I think Mickey appreciated that. He cleaned up his act when he left the A's, taking control of his drinking and becoming a power-hitting first-string catcher with Baltimore and then with Detroit. Knowing him better now, I feel that I wasn't in any physical danger that night at the Pontchartrain.

But I thought about that night years later, when men said of the victim in the Mike Tyson rape case, "What was she doing in his room, anyway?" In college, men would come to our rooms to study or to watch TV or to drink. We didn't have to worry that they expected something more. But, in the real world, we have to assume the worst.

And in the real world, we sometimes don't learn from our mistakes. The following winter, I interviewed Golden State Warriors rookie Chris Mullin for a feature story. He's from New York, and we talked about missing our families and friends in the East. He was living in my neighborhood in California, so I gave him my phone number and said, "Let's go have a beer sometime." He called me, but I do not think he had beer on his mind. He called me at seven one morning, at first asking if I'd meet him for breakfast and then suggesting I come over to his house and give him a massage. I declined.

Mullin later sought treatment for alcohol abuse, which may have explained his behavior. But I finally stopped taking chances like that with *anyone* I did not know well. Instead, I found friends. Over the years, I delighted in the company of writers like Kit Stier, David Bush, John Hickey, Bruce Jenkins, and Bud Geracie. There's no better accomplice in the drinking of mai-tais at Trader Vic's than Mickey Morabito. A's coaches, especially Dave Duncan and Jim Lefebvre, provided safe haven and even bought drinks once in a while. (Just kidding, guys: I'm sure I owe you a few.)

At first, though, I felt most comfortable with players. I was 27 when I started covering the A's, and I'm sure they felt at ease talking to women my age. The writers still disdained me, perhaps because they thought I didn't really know what I was doing — far be it for them to help — or perhaps they thought I wanted to marry a player. The more I learned, and the more I talked about my boyfriend, the clearer it became that I was as they were, simply lonely.

Some players welcomed me from the beginning. I owe a great debt to Dwayne Murphy, the A's centerfielder and team captain in those early years. I can still see him presiding over his corner of the clubhouse, cigarette in one hand, coffee in the other, allotting even the worst of questions far more deliberation and thought than they deserved. The team was awful, but Murphy could always find some subject or issue worthy of lengthy, humorous discourse. And he'd always ask how you were doing. We'd send each other margaritas from opposite ends of the bar and compare hangovers the next day.

He was friendly and respectful to me. And, as team captain, his was an example to be followed by his teammates. I always thought that if he had been in the clubhouse in Kansas City in 1986 and not at home with a knee injury, Dave Kingman might not have shipped that rat from the clubhouse to the pressbox. Murphy said he would have wimped out when it came to player vs. media, but that was hindsight. I think it might not ever have come to that with his presence. One spring, he even let me tag along with him to the dog track, where other players, too, started to treat me as if I didn't have cooties after all.

It won't surprise women sportswriters to learn that Murphy is an African-American. Black athletes tend to know what prejudice feels like. They know what it's like to qualify for insider status yet be stuck on the outside looking in. I think this is why women have felt accepted covering the NBA, where most of the players are black. Ronnie Lott of the 49ers told AWSM that black athletes are on our side because they "know what it's like to walk into a room and be instantly hated." They empathized with us. And sometimes, they rescued us.

Dave Kingman still belonged to the New York Mets in the early 1980s, when Helene Elliott was dispatched to Shea Stadium for some pre-game work. She had heard enough about Kingman to know that she ought to stay out of his way, so, she said, "I stayed as far away as I could." She soon learned, as I would, that staying away wasn't enough. Kingman decided to follow her as she conducted her interviews. He'd interrupt, he'd gesture, he'd yell loudly so she couldn't hear the answers to her questions.

"Finally, I went to the manager, Frank Howard, and I said, 'This is not fair. I'm not bothering him, yet he is going out of his way to provoke me and annoy me,'" Elliott said. Howard spoke to his players immediately, ordering "them" to treat Elliott professionally. The next day, Hubie Brooks called Helene over to his locker.

"Why didn't you come and tell me what was going on?" he said. "I'd have kicked his ass." Then Darryl Strawberry came over.

"Don't you worry about him," Strawberry said. "Don't you pay any attention to him. None of us do."

Brooks and Strawberry are black men. So is Dave Winfield, who stood up for Jane Gross when Jane, a Yankee beat writer in the early 1980s, had been harassed in the Cleveland Indian clubhouse. Winfield ordered her to go back in there the next day, scream profanity, and overturn the food table — then send him the bill! That wasn't Jane's style, but she appreciated the sentiment behind the suggestion.

Suzyn Waldman, who covers the New York Yankees for WFAN radio, told Ira Berkow of the *New York Times* about an encounter with the Toronto Blue Jays. George Bell, the bad-ass outfielder for the Blue Jays by way of the Dominican Republic, was talking to a group of men when Waldman approached. Bell cut off his interview and started screaming obscenities at Suzyn.

"It seemed like the entire clubhouse went silent," Waldman told Berkow. "I knew I had to leave, and didn't want anyone to see me break down. I started to go for the door — the room was still dead quiet — when I heard someone call out. It was Jesse Barfield."

Barfield said, "Hey, Suzyn. I went three for four today. Don't you want to talk to me?"

Waldman did not know Barfield, but she took her tape recorder to his locker for an interview. Later, she was told that he had turned to someone during Bell's tirade and asked her name.

Barfield is a black man.

So is my hero with the A's, Dave Stewart. Nobody calls him Dave and nobody calls him Stewart. He is David to family and women, Stew to teammates and buddies. I never knew what the hell to call him and usually alternated between Dave over lunch, Stew in the clubhouse, and David in an argument.

We met in May of 1986, just a few weeks before Kingman sent me the rat. He was a frightening-looking man, so muscular and dark, with an intense look in his eyes that — along with his past — scared me from interviewing him until I absolutely had to.

About that past: All we in the Oakland media knew of Stewart was that he had compiled mediocre stats as a relief pitcher and had been arrested two years earlier on a misdemeanor sex charge in Los Angeles that involved a male transvestite prostitute. So we expected a poor-pitching pervert.

Ooh, I was nervous. Then he opened his mouth to speak, and this comically high, shrieky voice rang out. And then he said something funny, and his face relaxed into this beaming, mischievous grin. This was no one to fear, unless you were standing at the plate awaiting his fastball.

*The Colts were still in Baltimore and the News American was still in business when quarterback Bert Jones sat next to me on the press couch to clown for this candid shot. My boss didn't like this too much. (photo by Gene Boyars)*

*This photo of me with A's manager Jackie Moore, one of the game's all-time good guys, was taken in Baltimore in 1986. (photo by Janice E. Rettaliata)*

*ruce Jenkins left the 's beat after the 1986 ll-Star break, so we rew a little party for m on this night in oronto, just a few eeks after Klingman d sent me the rat. es, that is shaving eam on Kit Stier's face eft to right: Kit Stier, ruce Jenkins, Bud eracie, and King hompson).*

Mark McGwire was the first player who posed for my farewell tour photo album in spring training of 1989. We had just finished a cordial interview, and I wanted a picture of his ever-expanding biceps. He was embarrassed.

Dave Parker was great fun in his two seasons with the A's, and I always thought he had one of the greatest smiles I'd ever seen. This was a spring training interview.

Jose Canseco
spent a lot of time
in the dugout
during the spring
of 1989. He'd sit
there every day
shaving the
handles of his
bats.

Here's me with Ken
Picking just before
Opening Night of
1989. He's the USA
Today writer who told
me in 1985 I'd have a
good time covering the
Oakland A's. Ken was
there the night
Kingman sent the rat,
and he wrote about it.

Jon Miller, who does ESPN baseball and Orioles radio, knew I was from
Baltimore, so he'd always put me on the air during a rain delay or
pregame show so that I'd get a gift certificate for a restaurant. Then, at
Christmas, I'd take my best friend Debbie out to dinner with the prize.

*Tony La Russa looked so good in this tuxedo at a banquet in Chicago that I had to get my picture taken with him in the hotel bar afterward. Pitching coach Dave Duncan took the photo.*

*Somehow it seemed we always saw the longest games in Chicago's old Comiskey Park. On this particular night, I was abandoning all hope of surviving a rain delay in time to have some fun on the town.*

*Here are two of the co-founders of the Association for Women in Sports Media pow-wowing during the Baltimore convention of 1989. That's Kristin Huckshorn of the* San Jose Mercury News *on the right, Michele Himmelberg of the* Orange County Register *on the left.*

*I rushed from a shopping spree at Filene's Basement to meet Dave Stewart for lunch at Turner Fisheries in Boston. I love this photo, because it's the side of him opposing hitters never see.*

*We were in Cleveland when Dennis Eckersley posed for my camera. I think he's the best-looking player in baseball, but this photo doesn't do him justice.*

Women friends are always asking me for a copy of this picture, taken in the lobby of the Hyatt Hotel in Minneapolis on my last regular-season trip as an A's beat writer. That's Storm Davis and Bob Welch to my left, then Dave Stewart and Dennis Eckersley. A fifth pitcher, Jim Corsi, was behind the camera. Aren't they well-dressed?

On September 29, 1989, the A's clinched their second consecutive division championship. Of course, they had to get me soaked in a spray of sparkling wine and beer downstairs before I could finish my story upstairs.

Here I am at the playoffs in Toronto with one of my favorites, A's pitcher Gene Nelson. "Geno" is the player to whom I accidentally said, "You're not very hung, are you?"

Claire Smith of the New York Times *must be the nicest sportswriter I have ever met, and she was the person I was looking for after the big earthquake shook Candlestick Park. Here we are at that 1989 World Series.*

*The night before the A's visited George Bush at the White House in November 1989, I whisked Kit (left) and Mickey (center) off to Filamena's in Georgetown. We emptied some plates—and some bottles.*

*Giants manager Roger Craig always made room on the bench for women writers. Here he is with Jackie Krentzman (left) of the* Santa Rosa Press Democrat, *me, and Robin Carr Locke of the Giants in 1991.*

*Dave Kingman played in the Giants' alumni golf tournament in 1991, and Robin Carr Locke pretended to be a bimbo so that he'd pose for this picture with her. He didn't know the photo would be presented to me later. Thanks, Robin.*

*The Bay Area chapter of the National Baseball Writers Association instituted a Bay Area Player of the Year award after the 1991 season. Will Clark was our first winner, and I got to make the presentation at Candlestick Park because I was chapter chairperson that year.*

Still, Stew kept a low profile for a while. He had thought his career had ended when the Philadelphia Phillies released him May 8. Nobody signed him until the A's took a look at him on May 23. He was a native of Oakland. They were desperate for pitching. So he signed a minor-league contract and went to Triple A Tacoma for six days, rejoining the slumping A's on May 29.

I do not remember talking to Stewart much during his first month with the team. But I will never forget the day I realized what a special person he is. We had returned home to Oakland after the trip that ended in Kansas City with Dave Kingman sending me the rat and manager Jackie Moore getting fired. And, one day, in the Oakland clubhouse, Stewart said to me from a few cubicles away, "Hey, I'm really sorry about what happened to you in Kansas City."

He was talking loudly enough for any of his teammates in the room to hear. And he looked serious. He went on, "I was new around here, so I didn't really know what was going on. But that wasn't right. I'm sorry."

I managed to say, "Thank you," and nod at him. But my eyes were filling with tears, and I turned away. I could not believe that a player, a teammate of Kingman's, was taking my side in front of the rest of his team of one month.

Dave told me later that he would have spoken sooner, except that he had been unaware of Kingman's intent with the rat until he came home and read the newspaper accounts establishing Kingman as instigator and me as victim. I'm sure his mother, Nathalie, said a word or two to him about it as well. She had raised her son to stand up for what he believed to be right and against what he believed to be wrong. And to mistreat a human being because the human being is a woman or black or Asian or fat or ugly would not sit right with the Family Stewart, David's brother and six sisters.

Speaking up did not hurt Stewart's career. When Tony La Russa became manager July 7 in Boston, he asked Stewart to take the mound for his managerial debut. It was Stew vs. Roger Clemens, a matchup that would become a dynamic duel for the next few years. And Stew won the first, as he would win the most.

In 1987, Stewart started a four-year string of 20-victory seasons. We became friendly that summer, with a lunch here or a dance there. He turned me on to his favorite restaurant in the East Bay, Skates by the Bay, and one night we ran into each other there in the bar. He had some friends with him and I was meeting Kristin Huckshorn, my sportswriter buddy at the *San Jose Mercury News*. When the hostess called Kristin and me to dinner, we invited Stew and his friends to join us, but they had other plans.

"Why don't I just send over a bottle of wine?" he said. "What do you like?"

I waved at him as if to say, "Thanks but no thanks."

"Anyway," I joked, "we only drink Dom Perignon."

Kristin and I went to our table and, as usual, stuffed our faces right down to the chocolate whiskey cake. During dessert, the waitress came over.

"Your friend David sent this over for you," she said. It was a bottle of Dom Perignon!

We were thrilled, and we asked if he could come and help us drink it. The waitress said he'd left already. So we decided to save it for another time when he'd be able to join us, and we asked for the check.

"There isn't one," she said.

"No, the dinner check," we explained.

"He took care of it," she said. "The *whole* thing." He'd bought our entire dinner and even tipped the waitress well, she indicated.

Kristin was stunned. "What's with this guy?" she said. "What's his motive? What does he want? Is he after you?"

"Nope," I said, smiling and shaking my head. "He's just a nice guy. That's all."

And that's the truth. I asked him about it later — we sent flowers to his hotel room in Minneapolis to thank him — and he told me he liked to surprise people that way. And this was before the day he had more money than he knew what to do with — he was "only" making $500,000 that season.

Stew is 15 days short of a year older than me, and he was, I always thought, single by divorce. He'd talk to me about his latest girlfriend and I'd tell him about my love life. We built a brother-sister relationship that always had a little bit of chemistry.

The amazing thing about Stewart was that he did not care what anybody thought about our friendship. He never pretended we weren't friends, and he was completely unself-conscious about meeting me publicly. I guess it didn't matter that teammates thought there was something more between us when we knew there wasn't.

I was more protective of our relationship than he was. When the A's swapped some players for Dodger pitcher Bob Welch in December of 1987, Welch came to town for a press conference on a day Stew and I planned to have dinner. Stew invited Welch and Kathy Jacobson of the A's to join us.

"Are you sure this is OK?" I said to Stew. "I mean, I don't know this guy. Will he feel comfortable with a sportswriter around? Will you? Will he have a lousy time because I'm there? Will you?"

Stew assured me I had nothing to worry about, and he was absolutely right. Welch is one of the least judgmental men I've ever met. We ended up at the Hot Rod Cafe that night in Alameda after Kathy had gone home, and I danced with Welch to the rock numbers and Stew to the funk numbers. (They liked each other OK, just not each other's musical taste.)

Dancing with the pitchers went against all of the AWSM ethics guidelines. But, professionally speaking, it was a good thing for me to have done. Welch was so uncomfortable in that first season with the A's, few in the media could get past the mini-syllable answers he'd spit out with his huge hunk of postgame chewing tobacco. But I had glimpsed the lively personality behind the chew, and I refused to settle for his evasive answers. It got so that the rest of the writers would let me ask him all of the questions.

They probably thought I got answers because I'm female, but I think I got answers because I had gotten to know Welch personally and he had gotten to know me. Lots of editors and writers think that the people we cover should stay on one side of the room and we should stay on the other side. And they believe this to be true especially of women sportswriters because of what people will think!

Christine Brennan of the *Washington Post* and I presented an ethics question to an AWSM group once. We asked if it was OK to date:

A.   A tennis player who was in town for a tournament that week if you're the tennis writer,

B.    A New York Giants football player if your beat is the New York Mets baseball team,

C.    The son of the owner of the team you cover.

The group of women screamed, "No!" on the first count, mumbled on the second, and shook its head No on the third. George Solomon, the sports editor of the *Post*, moderated the discussion, but he didn't want to get specific on these.

"It all comes down to integrity and common sense," Solomon said vaguely, sounding so much like the parents who don't want to think about what the kids are doing now that they've gone off to college.

The group decided unanimously that it's not OK to date someone you cover regularly. You shouldn't do it. I dated Dave Stewart — briefly and inconsequentially — sometime after I left the baseball beat, but we both knew better than to ever even think of such a thing when I was around the team every day. Maybe you can do it and somehow maintain your objectivity, but probably you can't. And if you feel you must do it, you ought to either tell your editor so that he can switch your beat or keep it a secret so as not to appear to have a conflict of interest — and so as not to lose your football beat when the editor finds out you are dating the quarterback.

But this discussion led our group to, "What about lunch/dinner/a movie?" Brennan said, "People see you with an athlete and immediately assume, 'It's a date!' Do we have to be beyond reproach this way?"

I already had learned that people would say whatever they wanted to, anyway. So I would openly go to lunch with players and writers and openly have drinks with them, thinking that if you didn't try to hide anything from people, then maybe they'd believe you had nothing to hide. One spring, some A's pitchers told me that reliever Gene Nelson had a crush on me. I think of Geno as an uneducated but intelligent country boy who loved to talk to women, especially about his wife and kids, and I was glad he liked me. Once, in Chicago, we made a "date" and met in the bar and went out drinking and then to breakfast. That's all. It was a harmless crush, and we handled it as such.

That was one way to appear to be beyond reproach. Another was to avoid socializing or even the appearance of socializing with players and coaches, but I was too bored and lonely to adopt this approach. Besides, I wanted to have fun.

So, I let my editors know that Dave Stewart and I were good friends, and sometimes I'd pass along some baseball gossip I heard from him — not to be quoted, of course. At one point, Stew and I talked about writing his autobiography, and I heard the whole story about the male transvestite prostitute.

"I did it thinking it was a woman," he told me. "And it was something that I was going to do, something that I had set out to do. When I left the nightclub that night and got into my car, I said to myself, 'This is the first time in my life that I'm going to interact with a prostitute.' I was 27 years old and it was something I wanted to do."

Stew even managed to be funny talking about this. He said he saw "what appeared to be a woman," and said, "Hey, she doesn't look bad." I guess in the jail cell he found out "she" was a he. Stew pleaded guilty to a misdemeanor, paid a fine, and received a suspended sentence.

Two days later, Stewart was to receive the Texas Rangers' Good Guy award at a banquet. He surprised the people who thought he wouldn't have the nerve to appear. Then he surprised the people who didn't think he would dare to speak. He told them: "I am human, just as you are human. And good guys make mistakes."

"I think there were a lot of people who, from that day on — if nothing else — respected me for the fact that I was a man about it," he told me. "I came. I stood up. I didn't have to talk about it, but I did: 'This is what happened, I embarrassed myself, I embarrassed my family, I embarrassed my friends, and the one thing I never want to do in my life is cause embarrassment to my loved ones.'"

It was a poignant story, but Stew told me another once that made us both cry. We were celebrating our birthdays (separated by 15 days in February) one night at a restaurant called Avanti's in Phoenix, and I had asked him how he had escaped the traps of crime and drugs that had ensnared so many of his childhood friends. He told me of a night when he was a teenager joyriding with four of his buddies. He sat in the back seat, on the passenger side, with one friend in the middle of the seat and another on the driver side. The group, he said, started "messing with" some of the prostitutes on San Pablo Avenue, and a shot was fired from another car. Stew said it entered the head of the boy in the middle of the back seat. Stew said the boy later died, and no one was charged with the killing. The shooting led him away from those friends and that life, he said.

I badly wanted to write this story. I thought that young readers would find a wonderful moral lesson here, told to them by one of their sports heroes. Maybe if they read this story, they wouldn't wait for something like it to happen to change their lives. But Stew decided he did not want to revive the painful memories for the boy's parents, who he said still lived in the area. I asked him if I could search for the parents and see if they thought the story might be worth retelling. He consented. But I never could find a record of the murder in the records of the Oakland or Berkeley police departments — maybe this stuff was out of my league — and I dropped the quest. Anyway, I think the memories are too painful for Stew.

And there are more where those came from. We dated for what seemed like about five minutes, after I wasn't covering the team day in and day out. I had left the baseball beat — mostly out of loneliness and exhaustion — after the 1989 A's trip to the White House, and was traveling with the A's and with the Giants for just one roadtrip apiece in 1990 and again in 1991. Stew and I were both unattached that last spring training and said, "Well, is there anything here?"

During that time, I learned that he hadn't yet divorced his wife and had driven his last girlfriend nuts — not to mention confused his children — with the ambiguity of his personal life. He had married his high school sweetheart when he was 20, and they had two children. I think he was trying to clear up the family situation, finally, that year.

For us, dating wasn't a complete disaster, it just wasn't much better than that. It wasn't even heartbreaking, more like losing a game after falling behind 10-0 than getting beat 3-2 in the bottom of the ninth. I feel fortunate that we didn't wreck a good friendship for a lousy romance.

I found that he prefers to keep his loved ones at a comfortable distance, especially when things are going as badly for him as they did in the 1991 season, and when I suggested that maybe he could turn to his friends for support during tough times — as he likes them to feel they can turn to him — he angrily replied, "I've been on my own since my father died, and I don't need anybody now."

Something clicked when he said that: I remembered him telling me how he had sat in his condo, alone and in the dark, for days after the Phillies released him in 1986. And I thought that this was truly, for all of his loving friends and fans and family, a lonely man still lost in the insecurity of his tragic childhood.

Unfortunately, we never said, "This isn't going to work, let's just be friends." We just drifted apart, until, finally, about a year later, I wrote a column that he hated. It was about his request, during spring training, to negotiate an extension to the A's contract that was to pay him $3.5 million for the upcoming season. He was coming off his worst year with the A's, and he wanted them to give him more money! I criticized his timing and offered him more money from my own wallet . . . a buck.

He left me an angry message. I left him a conciliatory message that went unanswered. Then, when a friend told me that he'd been angry because I hadn't talked to him before the column appeared, I left a more apologetic message. Still no answer, and I avoided any direct conversation with him when I visited the A's.

Finally, a mutual friend of ours, Sylvester Jackson, died of cancer at the age of 37. I saw Stew at the memorial service, and we resumed our friendship soon after, when he was agonizing over his decision to leave Oakland for Toronto. Life is too short and good friends too few, we agreed, to waste time bickering. I'm sure one of these days we'll yell at each other about that column (or this book!) and then forget about it over a scratch margarita at Skate's.

Maybe he'll start telling me about his ladyfriends again, the way he used to. I always kidded him about how many pretty girls he knew in every city. He'd tell me they were "just friends."

"But you're a man," I'd tell him.

"Oh, and men are whores?" he'd say, teasingly.

I nodded, laughing at my own commission of sexism. But I went away from the baseball beat with a low opinion of man's morality. It made me laugh to hear that The Wives (there are some women who manage to have lives of their own despite having married baseball men, and I do not include them in this category) didn't like me because I was on the road with their husbands. But they had so much more to worry about than women sportswriters in the locker rooms.

Don't get me started on the human male animal, though.

Well, OK, if you insist . . . Let me share a few revealing anecdotes that might equal a point or two.

One night in Milwaukee, Stew told me he'd been in a bar with three veteran teammates. A woman there greeted each of them warmly. According to my buddy, they then discovered that each of the four players had been with this woman when they had played on four separate teams.

I didn't ask whether this woman possessed special talents or uncommon beauty. I just figured, "Ah, loneliness again." But what struck me was the way these men discovered they had all had sex with this woman — someone bragging, and the next guy saying, "Me, too!" on down the line. I could not imagine a group of women swapping notes on a man this way. But these athletes did not sit around in the clubhouse and brag about how long they had been faithful to their wives. Fidelity is just not fair game for locker-room banter.

Not that it wasn't ever acknowledged as a potentially good thing, in extreme circumstances. In a basement bar in Chicago on the night before the last day of the 1987 baseball season, the married pitcher on the barstool next to mine was reminding me how he had tried to get me to take his room key on another night in that city. It was another of those events I had so conveniently forgotten. Then the player said, "Sue, I've been true (to my wife) all season. First time!"

I sat there thinking, "Wait a minute — isn't 'forsaking all others' a standard clause in the marriage contract?" But then I thought, "Well, what do I know about that? I've never been married. Anyway, he seems so proud of himself. I might as well go along with him."

And I asked him, "So, how did you do it? What was your secret?"

"Fear of AIDS," he replied, somewhat sadly. So much for bragging about fidelity.

I learned more about that on another night, from A's manager Tony La Russa and several of his coaches. Tony and I had made a bet, because I had tired of the long games early in the

1988 season and told him I'd buy him and Mickey dinner if he'd get a game over with in under two hours and 38 minutes. We made several of these bets in the next two seasons, and it was after I had collected on one of them that Tony, Duncan, and I stopped in Seattle's beautiful Garden Court for drinks and, gulp, dancing. Not the kind of thing you tell your boss about. I did get a scoop, too: La Russa has a death grip on the dance floor.

I lost the first bet, however. Miraculously, with Stew pitching in the Metrodome, the A's and Twins finished in under 2:38, and dinner was on me at a stuffy men's club restaurant in Toronto. Tony kept inviting others, though, and soon I was the only woman in a group of eight. There was not much baseball conversation at the table that night; instead, Tony charmingly presented several mind-teasing questions for each of us to answer in turn. (The team was winning that summer, a condition that seemed to be a prerequisite for that La Russa charm. With the team losing, his only question to us would be a gruff, "What else?")

The first question that night at Hy's was, "What was the most scared you've ever been?" The highlight of the round of answers came from hitting coach Bob Watson, who described a "parade" he and a teammate stopped to watch when he was a minor leaguer playing in the South. When the paraders stopped, pointed, and shouted, "There they are!," Watson and friend — both of them black men — realized they were facing a Ku Klux Klan "parade."

Another of the questions was, "What would you do if you had just one week left to live and you could do anything you wanted?" As the question went around the table, each of the men talked about which beautiful woman/women he'd like to spend a night with. I squirmed at first, then I fumed. Finally, Dave Duncan said, "Well, I have some children I'd like to spend that week with." I practically screamed, "Thank you! What is wrong with the rest of you guys, anyway?" They could not believe that I wasn't envisioning wild sex with some male hunk in my last week on earth, and I could not believe they weren't thinking of family and friends. Either I took this question more seriously than they had, or I had encountered another closed locker room door.

I think it was the latter. Here, the "big locker room" mentality had surfaced again: I could go into the locker room now, but I could not participate in these conversations about sexual conquest.

Not that I wasn't invited. One night at my favorite bar in the world, the Lodge in Chicago, I met a gorgeous man whose personality and sense of humor turned out to be even more appealing than his looks. Across the room, A's pitcher Rick Langford kept gesturing for me to come over to him. I kept shaking my head at Langford, mouthing, "No way." I wouldn't budge from conversation with my new friend.

The next day, I asked Langford, "What did you want?" He said he had just wanted to congratulate me. Apparently, even he had admired my friend's beauty and thought him to be, as he put it, "a nice catch" for me.

I did talk to these men about my relationships, but I don't think any of them gave me much useful advice. No wonder: lots of the players had hardly dated! They'd married their high school sweethearts or found a wife when they left home for some midwestern small-town rookie league team. One of them spotted me out one night with a boyfriend of several months and shared this observation with me: "He doesn't look like your type." I showed tremendous restraint in not replying, "Well, your wife doesn't look much like YOUR type."

An exception was Dennis Eckersley, whose wife looks exactly like his type: Nancy is beautiful. She won my appreciation when we met in the spring of '92 and she said, "I've heard so many great things about you." None of the other wives had ever expressed anything other than curiosity toward me. I guess Nancy knew that we agreed on something important: Dennis is wonderful. He's the rare secure person who can turn an interview around on an interviewer, asking personal questions and offering personal insight. He'd talk frankly about how he'd failed at his first marriage and then nearly lost Nancy, who left him three times because of his alcoholism.

Once, Dennis confirmed what I had already heard — that he had been quite the ladies' man in his younger days. "I thought I was so great I ought to spread it around," he said.

We laughed at that. He added that he'd reformed, and that his marriage was better than ever because of his on-going recovery from drinking. Eckersley, unlike fellow recovering (but still dancing and partying) alcoholic Bob Welch, made a point of

staying out of the bars except for rare occasions like team meet-
ings or visiting friends, and once I listened to him debating with
Gene Nelson about the right way to handle "temptation:"
Eckersley clearly thought temptation was best avoided.

I became such a fan of Dennis the pitcher and Dennis the
person that I was crushed at cheating allegations I heard after
Oakland's 1989 playoff series with Toronto. Blue Jays manager
Cito Gaston had had the umpires inspect Eckersley before the
final inning of the series, won by the A's, because he suspected
Eckersley of doctoring the baseball. Gaston and Eckersley traded
wicked insults while the umpires found nothing. Afterward,
though, I learned that Gaston was acting on reports from one of
the clubhouse kids, who had seen an emery board taped to the
inside of Eckersley's glove.

Eckersley was such a dominant pitcher that year, and he
seemed so honest — this idea that he was cheating disturbed me.
I knew he couldn't really talk about such things on the record, so
when I was standing next to him in an Arizona hotel bar during
the earthquake break in the World Series, I raised the subject.
Dennis looked directly at me as he listened, then he said, "I can't
really say anything about (what the clubhouse kids reported).
But it wasn't what it looked like. I didn't . . . cheat."

His answer made sense to me, because Eckersley's pitches
were almost always strikes. Cutting or marking the ball would
not have affected their velocity — more likely, it would have
moved them out of the strike zone. So I can only assume that
Eckersley or one of his teammates may have planted the emery
board as a bad joke on the Jays. Eckersley even apologized, a few
days after the incident, for the language he had spit back in
Gaston's face.

Being around Eckersley used to remind me of my Aunt
Annie's line for handsome young men: "Do you have a father?"
Except I would have asked, "Do you have a brother?" I never did
ask, and later I learned that his brother Wallace would be spending many years in a Utah prison on a kidnapping-attempted
murder rap. Glad I didn't ask.

Another player actually set me up with a reporter-friend
of his, and what a disaster that turned out to be. Maybe he was
mad at me about something I'd written, because I'll bet he
wouldn't have let his sister get anywhere near this guy, who was

secretly pursuing one of my best friends the entire time he was seeing me. Once again, I reminded myself: The locker room is not a place to find a date, not even indirectly.

Unfortunately, the longer I stayed on the baseball beat, the more deeply I became entrenched in this big locker room. I would go off on a roadtrip for 10 days or two weeks, shopping and dining and partying as I worked my way through three cities.

Sometimes, I longed to sit down and have lunch or a drink with another woman. Claire Smith had begun traveling with the Yankees in 1983, and she told me, "My favorite trips were always the ones when other papers would send substitute writers like Jane Gross or Helene Elliott. The guys were not bad — they were just guys. They could never understand the times when I didn't want to do the big dinner with them and preferred just to stay in my room instead. They couldn't understand that sometimes I wanted to be away from the fraternity."

Elliott still laughs when she remembers coming home from one of her private dinners with Claire.

"We were in Detroit and had a wonderful meal at the Pontchartrain Wine Cellar," she said. "Afterward, we're walking up to our hotel, which had this fountain in front of it. In the fountain were two people doing something two people shouldn't be doing in a fountain — or anywhere in public. We did a double-take, and I said, 'Claire, I think it's so-and-so (a Yankee player),' and it was. So we started doing a detour so this player doesn't see us seeing him. In the middle of it all, he looks up and says, 'Hi! How ya' doin' tonight, ladies!' He didn't say a word about it the next day. He probably didn't remember."

The volatility of Billy Martin, three times the manager of the Yankees Claire covered in the 1980s, forced the women to bust out of their sorority and join the fraternity more frequently than they might have liked. Billy was always getting into squabbles or confrontations, sometimes even fistfights, with players or coaches, and sometimes even strangers. Many of the Yankee beat writers cruised the bars with Billy and stayed awake until he was safely put to bed — all of this so that they did not miss any potential stories.

"Being a woman probably cost me some stories," Claire said. "I missed one fight, the famous Cross Keys fight (with

Yankee pitcher Ed Whitson in Baltimore). But I'd heard that Billy had gotten into a confrontation with a bride and groom in the same bar the night before, because one of the other writers told me about it and said, 'We didn't want to call you because we thought it was too late.' I told him not to worry about that, just to call me if something else like that happened. The next night, I got a phone call: 'Claire, Eddy Whitson is trying to kill Billy Martin. You might want to come down here.'"

Claire made a point of making all of the team charters in case of similar incidents on airplanes, but she told her editor she did not consider bar-hopping an integral part of the beat, or, as Claire said, "I don't do the bars." She preferred to visit with friends who were unconnected with the businesses of sports and journalism when she could. When I'd get really lonely, or when I simply tired of the locker room mentality and humor all around me, I'd take myself out to dinner alone.

Once, my editor asked me, "How could you spend $50 on dinner? I can't believe this." I remember the night well. I was burned out in Cincinnati, near the end of my first roadtrip with the San Francisco Giants, and I decided to treat myself to lobster, with an appetizer of prawns and crab legs, a small bottle of wine, and, probably, dessert. Other writers overdosed on obscure sporting events, like traveling crew member Steve Sneddon from Reno, or free-lance assignments, like the *Oakland Tribune's* Kit Stier. Other writers — I'm going to protect their identities from the IRS — made money off their expense accounts by living cheaply and billing their papers lavishly. Me, I spent as much of my own money as my newspaper's, wining and dining myself, probably wearing some new outfit I had bought out of loneliness and boredom that afternoon.

When the trip finally ended, I would come home with nothing more expensive or taxing in mind than reading a good book or doing some sewing. I didn't want to go out and make friends and meet people — I had just done that constantly for 14 nights running. So I would rest and start the cycle again the next time I boarded a plane.

I always joked with girlfriends about wanting to have a "phone number" in every American League city. The sad truth was that I had phone numbers in just about every city but my own. Whenever I did luck into a fun date at home, it would end with him asking, "When can we get together again?" and me saying, "How about two weeks from Tuesday?" I could never seem to get anything started. At least the ballplayers had the money to import their dates, or they had ready-made dates in their wives. Me, I could not imagine being married and covering baseball.

Neither could Claire Smith, who recently became a single mother with the adoption of five-year-old Joshua. She's now off the Yankees and on the national "business of baseball" beat.

"Covering baseball probably prohibited certain things," she said. "Maybe I could have been married. It is so all-consuming. But, then again, I just took control of my life." She had to leave the traveling baseball beat to do that, though. I don't know of many sportswriters, even men, who could successfully combine the baseball beat with the family life.

Not that I wanted to be married and have kids! In 1988, the local public television station did a special live broadcast of an A's-Red Sox game, interviewing various characters during the game. One of the characters was me — one very happy sportswriter that night because she was getting paid to watch Stewart-Clemens in a scoreless pitchers' duel at the Coliseum. I was enjoying the season, too, my first covering a winning baseball team.

But I remember my surprise as I answered the interviewer's question about how a single woman can maintain any kind of social life in a job like this one. "I'm single, and things are pretty slow from spring training in February until the World Series in October," I told him, slowly. "But I can't imagine being married and trying to do this. In fact, I wouldn't even try it. But, at the same time, I'd rather be doing this."

As soon as those words came out of my mouth . . . "I'd rather be doing this!" . . . a look of realization crossed my face.

Had I really *said* that? Yes, I thought, I really had.

Did I really *mean* that? Yes, I thought, I really did.

And that look of realization turned into a small, surprised smile. I really, really loved what I was doing that summer.

No, it wasn't marriage I missed. But I was finding it harder and harder to cultivate a support network independent of my career. All of my life, I had had lots of friends for whom I'd organize outings and dinners. I still had lots of those friends, but now they were on the other side of the country. All of my California friends were sportswriters and baseball players. When the off-season came, I just got so bored that I'd go off on a series of vacations until spring training renewed my nomadic cycle.

It had gotten so those flight attendants didn't really need to single me out as the lady with the gentlemen. I had become one of the guys. Sort of.

# 8

# What's So-and-So REALLY Like?

Bud Geracie hunched over his Jack Daniels double one night trashing player after player after player.

"So-and-so is so obnoxious his own teammates can't stand him," Bud would say. And, "How'd you like to be stuck in an elevator with so-and-so?" And so on.

Bud spent four years on the A's beat before he was promoted to columnist at the *San Jose Mercury News*, and two of those years were pretty horrendous ones for the Oakland A's. The team was a collection of raggedy-armed pitchers supported by a succession of hitters who proved to be either unthinking, unproven, or just plain undone. The Haas family, which had bought the A's from Charlie Finley in 1981, opted not to spend money on talent until after the so-so 1987 season, when Tony La Russa's managerial genius and Jose Canseco's one-man slugfest began to hint that the A's might be a bet worth placing.

Bud was one of those hip, young, white, male writers whose wonderful ability to relate to anyone made him popular with the players. But it was in those early days that he ticked off the names on the A's roster and concluded, "I don't think there's one guy here I'd want to have even one drink with." I was horrified to realize, as Bud went down the list, that I wanted to have at least one drink with *every*body!

It wasn't multiple drinks I was after — I just believed there was something redeeming, something worth knowing, about almost everyone. I even believed that if I'd sat down and had a drink with Dave Kingman in 1985, he would not have sent me a rat in 1986. He might still, gulp, be playing, and I might have found something to actually like about the man had I had the chance to get to know him.

This belief of mine led me into all sorts of relationships with my sources and put me into some rather compromising positions. People told me things I didn't really need to know — one of the blessings out of the mixed bag that women carry into sportswriting.

Tony Phillips was a troubled man in those early years with the A's, a talented infielder who couldn't untangle his career from his unhealthy hobbies. His marriage to his childhood sweetheart was crumbling, and one day, during a weather delay in some airport, over drinks he told me about his misery.

When he had finished, Phillips fixed his bloodshot eyes on mine and said, "You know, it's so much easier talking to you than it is talking to the guys. I could never talk to them about something like this."

It was a recurring theme in my career as an A's beat writer. I was always toeing this delicate line between confidante and reporter, listening to secrets and then deciding what to do with them. Write it? Tell it? Forget it?

I saw private sides of Canseco, La Russa, Reggie Jackson, Mark McGwire, and others that were contrary to the images readers saw in newspaper accounts — even the ones that carried my own byline. I didn't always write what I saw or even knew.

Not that I knew much in the early years. I had a lot to learn, and I appreciate Phillips for observing later, "You sure have come a long way." That was after 1987, the season when La Russa made his mark and we writers were placed on alert. I *had* to come a long way.

I learned more about baseball from those daily talks with La Russa than I learned from all of the books I'd read. The man is incredibly, obsessively thorough when it comes to his preparation for the game of baseball, and I felt like a puppy pleasing its master when, in a 1989 interview with *ABC News*, he said of me: "From early on, she's always been among the best prepared (and) asks as good a question as anybody. We've all come to respect her a great deal."

Prepared, me? Here's a man who knows preparation. Tony made use of information you can't even find in the *Elias Baseball Analyst*, a compendium of useful and useless statistical information. *The Analyst* ranged beyond the realm of most managers, but it was a nursery rhyme for Tony.

He'd relax over drinks, all the while filling cocktail napkins with scribbled lineups for the next day's game. He'd organize his 5 1/2-field, stopwatch-timed spring training drills so precisely that he could find anyone, anytime. New coaches marveled at La Russa's preparation and organization.

Another of his pet peeves led to the dismantlement of the A's team he inherited in 1986. Those guys were always hurt, and Tony *hates* injuries. It's not so much that he feels badly for the hurt player as inconvenienced by the changes he has to make. I think La Russa takes it personally when a good player gets hurt over and over again. He'll phone in the off-season to tell the guy he'd better get healthier or stronger or whatever it is he needs to do to stay in the lineup. And if the player can't stay healthy, his stock falls.

This is one reason why Tony loved Mike Gallego, a hardly hitting infielder who stayed in La Russa's revolving lineup throughout the 1991 season. I think it's also why he traded Jose Canseco, a blockbuster player who couldn't be counted on in Tony's eyes after back injuries sidelined him in 1990. And I think it's why the A's gave walking papers to Walt Weiss, a great-fielding shortstop who was Rookie of the Year in 1988, but hasn't played a full season since. La Russa loved the guy four years ago, but now would rather take his chances on Mike Bordick, because Bordick stayed healthy for all of 1992.

In 1987, La Russa was adjusting for injuries all of the time — his center fielder, his right fielder, his pitching staff. He was also schooling a team that lacked fundamental baseball sense (how many outs were there? who was the cutoff man? what was the count? when to run? when to retreat?), another violation of his sensibilities. Twice, he threw tantrums highlighted by his upheaval of the clubhouse food table. And this was just an appetizer for the biggest upheaval of them all, an 11-player off-season turnover to reconstitute the World Series-bound 1988 team.

The 1987 team won only half of its 162 games, and finished third. But I remember it fondly as our last season of intimacy. By the next spring, the rest of the world had turned the A's and their trademark forearm bashes into media darlings. On the last day of the 1987 season, I was the only reporter left in the clubhouse minutes before the first pitch as players, coaches, and former A's owner Charlie Finley hugged Reggie Jackson and wished him well in his final game.

Jackson had replaced Kingman that spring as the designated hitter for the A's, and, for that alone, I appreciated him. He was 41 that year, but he would not announce his retirement during his final season — or ever! He made the rounds of all of the ballparks as if they were his last, yet he refused to make it official with the media and public. I thought it was because Reggie needed the money and wanted to keep the option year on his contract plausible; he said that he did not want to create hoopla that would detract from the team.

Lots of luck. Reggie made a fuss just by being Reggie. Mark McGwire hit a rookie record 49 home runs that year, yet, somehow, Reggie was there sharing the credit. He befriended Jose Canseco and was quoted in every story about the so-called "Bash Brothers." Reggie referred to McGwire and Canseco as "my sons."

He courted the media, and that included me. He'd flatter me, apparently thinking that the way to manipulate any woman was to tell her you liked her hairdo.

But, here's the contradiction that is Reggie: One day, he complimented my outfit (nothing special, just slacks, a sweater, and pumps) in front of the other writers, then used my example to inform them in detail that they were slobs.

And, here's more of the contradiction that is Reggie: On the day the team honored his career, the baseball writers — represented by Bud Geracie — presented him with a plaque thanking him for all the years of colorful quotes. After the game, Reggie started making unkind fun of a writer from the *Sacramento Union*. By now, I had tired of his act.

"Give back the plaque," I said under my breath. Reggie looked as if he hadn't heard. I think he did. So did Bud, who was laughing.

Sometimes, like that time, I despised Reggie. But sometimes I felt sorry for him. He seemed so in love with himself, and

I thought that must feel lonely — especially when he obviously wanted desperately to finish his career dramatically, yet couldn't stay healthy enough to help his team into the spotlight of postseason play. He had stringent superficial requirements for his women — they had to be under 30 and, until recently, blond — yet seemed to have no intimate friends.

After the A's chose not to re-sign him for 1988, Jackson did not know what to do. He wanted badly to stay in the game in some capacity, but no team knew what to do with him. He was too "big" to be a coach, it seemed, but not experienced enough to manage. Whatever he did, he would be misdirecting someone else's spotlight so that it shined on him.

In the spring of 1989, Jackson gave a speech in A's camp — subject: repeating as champions — and spent a few days working out with McGwire. One night in the hotel bar, he expressed his frustration about not being able to find a postplayer niche. I had an answer for him.

"Reggie," I said, "you're just too big. Nobody knows what to do with you."

He looked at me sadly, but agreeably. He liked thinking of himself as "too big."

The best description of Reggie that I ever heard came from Jose Canseco. Reggie was in the A's TV booth one night in 1991, after he'd finally found a job in broadcasting, and Canseco happened to strike out a time or two (or three) that night. After one of the strikeouts, Reggie looked over at me and saw me smiling through the glass windows in the direction of his booth. So, he told his "son" Canseco later that I had been laughing at Jose's strikeout.

It was a classic case of making a problem when there wasn't one. I certainly didn't know I had been laughing at Jose's strikeout, until Reggie told me so. Reggie also told me that Canseco was avoiding me now, so I went to Canseco about it. He listened to me patiently, then told me not to pay any attention to Reggie Jackson. Contrary to what Reggie told me, Jose wasn't avoiding me.

"You know what?" Canseco said. "Reggie's weird. Weirder than me. And that's weird."

In some weird way, I felt better. But I feel weird about something, too: In my five years on the A's beat, I collected only one autograph... Reggie's. I asked him to sign the scorecard I had kept of his final game that day in Chicago. He did ("Sue, it's been great and fun... Mr. October"), and it hangs on my bulletin board under a photo I took of him in the spring of 1989. I always did love watching Reggie play, even after I knew him and was then reminded constantly of one of La Russa's favorite maxims: "The bigger the pain in the ass you are, the bigger your talent had better be."

Reggie was elected to the Hall of Fame in his first winter of eligibility, which meant he could afford to be a Hall of Fame-size pain in the ass — and he remains so. His decision to be inducted into the hall as a Yankee was insulting to the A's, the team that employed him for the earliest and last years of his career and then gave him a job after he'd retired. But the A's weren't retaining Reggie for their 1993 telecasts, so he probably figured he ought to kiss up to the Yankees for his next job.

Do I sound disrespectful? OK, so I would like to see inscribed on Reggie's plaque at Cooperstown, "Hall of Fame pain in the ass." Ironically, Reggie first returned to the A's for 1991 to serve as what I described, to his amused chagrin, as "The Jose Coach." Oh, Sandy Alderson said Reggie was hired to do TV and also to bring a "winning attitude and work ethic to the 1991 A's." But you could hear that Canseco name between all of the lines — the A's wanted Reggie, their retired Hall of Fame-size pain in the ass, to instill a Hall of Fame attitude and work ethic in their current All-Star player.

It's still hard for me to believe that Canseco ultimately inflicted more pain on his manager's rump than his bat did damage to opposing pitchers. I would *never* have traded him.

Canseco first joined the A's in the September of my rookie year, 1985, and became Rookie of the Year with his 1986 campaign. I loved to watch him swing his bat. Canseco hit so many kinds of home runs, you could not pick out his single best without first specifying a category. You'd have to remember a line drive that never seemed to rise more than 10 feet off the ground before leaving Anaheim Stadium (freakiest?) . . . and the fifth-deck homer they're still sighing over in the upper left corner of Toronto's SkyDome (tallest?) . . . and the did-you-see-what-I-saw shot that cleared the 36-foot-high center field fence 420 feet from home plate at Tacoma's Cheney Stadium (longest?) . . . David Letterman could come up with a Top Ten, no problem.

I also — and this is not a misprint — *liked* Canseco. I liked his sense of humor, the way he could go 0-for-40 and joke about it. I liked the way he turned himself into a complete player in 1988, after his teammates had criticized his defensive techniques. And I thought he had a good heart. There was a gentleness about him, a mild-manneredness that manifested itself in his love of pets like turtles and puppies.

Jose was always the guy who'd sign 20 autographs and then get photographed waving, "No more," as he walked away. He'd talk to five cameras and 10 writers and get ripped for walking away from the visiting writer just strolling in from the opponents' locker room. I heard stories of how he stiffed other media people, but I never had this experience with him. Once, in 1988, just before the All-Star break, I did ask him if I could have some time with him for a special All-Star feature.

"Like, how much time?" he said.

"Half an hour or so," I told him.

"What? Half an hour? Are you kidding?"

I think he was kidding, but I was so mad, I told him to just tell me to forget it, because, "I didn't want to do the story anyway." The next day, he talked to me in the clubhouse for longer than half an hour. And when he achieved his 40-homer, 40-steal goal on a cold night in Milwaukee at the end of the season, he came out of the clubhouse while the game was still in progress, in extra innings, so that the team's writers could get some quotes into their stories.

There was a good-bad contradiction within the man — a lot like there was in Reggie. Both men make themselves difficult to like. No one ever questioned Jackson's effort on the field as they did Canseco's. But I think Reggie was much more manipulative; Canseco was just being himself, whether that meant motivated or lazy, for better or worse.

Of course, this was often for worse. The public must think he's a cocaine addict or a bad drunk, for all of his encounters with the law. But he was neither. Once, on that long bus ride to Yankee Stadium, he told me about having experimented one time — and only one time — with cocaine. "I didn't like it," he said. "It made me too hyper. I'm hyper enough."

I wanted to write about that, thinking it would be nice to hear from a real live hero who had just said no. I even told him I had tried cocaine once, too, and liked it so much that I thought,

"I can never do this again," and didn't. But he feared people's reactions if they read something like that about him.

They were going to read plenty anyway, after he embarked on his post-season meet-the-police tour in 1988. That fall, Canseco married Esther Haddad, after a season-long engagement. He had one "fiancee" in 1986 and another "fiancee" in 1987, so when he reported to spring training in 1988 and told a roomful of reporters, "I'm engaged," I was the smart aleck in the back of the room piping up with, "Again?" Yes, he laughed. Then, he made a $10,000 bet with Dave Stewart, who, speaking for the rest of us skeptics, said, "No way you're really going to get married."

I don't think Canseco married Esther for the bet, but I think he did want to prove everyone around him wrong. Esther seemed so down to earth — she was one of travel director Mickey Morabito's favorite wives for the grace with which she accepted travel and seating arrangements — and they were a beautiful couple. But they did have their problems. I think Jose just never grew up. I don't blame him for that. I and my colleagues probably contributed to that.

He was 24 when he won the Most Valuable Player award, unanimously, on his honeymoon in 1988. That off-season, on February 10, 1989, he and his new Porsche were clocked at 125 mph in a high-speed chase with Miami police, who ticketed him for speeding. He was a no-show at a prestigious banquet in Baltimore and skipped an autograph signing session in Rochester. As usual, he reported late to spring training — and then was stopped, in the Porsche, by Phoenix police for running a red light.

Moving on to Oakland for the 1989 season, Canseco was arrested and charged with a felony for having a gun in plain sight inside that same Porsche when it was parked on university property. He said he was protecting his wife. The court suspended his six-months' sentence and placed him on three years' probation. It was not a good year for Canseco: he missed the entire first half of the baseball season with the wrist injury that had taken him to that university property in April for an MRI exam.

But Jose was tearing up the league again in 1990, and the A's signed him to a five-year, $21.5-million contract before the All-Star break, when he led all players in the balloting. So he was a well-paid scapegoat in the 1990 World Series, combining his lone hit with several miscues in right field to accidentally help the Cincinnati Reds to a four-game sweep.

Esther made headlines of her own in the fall of 1990 when she called Tony La Russa a "punk" for criticizing Canseco's play and then benching Canseco in the final game of that World Series. She said she wished she'd worn a red dress to the final game between the green-and-gold A's and the Reds.

Just a few weeks later, in January 1991, the Cansecos filed for divorce in Florida. Jose committed his seemingly annual traffic infraction on February 13, this time being clocked at 104 mph in his new Porsche, in which he claimed to be testing aviation fuel.

Never a dull moment.

He and Esther reunited in the spring of 1991, but in May Jose was photographed exiting Madonna's Manhattan apartment. The team went from New York to Baltimore, where I was vacationing with my family and found out one more thing I'd rather not have known. I was sitting in the stands with my handsome younger brother, Bob, who found himself flanked on the other side by a provocatively dressed young woman. Our seats were in the visiting team's section, but this bimbo did not look familiar to me. She told Bob she was in town from Miami (an "import") to visit with Canseco.

We were heading from the ballpark to the team's hotel to have drinks, so my brother offered her a ride. He lost her somehow, but she found us after she had gotten into a taxi with yet another man, and we had started the long walk back to Bob's car. She stopped the taxi and had it give us a lift. Once we reached the hotel, there she was again — now boarding the elevator to, she said, go to Canseco's room. Then we saw Canseco, in the bar, with yet another honey. It wasn't Madonna and it wasn't Esther. My brother was beside himself thinking that woman he'd met was upstairs waiting for a man who had another date downstairs.

Of course, I didn't write any of this. I did suggest to Canseco, the next time I had a private moment with him, that he might want to be a little more discreet. I told him exactly what had happened and that another reporter might have had some fun with the woman.

It turned out that another reporter did. The woman, apparently a graduate of the Gennifer Flowers school of discretion, turned informant for one of those entertaining tabloid talk programs on TV because she was upset that Madonna was calling Jose's room all night. Apparently it was OK with her that Jose had a wife, just not another girlfriend.

Jose, by the way, told the show's reporter the woman was lying about everything. I'd love to have been a fly on the couch at Jose's appointment with a court-ordered psychiatrist. Jose was ordered to see the shrink after his next arrest — again in Miami, again on February 13, this time 1992, for ramming his Porsche into Esther's BMW at 4:30 in the morning and then spitting on her windshield when police arrived. Jose never publicly owned up to his mistakes or crimes, never seemed to grow up. He thought that the only reason he kept getting those speeding/gun possession/ aggravated battery charges was some flaw in the law.

Every time Jose would get arrested or injured, I'd say to friends, "This is it. This is what he needs to straighten out his life. He just needs some hardship." Some of his teammates felt this way, too. Dennis Eckersley saw his misguided younger self in Canseco and kept waiting for Canseco to be transformed the way HE had been after watching a video of himself, drunk, in front of his daughter on Christmas of 1986. The video opened Dennis's eyes, prompting him to enter a rehabilitation facility for six weeks that January. Jose, it seemed, needed only emotional rehabilitation. But it never happened. By 1992, Eckersley would describe Canseco as the biggest jerk he'd ever met.

Dave Stewart liked Canseco, more socially than professionally. And he would tell Canseco when he had messed up in the field or was rubbing teammates the wrong way. But Canseco had reached a point when he had heard so much from so many angles, he wasn't listening anymore. The man had stopped improving, maybe even started atrophying, as a player and as a person, and La Russa decided he had become a Hall of Fame pain in the ass who hadn't compiled Hall of Fame playing credentials.

Still, it was a shock when Canseco was called back from the on-deck circle in the first inning of a 7:05 game against Baltimore August 31. I was the official scorer at the game that night, and the press box began buzzing. There had to be something wrong with Canseco.

But no one called from the dugout with an injury report. And then a press conference was scheduled for 8 p.m. In my seven years in Oakland, there had never been an in-game press conference.

So, we knew. The press box emptied, and I watched the TV monitor as Sandy Alderson announced Canseco's trade to the Texas Rangers. Canseco appeared to be in shock. Later, he would have harsh words for his manager's team politics and for management's abrupt handling of the deal. That's what happened when he had time to bat things around in that young head of his. But, for now, he was instinctively gracious. Stunned and gracious.

I went home and cried. I lived eight miles from the Oakland Coliseum, and I had thought that I would have another 10 years or so to drive across the Estuary and watch Canseco invent yet another home run category. I had always described my greatest thrills in covering the A's as "watching Mike Gallego field ground balls, Dennis Eckersley save games, and Jose Canseco hit home runs." Gallego already had left for a free-agent deal with the Yankees. I knew Eckersley might retire in a year or two. But I could not imagine the A's without Canseco.

And there they were, the next day: the A's without Canseco. Everyone looked as if there'd been a death in the family. I remember arriving at the park and seeing a couple of the ticket attendants in tears. "He just left," one of them said. My disappointment at missing him quickly turned to relief at not having to say good-bye. I know I would have cried, too.

Of course, now I began hoping once more: "This is it. This is what he needs to straighten out his life. He needed a trade, a change of scenery."

At least he doesn't have a drinking problem. I don't think he drinks much at all, and I certainly never did have a drink with him. Closest I came was on the night before the team's (and Reggie's) last game, in 1987. I wandered from my favorite bar in the world, the Lodge in Chicago, across the street to a downstairs bar that had dancing. Several A's players were drinking at the bar, and others — among them, Canseco and Tony Bernazard — were near the dance floor. I guess some guy made the mistake of hassling Canseco, then relatively unknown, while he was dancing. Finally Canseco turned around and punched the guy.

The players I was sitting with jumped up and escorted Canseco, who was somewhat surprised but quite proud that his one punch had floored the deserving fellow, up the stairs. I went along with them. Meanwhile, Bernazard stayed behind to take the fall. The cops cuffed Bernazard and put him in a wagon as we watched sympathetically from the street. Bernazard kept smiling and telling us not to worry. But I went to a phone and called A's travel director Mickey Morabito.

Mickey had joined the A's from New York in 1981, when Billy Martin, the great infielder and manager known best for his feisty years with the New York Yankees, was managing in Oakland. Mickey, a former Yankee bat boy, had befriended Martin and his wife, Jill, and served as a pallbearer when Martin was killed in an accident on Christmas Day 1989. I knew that Morabito's experience with Martin served him well when it came to matters of pugnacity and law — Billy was always getting into something or other — and so it was Mickey I called when the paddy wagon took away an Oakland Athletic.

Mickey had been assigned by La Russa to throw a little end-of-season party for his coaches. There was an exotic dancer in the suite doing exotic things, and my call had interrupted the proceedings. They all came down to the Lodge and got things straightened out. I don't think the cops took the smiling Bernazard too many blocks before letting him go.

I never wrote about this. I didn't write about it mainly because I was several drinks into the evening myself and felt I shouldn't be throwing stones from my glass house. I didn't write about it because there were no charges filed. I didn't write about it because I wasn't carrying my notebook. I didn't write about it because it seemed to me that the guy on the floor had gotten what he had asked for, and I don't think he knew who or what had hit him.

I didn't write about it, and I've had to defend that decision to other writers ever since. In an AWSM ethics panel discussion, I raised the subject and was told by *Washington Post* sports editor George Solomon, "Write! That's why you're there."

Then Chris Brennan told a similar story of what had happened to a Redskin player with whom she had a drink in Georgetown. He must have had a couple of drinks more than she did.

"We had met to discuss some off-the-record information he was giving me about another player, and some contract information — very valuable," she said. "We had, I think, two beers. I paid for the beers, and we went our separate ways.

"I get a phone call at three in the morning from this player. He's been arrested, DWI. I said, 'Why are you calling me?' He said, 'Well, I didn't have anyone else to call and I'm really upset . . . ' What can I do? I said I was sorry, asked if he was OK . . . He was very upset, obviously. Then we hang up, and I go back to sleep.

"The next morning, I wake up and just think, 'Oh, my God.' I mean, here's a big-time player for the Redskins, (and) I actually paid for a couple of the beers that ended up getting him drunk. Now, he had been out all night with some friends before he met me, so I didn't feel too terrible about that, but what do you do?"

Chris called a friend, who advised her to think about what the *Columbia Journalism Review* would report if it ever got the tidbit about the *Post* reporter who paid for the drinks that got the guy DWIed and then covered it up.

"I think that's a good way to look at it," Chris said. "What if the worst possible thing happened? Immediately, I had my answer."

Chris called her *Post* editor Solomon with the whole story, and he passed the DWI info along to the metro desk for a brief that appeared in the paper the next day. Then she called the player and said, "First things first. Every relationship is first reporter and athlete. Any second relationship — acquaintance, friend, whatever — is completely secondary."

I'm sure that's the proper, ethical approach. It's not mine. If I had to go back and do it all over again, I still wouldn't write about Canseco's right to the chin. The punch he threw at Chicago's China Club in December 1992 was different — the bouncers didn't let him sneak out the side door, blood oozed from the victim's face, and charges were filed that probably will wallop Canseco's wallet. But this early incident wasn't a big enough story to violate confidences and the code of the road.

I wouldn't have written that Arthur Ashe had AIDS, had I known. I wouldn't violate the privacy of a man who had a fatal illness, unless he was a public official whose illness was interfering in his ability to do a competent job. If I had AIDS, I could choose the way I wanted to spend whatever time remained for me. I think Arthur Ashe deserved that right, too. He lost it when his illness became public.

I think I made a big mistake, though, in the summer of 1989. We were in Kansas City — why did things always seem to happen to me in Kansas City? — for a three-game series with the Royals. One night, a whole gang of players and reporters was drinking in Quincy's, the downstairs bar in our hotel across from the stadium. By now, I knew I was in my last season on the full-time A's beat, so my hair had fallen. I remember dancing with Dave Henderson, among others, that night. Then somebody pulled me out of the elevator at last call and dragged me along to the all-night breakfast spot across the street.

Several players ate there with their dance partners, and it was an animated group, without any other writers or club officials nearby. When we finally crossed the lawn back to the hotel, it must have been four in the morning. I walked with relief pitcher Greg Cadaret. And as we strolled through the wet grass, he told me he had heard that he, outfielder Luis Polonia, and reliever Eric Plunk were about to be traded to the New York Yankees for Rickey Henderson.

WOW!

Rickey Henderson had been raised by the A's, until they traded him before the 1985 season because they couldn't afford to pay him $8.6 million for five years. How times have changed. Rickey wouldn't sign for *three* years at that price in 1989. So the idea that he would return to Oakland — his home — was mind-boggling, especially at 4 a.m. crossing the parking lot between Denny's and the Adams Mark with my mind already boggled by many rounds of some red shooter called a "WooWoo."

I entertained the possibility of the deal for about 30 seconds after my boggled mind hit the pillow. Next day, I awakened and put in some late-morning pool time before lunching at a favorite restaurant in Westport.

Back in my room, after noon, the phone was ringing. It was Cadaret. "About what I told you last night..." he said.

I wondered what he was talking about. What had he told me? Then, I remembered. "Oh, *that*," I said nonchalantly.

"Listen," he said, "it could get me in a lot of trouble if you wrote that." I told him not to worry. I didn't tell him I could barely *remember* "that."

But the elements came back to me in the next day or two, and I began scouting. I asked Claire Smith, my friend covering the Yankees, to try to get a private moment with Rickey. I could have done that if I had dragged myself to the ballpark on the off-day that followed the series in Kansas City, but we were in Baltimore and I was with my parents and brothers. Some of the coaches realized I knew what was happening and started to tease me about it.

"There's something big going on," they'd tell me. But they wouldn't really tell me. And I could not find the confirmation I needed to turn the 4 a.m. coffee shop talk into a story that weekend in Baltimore without violating the confidence of my source.

On June 19, I flew home. It was one of those days when the airlines jerked me around, and I got home depressed and exhausted, just trying to salvage some time to myself on June 20. But by then the trade had been made. It had been made exactly as Cadaret had said it would be.

It was the biggest story I ever failed to break. I wish I could have confirmed the rumor Cadaret presented me. I wish that, in that instance, I had not been so considerate of the people I covered day in and day out. Why did I have to treat them like human beings *all* of the time? Why didn't I pick my spots more efficiently?

I guess it was purely logistical. I interacted with Tony and his players, coaches, media, and staff every day. I drank with them in bars, slept with them on airplanes, ate with them at Denny's (and other establishments more conducive to exhausting expense accounts). I saw much, much more of them than I ever saw of my readers and my editors. It was them I had to live with — them and me, not all of those other voices on the telephone.

I wanted *their* respect, *their* trust. My readers bought my paper. My editors mailed me my paycheck. But I had to live in a world, day in and day out, with men who wore identical uniforms on the job and matching sportcoats on the plane. I shared cabs with my rivals, swapped compact discs with the hero of the game. I know I sacrificed some stories for what I considered to be a matter of integrity to those with whom I had to have daily contact on the baseball beat.

"Reporter first" — that wasn't the only journalistic commandment that's ever been broken. I know, because I broke another one — and on this violation I had lots of company. I misrepresented people. Mostly, I ignored their flaws and engaged in newsprint hero worship. It's a much more subtle sin than deciding not to write about a punch to the jaw. It's also much more universal — an offense routinely committed with the full complicity of sports editors. Simply put: It is encouraged to report on a player's clubhouse presence, his community involvement, his family devotion — but only when those elements are positive.

Once, before I had any problems with Dave Kingman, I tried to convey in a story that the A's tolerated his dubious character because he was such a strong hitter. I was told by my desk that this was unnecessary, and the inference was removed. And when Kingman sent me the rat after harassing me for months, the public couldn't understand why the other writers had not published his previous actions or at least clued the readers in to his behavior.

Another A's player had a drug problem so obvious that the writers knew about it. He was well-liked, and we'd talk with concern about what might happen to the player if he didn't get his act together. I'm certain that the drugs were interfering with his performance and preventing him from becoming an everyday player. Yet it was never a story because the player was never arrested. He eventually underwent rehabilitation and righted his career, but I am not sure that the entire story has ever been reported.

That's not necessarily unfair, except when what is written instead is far from the truth. For instance, in an on-the-record interview, the player could say to me, "I don't want to talk about that," and I'd end up writing about how his new stance added 20 points to his batting average rather than how drug or alcohol rehab had turned around his entire life.

We spent an entire year writing about how an off-season aerobics program, plus a new role as a relief pitcher, had rejuvenated 33-year-old Dennis Eckersley's career. In fact, Eckersley had overcome a list of personal problems that included alcoholism. But he asked us not to write about that until he was ready, which wasn't until after the 1988 season, to use the "A" word.

Mark McGwire snowed the public in 1988 — or, rather, we snowed the public on his behalf.

McGwire had batted .289 and hit 49 homers in his rookie year of 1987. A freckle-faced, red-haired 23-year-old, he had barely made the team out of spring training and then captivated the critics with his fluid swing and his happy-to-be-here approach. McGwire seemed so fresh and innocent in comparison to his shyer '86 counterpart, Canseco. He'd talk forever to the writers after his games, and the talk soon included his wife, Kathy, who was expecting their first child that autumn.

Kathy, he'd tell us, would keep him in line. She wouldn't let 49 homers go to his head. Maybe he was right. But by the time his son Matthew was born on the final day of the season, McGwire had another woman in his life. His marriage soon hit the rocks and took a pounding there throughout the 1988 season. The other woman was appearing on roadtrips, and once I saw them openly holding hands in a tourist area of Kansas City.

Meanwhile, McGwire's batting average fell by 29 points, his home run production fell by 17, and his runs batted in dropped off by 19. "What's wrong?" we'd ask him.

"Nothing!" he'd say irritably. "I'm just not going to have a year like last year all of the time." He refused to talk about his marriage with the media and told even his teammates that his personal problems were not affecting his play.

McGwire's marriage ended after the '88 season, and he was newly engaged shortly after that. A's wives — liking his bright and bubbly ex, and no doubt feeling territorial about their own husbands — ostracized the newcomer, though, and she, too, had moved on by the start of the 1992 season. In 1991, when presumably their relationship faltered, McGwire had his worst season. In 1992, McGwire had his best season since his first season, five years earlier.

Serious journalists would, I believe, report on the possibility that McGwire's personal problems were affecting his play. It was an easily documented theory and one with which the everyday reader, male or female, probably could empathize. We were not supposed to report on such matters, though, unless the subject decided to discuss them. The players didn't want us to, and our editors didn't want us to. We were not supposed to alienate a source who might hit three homers the next afternoon and then decide not to talk to anybody from the such-and-such newspaper.

Sportswriters always bring up Babe Ruth at times like these. I'll say that we should have reported on the breakup of McGwire's marriage in a season when he had to put up such a struggle to be professionally productive, and some guy will say, "But, Babe Ruth . . ."

Babe Ruth, the most famous and beloved baseball player of all time, was no milk advertisement. He drank himself into trouble and womanized excessively, and the sportswriters neglected to report this to the public.

But he also hit 714 home runs in his career. He brings to mind, again, that La Russa proverb: "The bigger the pain in the ass you are, the bigger your talent had better be." Maybe the journalists should add, "so that we don't have to write about what a pain in the ass you are."

There was no reason to report on the Babe's swinging adventures if he could still connect with a fastball. There was no reason for me to report on a punch thrown by Jose Canseco if he could still throw a baseball the next day. I don't think there's even a reason for a sportswriter to report on a player's arrest on drunk driving charges unless it gets the player into hot water with his team or league.

But in a case where a player's off-field activities retard his performance, and where that player is earning millions of dollars from his team to deliver for its fans, we should dip deeper. It's an impossible situation for a beat writer who always travels with—and thereby virtually lives with—a team, but it is certainly not an impossible situation for a columnist who never travels with a team. Yet the boys will be boys, big locker room attitude prevails.

Canseco seemed to feel excluded from this particular locker room by his Cuban heritage. He'd say that the all-American players on the team (read: McGwire) did not undergo the intense scrutiny on their careers or marriages that he did. But Canseco would answer any question you asked, while McGwire would deflect a question that delved too deeply. And once the waters get deep, the sportswriters are heading for the beach.

Maybe they just don't want to know too much. Consider the misrepresentation of A's manager Tony La Russa. Tony's wife, Elaine, told me she laughs every time she reads about the way Tony organizes his team. At home, she said, he is constantly losing the keys, his sunglasses, their checkbook.

But that's not all. Tony talks so much of Elaine and their two daughters, he seems to be the ultimate family man among baseball managers. The girls were being schooled by Elaine at home — an oddly interesting woman who speaks with such fluency and passion about their home life and pets — just so the family could spend more time together. And the La Russas took advantage of their prominence to promote their special cause, animal rights. They say they don't eat meat or sugar or white flour at home, and they don't watch television. Reporters dutifully write all of this down, except that if they'd hit the road with the manager they'd have seen him scarfing up a burger or a chicken burrito from the post-game spread.

Annually, or at least when the playoffs arrive and the A's are involved, stories appear in the paper describing the close family unit of the A's manager. The *Sacramento Bee* even reported, in 1990, that the La Russas all sleep together in a king-size bed.

The La Russas have been married since New Year's Eve 1973, but here's a secret: Elaine is La Russa's second wife, and Devon and Bianca are actually his third and fourth children. Once, Ron Bergman, a writer who remembered La Russa from his playing days, had the nerve to inquire about his first wife and family. The writer reported that La Russa abruptly told him that that was another life that no longer existed.

"I was covering his first press conference, when he was named manager, and I said to him, 'It says here (on the press release) that you have two children. But you have four children,' said Ron Bergman, who had covered the A's for the *Oakland Tribune* when La Russa played. "And Tony said, 'That was a previous life.' I never raised the subject again. But I always wanted to ask him, maybe over a beer, what that was all about."

In 1989, around the time of the Bay Bridge World Series, several of the Bay Area newspapers received letters from Tony's "previous life." And, most springs, Tony's ex-wife or children contact the *New York Times* to say, "Why doesn't somebody write about this?" The New York editors reply that the off-field foibles of the Oakland A's aren't part of the *Times*'s territory; the local editors answer that this isn't a story they want to run.

Is the former family a story? I don't think it's a sports story. I do think it belongs, even if only a paragraph or two, in a profile on the man who is one of baseball's best managers.

La Russa's past "life" did not seem to have any adverse effect on his management of the A's, and Elaine's strict management of their life at home probably helped him focus on his job. I suspect, by comments he made about Devon and Bianca to Mark Naman of *The West* magazine in 1989, that he felt he had married too young the first time. "I kid our children they're not going to date until they're 25, and then it's only double-dating with their father," he said then.

It's not far-fetched to infer that Tony believed his first marriage to be a mistake attributable to his youthfulness. And he is not a man to say, "I made a mistake" — thus, the secret. We're all entitled to forget our mistakes. But it was unfair and misrepresentative for newspapers to write stories about La Russa, the family man, without pursuing the subject of his first family, if only to say, "La Russa refuses to discuss his first marriage." Evidence was right there in the 1968 Oakland A's media guide: "married (Luzette), one child."

They did ignore the matter, though. The obvious explanation: no sports editor and no sportswriter wanted to risk losing La Russa's cooperation throughout the course of a long baseball season. They wanted him to like them. My companion theory: male sports editors and writers did not know how — much less want — to approach a story that could denigrate the character of one of the members of their men's club. The story made them nervous.

It made me nervous. I would not have wanted to investigate or write that story when I was covering La Russa's team. But I certainly would not have wanted to ignore it and write another story portraying La Russa as Ozzie Nelson. Sports page strategists need to make up their minds: either address the at-home and off-the-field stories completely or not at all.

For a proper perspective, I'd love to see major sports sections running weekly gossip columns like this:

> Oakland's pet-loving power hitter was spotted in an East Bay shop specializing in pot-bellied pigs. Told the owner he'd be back with his missus. ... The kooky quarterback won the

karaoke contest at the Pierce Street Annex last Monday with his rendition of "Feelings." First prize was a trip to Las Vegas next weekend, though — and he's expected to suit up for a game in New Orleans. Wonder who he'd take with him, the wife or the new girlfriend. . . . Wife of one East Bay baseball player got expelled from the local health club for indecent exposure. Officials there deemed her outfit too scanty for working out (in their establishment, anyway).

Just a thought. This way, the sportswriters could cover the games and the gossip experts could cover the personalities. The *National* tried something like this, but the scale was too big. It would fit a local scene — particularly a sports-rich one like New York, Chicago, and the Bay Area — more snugly, and readers would love it. Mike Conklin of the *Chicago Tribune* does something like it, but, perhaps because he's in the big locker room, it rarely imparts any really juicy or possibly negative gossip.

My next career, maybe?

# 9

# Save 1988 For Me

When fans begin thinking past the locker rooms onto the fields, they often ask: "What was the most exciting moment or event you've ever covered in sports?"

I think about Jack Nicklaus's U.S. Open victory at Baltusrol in 1980, the year he had turned 40. I think about Jose Canseco's 40-40 season. I consider Brian Holman's near perfect game that was spoiled only by a two-out home run in the bottom of the ninth inning. But I always answer, "Kirk Gibson's home run in the 1988 World Series."

It is an answer that usually silences a roomful of A's fans, who still seem to remember only the awful pain of that moment and none of its drama.

Me, I remember the silence that hit a press box packed shoulder to shoulder with sportswriters pecking away on their computers. They were putting the finishing touches on their stories about the formulaic way that Jose Canseco's first grand slam, Dave Stewart's start, and Dennis Eckersley's finish had led the heavily favored A's to a 4-3 victory over the Dodgers in Game One of the World Series. Suddenly, Kirk Gibson limped out of the dugout, the pain in his knee dulled by shots, to hit a two-run homer that beat the invincible Eckersley 5-4 in the bottom of the ninth at Dodger Stadium.

The press box had become the eye of a hurricane. All around us, it was bedlam. But, where we sat, stunned, it was silent. We had slaved for 8 1/2 innings over stories that had just been rendered fiction, to be replaced by a moment so dramatic that it sounded less believable than what we had already written. The movie capital of the world had just shredded another script.

Usually, at times like these, the writers roar. "Nooooo!" they cry, with deadlines so close at hand. But, in this case, they just sat calmly, many of them shrugging and smiling at each other. They could, even at such a pressure-packed time as this, put aside their professional concerns to appreciate a special moment in the sport they covered.

That entire 1988 season was a special moment for me and for the A's. It was an efficiently directed team that led all of baseball with 104 victories and won its division 13 games ahead of the Minnesota Twins. But I remember it so fondly for the joyous novelty that winning presented the players, the management, and the fans.

It was the first year the A's had ever drawn two million fans — an achievement that had been thought to be impossible in the recreation-rich Bay Area when the Haas family bought the franchise in 1981. And it was the first year the team had won a division (except the split-season strike year of 1981) since the end of the Charlie Finley A's dynasty in 1975.

The heroes and heroics ranged so far and wide, I remember agreeing with infielder Mike Gallego when he said: "I'm so excited, I can't wait to get to the ballpark tomorrow. I can't wait to see who's going to do something exciting tomorrow, so we can watch it, so we can win." Except I replaced "so we can win" with "so we can write about it."

There was always a story. That team was so special, it already has spawned three major-league managers: Jim Lefebvre of the Chicago Cubs, who was the hitting and third-base coach, Don Baylor of the Colorado Rockies, who was the designated hitter, and Rene Lachemann of the Florida Marlins, who was the first-base coach. Pitching coach Dave Duncan would be a manager by now if he wanted to be. The team's top advisor in 1988, Ron Schueler, went on to become the general manager of the Chicago White Sox. Another coach of that team, Bob Watson, is the assistant general manager of the Houston Astros; his name has now entered the general managerial rumor mill. Catcher Ron

Hassey was named to Baylor's coaching staff in Colorado. And outfielder Dave Parker should show up on somebody's coaching staff — the A's wanted to name him hitting coach for 1993 — as soon as he accepts that he's not a player anymore.

There was a magnificent chemistry on the 1988 A's, a blend of young players unspoiled by contracts and veteran players hungry to win just once more. Jose Canseco and Mark McGwire represented unspoiled youth of unlimited potential, Canseco earning just $320,000 that year, McGwire $240,000, yet Canseco hitting 42 homers and McGwire hitting 32. Baylor, 39, and Parker, 37, had won the World Series before and could show the way back, if not with their bats then with their spirit.

These were the big men. The little men played big roles, too — outfielders Stan Javier and Luis Polonia, infielders Gallego, Tony Phillips and Walt Weiss. There was a practical-joking veteran second baseman from Atlanta, Glenn Hubbard. There was a hit-to-all-fields third baseman and unofficial team captain in Carney Lansford, a young-old platoon of Terry Steinbach and Ron Hassey behind the plate, and a center fielder, Dave Henderson, who seemed incapable of catching a fly ball in spring training but seemed unable to miss one during the season.

The chemistry of the pitching staff blended the best bullpen in baseball around a starting four of Dave Stewart, Bob Welch, Storm Davis, and Curt Young. Gene Nelson was the long man, Greg Cadaret, Eric Plunk, and Rick Honeycutt the short setup men for Eckersley, who saved 45 of his 54 opportunities.

The team's roster seemed so stacked with talent, A's manager Tony La Russa started jokingly calling himself, "The push-button manager." He was feeling the pressure in January, when general manager Sandy Alderson met La Russa's requests by trading for or signing seven newcomers: Matt Young (a left-handed pitcher who was hurt all year), Welch, Parker, Henderson, Hubbard, Hassey, and Baylor.

Those were enough new faces to make a veteran woman sportswriter feel at home in the clubhouse on the first day of spring training. I remember feeling so "arrived," I wore shorts in training camp for the first time ever. I wasn't the nervous outsider any more, I was the smug old-timer.

At least I knew how to *find* the clubhouse, unlike Baylor, who nearly reported late for spring training for the first time in his career. I think the Arizona cacti threw him off — he had been a Florida palm tree spring trainer for most of his 17 years.

It was Baylor's second go-round with the A's: he had first joined them from Baltimore in 1976, when Finley traded Reggie Jackson for him. The other newcomers were donning the uniform for the first time, and we writers wandered around in the cramped clubhouse quarters uncertain of whom we ought to talk to first.

At least we didn't have to spend any time with Canseco that day. He never reported punctually to spring training. His excuse in 1988: He had contracted to appear at an autograph show. "I think I'll send him to Triple A," La Russa mumbled. Canseco's teammates — Baylor and Parker leading the rounds — collected change and dollar bills for him, since he obviously needed the money, in a huge jar that greeted his arrival. And the new A's began to mesh.

They showed their swagger in the opening game of the season, defeating the Seattle Mariners' ace, Mark Langston, 4-1 behind the pitching of Stewart. Eckersley made the emotional, fist-pumping save, and Henderson and Canseco homered.

Henderson had had a horrible spring training, but that didn't seem to humble the always cheerful "Hendu" a bit when the real action began on Opening Night. He angered his former Seattle teammates that night when he appeared to take a jaunty detour toward them at the beginning of his home run trot.

"I was looking for him," said Rene Lachemann, the A's first-base coach who wanted to shake Henderson's hand, "and he was in the Mariners' dugout!"

Lachemann, probably the clown of his class, tended to exaggerate —Henderson hadn't gone quite that far. But he had gone far enough to inspire the beginning of the American League's hate affair with the A's, who combined preen with their power and alienated even best friends with their struts. Henderson and Langston, the Seattle pitcher who threw the Opening Night home run pitch, were neighbors. A few weeks later, Eckersley angered a man who had been a member of his wedding party. He was Dwight Evans, the Boston outfielder, who struck out against Eckersley at Fenway Park May 16. Eckersley's final flourish: a pantomimed pistol fired at Evans.

"He didn't like that," Eckersley said after the game, sheepishly and regretfully. "I don't blame him. (The phantom firing) must be instinct."

Eckersley's antics were colorful, like the vocabulary of words and phrases that were so distinctly his "Ecktionary," or, as Peter Gammons called it, "DialEckt." There was "baboomba," a home run. There was "oil," the alcoholic beverages that had dragged him down, and "iron," the big money he was making after he signed a two-year contract extension in July. There was, now and then, a "walk-off piece," a game-winning homer by the opposing team host to send Eckersley and his fellows in the field walking forlornly off to the showers.

But normally it was Eckersley who walked off happily, sometimes too happily for his opponents. Again, this time in Cleveland on the Fourth of July, Eckersley angered Ron Washington by his game-ending display of excitement. On the fifth of July, Eckersley sought out Washington before the game and shook hands with him. "I don't want people thinking I'm a jerk," Eckersley said.

He didn't seem to be a jerk. He just seemed like a man who had been so far down, he couldn't see up, and, now, he *was* up! There he was! He talked, always, about the fear he feels, standing on the mound in the ninth inning with the victory of some other pitcher — probably a good friend — in his charge. I think the emotion he vented was the same that you or I would unleash should we realize, as we sit down to a pile of bills, that, yes, that is a winning lottery ticket at the bottom of the pile. Go ahead, say it: "YES!" And you, too, could be Dennis Eckersley striking out the side in the ninth.

Eckersley symbolized the intensity and excitement of that 1988 team. It was such a dominant, invincible combination that opponents could find little to criticize but its swagger. The managers in Texas and Boston tried accusing Eckersley of throwing a spitter or other illegal pitch ("a sinker of some description," Red Sox manager Joe Morgan said in his wry New England manner), but those accusations floundered. And the umpires hindered the pitching staff by implementing the largely ignored stop-and-set balk rule, but all that did was drag out the games and postpone the inevitable. The A's were going to win, no matter what their opponents called them and no matter what the umpires called on them.

That became apparent on an 11-game roadtrip that began April 21 in bitter-cold Chicago and proceeded around the Great

Lakes, to Toronto, Cleveland and Detroit. The A's were wearing, for the first time, team sportcoats — gray herringbone silk jackets bearing green-and-gold A's cap pins. The jackets might have doubled as Superman capes — the team wearing them compiled a 10-1 record on trip. By the end, players were vowing to sleep in the jackets, which they hadn't liked so much in the beginning.

But they extended their winning streak to a club-record 14 games wearing their home uniforms at the Coliseum. It was still April when pitcher Storm Davis whispered to me, "The feeling here is unbelievable. Know the last time I saw something like this? '83."

Davis had pitched for my favorite team, the Baltimore Orioles, when they won the World Series that year. With the A's in '88, he compiled a very strange 10-game winning streak late in the season. I say it was strange because he didn't pitch that well — the A's simply went out and scored an average of nearly six runs every time he started a game, and the bullpen cashed in on the two or three innings Davis invariably left them.

Stewart had started the season with an eight-game winning streak, and he was the man La Russa wanted pitching every important game. These included a June 3 victory in Minnesota, where the A's had lost all seven games in 1987 to the Twins, the defending world champions.

That night of June 3, the A's were losing 4-0 but fought back for an 8-5 victory that gave them a 10-game lead in the division. Afterward, in his office, La Russa poked his food around on his plate and mumbled about it being a 162-game season. But, in the hotel elevator, he told me, "This is the happiest I've been all year."

But La Russa wasn't smiling that night. It seemed he finally realized he had a team that could take him to his first World Series, and he took that possibility seriously. Bill Rigney, a 50-year baseball man who had enjoyed a long, successful managerial career before becoming an A's consultant, had never won the World Series. And there were so many others like Rigney.

But I don't think there have been many managers much better at squeezing so much toothpaste out of the tube. La Russa inspires loyalty and affection in the players he wants on his side. And his behavior inspires a tolerant sort of detestation in those he neither wants nor believes to be on his side. Carlton Fisk went from playing for La Russa, on the Chicago White Sox, to playing against him, and was surprised to hear La Russa accusing him, during one game, of "headhunting."

"I said, 'That's bullshit! I played for you, don't you remember?'" Fisk said.

But that no longer mattered. To Tony, there are two kinds of players: his and everybody else's. Silly was the pitcher who beaned one of Tony's players and expected to get away with it without a barrage of profanities, glares, and worse. Tony lost his control so completely when Terry Steinbach was hit in the head in Chicago in 1990, even the columnists at home in Oakland suggested he tighten his screws. He didn't like that one bit: If you were covering Tony's team, you were expected to support him as if you were one of his players.

To Tony, there is winning and there is losing. He could never understand why the length of the game mattered to me, when it was only winning that mattered to him. I hope he figured out, in the course of our wagered dinners that season and the next, that what mattered to me was having as much time as possible to conduct postgame interviews and write my stories. Our aims were identical: We wanted to perform well.

But I never figured out Tony La Russa. The man could be charming and conversational, and I adored him. He could be brusque and incommunicado, and I despised him.

I'm sure he didn't care what I thought. One night in August, at Fenway Park, the Red Sox defeated the A's 7-6 in a game that I thought La Russa blundered away. Now, I know he's a genius and all, but even Dennis Eckersley blows a save once in a while, even Jose Canseco strikes out once in a while, and even — La Russa has actually *said* this — Sinatra clears his throat once in a while. It seemed to me that La Russa made two questionable moves that night that cost the game. One was leaving a struggling Stew in the game after the A's had tied it 6-6 in the seventh inning, on back-to-back homers by Luis Polonia and Dave Henderson. The second was pitching to Mike Greenwell, the major-league RBI leader, with one out, a runner on third, and first base open. Greenwell singled to score the game-winner.

Afterward, I amiably tried to give La Russa the opportunity to say, "I stunk," or, "I didn't have my best stuff tonight," or even make some alibi as one of his players might have. But this was a man who couldn't even admit to having been married and divorced. He wouldn't bite on a question of tactics. He said only, "I regret that we lost the game. That's as far as it goes."

I'm not sure he ever second-guessed himself publicly. He is not a good loser. And I am sure that has something to do with why he is a winning manager. He needs to win to sleep, to smile, and so he does it.

I remember lots of smiling faces besides Tony's in that 1988 season. It was an odd collection of personalities united mostly by winning but also by joking.

Glenn Hubbard, the little second baseman from Atlanta, had observed of the A's in spring training, "These guys cuss a little bit too much for me." But he joined in the fun with a series of practical jokes, the last of which made him pause for breath, when he put a dollar on a string at San Francisco International airport and a man tried to pick it up. The man didn't laugh when he missed his flight, and he came back to blame Hubbard. "He kicked me!" said Hubbard, who shelved that joke for a while.

The jokes between Lachemann and Baylor reached the sky in late May, when some jet banners appeared over the Coliseum imploring, "Groove, Be home by 5, don't be late — Becky," and, "Groove, you forgot to do the dishes — Becky." Baylor's nickname was Groove and his wife's name Becky, but Becky, said Baylor, wouldn't have done such a thing. The culprit was revealed to be Lachemann. He was getting even with Baylor for having "Lori" printed on the back of Lachemann's team jacket. Lori was Lachemann's wife, who, so the legend goes, was wearing the Lachemann pants. If any of this sounds childish, consider that Baylor will be managing the Colorado Rockies, Lachemann the Florida Marlins, in 1993. Pranks are such a part of baseball that I'm sure they'll have something special planned for the first meeting of the league's two expansion teams.

By the All-Star break, the A's looked up at the scoreboard and saw themselves 20 games over .500, at 54-34. Eckersley observed, "You hate to scoreboard watch, but . . . they've got those scoreboards." And the A's topped the standings for the rest of the season with a big media entourage in tow.

It was no race for the division: What we were covering now was Jose Canseco in his quest to become the first player to hit 40 homers and steal 40 bases in a season. Some of the experts ridiculed this goal, saying it was contrived. And maybe it's not like hitting 62 home runs in a season or even like driving in 100 runs. Still, it was April when Canseco said he wanted to reach the following numbers: 40 homers, 40 steals, 130 runs batted in, and a .290 batting average. His bottom line six months later: 42 homers, 40 steals, 124 runs batted in, and a .307 batting average. He told me in April when he set his 40-40 goal, he thought he could "max out" some day at 50 homers, 50 steals, 150 RBI, a .290 batting average (here, he underestimated himself), and no errors.

Canseco's play — or, shall we say, misplay — in the outfield had been hilarious in his first year, 1986. Coach Joe Rudi helped him in 1987 by coaxing him into using a perpendicular ready position that made him look like a waiter pouring coffee, but it worked. By 1988 he was wowing his critics. "In his first year, he was terrible out there," Lansford said. "But, now, he's unbelievable."

By 1989, Canseco's teammates would begin complaining again about his play in the field. But in 1988, they raved. It was that kind of season.

Another shaky fielder, Luis Polonia, rose to the big leagues in June. A flashy, speedy, inventive hitter from the Dominican Republic via New York City, Polonia never saw a stop sign he liked. Time and again, he'd ignore the signal of the third-base coach, Lefebvre, and fly home. Time and again, he scored. I don't think I ever saw him called out at home after running through a stop sign.

Mike Gallego must have been Polonia's alter ego. Unlike Polonia, he couldn't run very fast or hit very well. Unlike Polonia, he could make a play on anything hit his way and lots of balls hit somebody else's way.

Gallego became one of my favorite players on June 12, 1987, when he gave new meaning to the cliche, "I'd give my right arm to catch that ball," taking off into left field to make a spectacular over-the-shoulder catch on a fly ball. As he fell, he tumbled into left fielder Stan Javier and broke his wrist. Gallego — "Gags" or "Gagman," his teammates called him — missed the next six weeks of the season. But he held on to the baseball.

I also liked being able to look Gallego in the eye, unless, of course, I (5-foot-7 1/2 inches tall, barefoot) was wearing heels

— he's that short, a condition to which he always credited his flawless fielding. "I'm close to the ground," he'd say.

Gallego was a good team player, too, who selflessly shared his knowledge with the least sung — yes, I said, *sung*— A's note, Walt Weiss. Weiss batted only .250, but he won the Rookie of the Year award with his fine fielding at shortstop. The A's had traded away Alfredo Griffin for Welch and rushed Weiss to the big leagues, but he proved he was ready with a 58-game errorless streak in the heart of the season. When it ended at the Coliseum on Sept. 21, he refused to acknowledge the crowd's standing ovation, because, he said, he wouldn't tip his cap for an error.

The team won back-to-back 16-inning contests on the road, in Toronto July 3 and Cleveland July 4, and lost Dave Parker to thumb surgery. I remember Parker wasn't even put to sleep for the operation, and then went out shopping afterward.

Hubbard hit three homers in three consecutive games in August, after which he said of his teammates' congratulatory whacks, "I don't like the (forearm) bash much. Some of these guys, they hurt."

The A's clinched the division title on September 19 and celebrated with a raucous display of champagne and beer spraying. I did not know, then, that the next ten days would be our last as baseball team and entourage. The daily contact among the writers would give way to sharing our expertise with out-of-towners. Our casual one-on-one repartee with the players would disappear into formality, behind cords, podiums, and security. The alienation was so pronounced, Tony La Russa generously held a daily briefing for the local writers, just so that we could stay in contact with the day-to-day doings of the team we had covered all season. The playoffs and World Series may be the highlight of a baseball fan's season, but they are the lowlight of a baseball beat writer's season. Not only are they physically dangerous—what with having to fight through dozens of reporters and minicams to try to get an interview—they are emotionally and professionally exhausting.

The only writers having fun are the ones whose teams finished out of the race. They can write one story and a notebook and actually watch the games; the rest of us are running around catering to the whims of some editor who has just come on the scene to assign this sidebar and that sidebar. Suddenly, the seats on the team's charter are filled with families and front-office secretaries. The team's hotel turns into a zoo where we writers should feel lucky to have a room. We weren't covering baseball anymore: we were covering an Event.

The pennant clinch on September 19 signaled the end of the baseball life's few charms. Eleven days later, Tom Boswell of the *Washington Post* appeared on CBS's *Nightwatch* program alleging that Canseco had used steroids to pump himself up, and the circus began. Canseco denied ever using steroids, and pointed out that he had undergone annual urinalysis and blood sampling that would have detected steroids. He and Boswell later discussed the matter, apparently to the satisfaction of both men, and it was dropped.

But then the playoffs began on October 5 in Boston's Fenway Park, where the fans in right field sang, "Ster-oids, Ster-oids," to Canseco. Canseco giggled at them and then homered in his second at-bat. The Boston fans — about the liveliest anywhere outside of Yankee Stadium — also got on Stewart that day in the bullpen about his arrest so many years ago. Stewart, firing away angrily, held the Red Sox to one run. Finally, Dennis Eckersley struck out Wade Boggs on three pitches to end Game One.

Game Two ended with the hawkers on Yawkey Way pitching Red Sox pennants in a going-out-of-business sale. The A's won 4-3 on Walt Weiss's two-strike, two-out game-winning single in the top of the ninth and went home leading the series 2-0. The odds of the Red Sox surviving three games in Oakland to take the best-of-seven series back east weren't good. They had won only once in their last 15 games at Oakland's Coliseum.

Game Three, Saturday night in Oakland, was the wildest of the series. It was the kind of warm, still night — more typical of Fenway Park in August than the Oakland Coliseum ever — that makes for home run conditions. The A's hit four of them to come back from a 5-0 deficit and win 10-6. Sunday's series-sweeping 4-1 win was just a formality that awed even the competition.

"I think Oakland has the best club in baseball," Boston outfielder Mike Greenwell said.

"I would feel bad if we didn't go all the way now, because I think we have the best team in baseball," said Eckersley, the

MVP of the playoffs with four saves in four games. "I'm sure we still have to prove that, because otherwise we're not the best team in baseball. Right?"

Uh, right. Too right. Now the A's would shave their bats and oil their gloves for five days, awaiting Game One of the World Series while the Dodgers wrapped up their seven-game series against the Mets.

It was a tedious wait. We writers were supposed to try to come up with something to say every day while there was nothing going on. The players tired of our questions about nothing; it was easy for them simply to avoid us. They made it clear to us beat writers, though, that they wanted the Dodgers to defeat the Mets. The coast-to-coast travel didn't bother them so much: It was the idea of going to Shea Stadium in October. They thought that would be cold and dangerous, and some of the players said their families would not be attending a World Series game there under any circumstance. Of course, the A's wives were cheering wildly when the Dodgers won Wednesday night.

By Friday, the A's and their massive entourage had moved to Dodger Stadium for an afternoon workout. It was a beautiful day, and pitching coach Dave Duncan asked me, "How come you're not at the beach?" I wanted to strangle him. I would have loved to have been at the beach. I had three or four stories to write instead.

I wasn't the only miserable beat writer, either. Bud Geracie, in his final weeks before he vaulted off the beat to a column, had turned out to be an off-day story. He had stopped by Don Baylor's locker Thursday morning, just before the A's boarded the flight to L.A., and heard Baylor fuming.

"He was ripping the entire Dodger organization, and so I started writing it all down furiously," said Bud. "But I couldn't really understand why he'd do something like that. So, on the plane, I'm in the back smoking with Hassey, who was the only guy there who smoked, and I asked Don why he had said those things. He went off on (Dodger reliever and former Athletic) Jay Howell in this brutal, vicious, horrible way, and said, 'And you can print it.'"

Bud got his notecards out, and Baylor repeated his statements for Bud to write when the plane landed. A nice little story, Bud figured—but it had been blown into a big deal by the next day, because Bud's editor had relayed the story to the *Los Angeles*

*Times.* I think Bud would have liked to have been at the beach along with me that next afternoon. With writers from all over the country asking Baylor why he was mad at Howell, Baylor answered that he had been told that Howell had made derogatory comments about him and theA's.

"Who told you that?" the writers asked Baylor.

"I don't remember," Baylor said.

As it turned out, Howell had said nothing derogatory, at least publicly about Baylor or the A's. So Baylor had embarked on his tirade based on false information. Naturally, everyone incorrectly believed that the bug in his ear had been Bud.

"It was a very bad episode for me," said Bud. "I don't even remember what Eck looked like the night Gibson hit the homer."

Ah, baseball. Yes, finally, Game One arrived. And, finally, there was Kirk Gibson hitting his unforgettable home run off Dennis Eckersley, a blow from which the A's would not recover. It was the ultimate "walk-off piece" against the Eck, who stood at his locker afterward and answered questions — the same ones over and over: What was the pitch? Did you think it was out? — as long as anyone asked.

The A's performed so poorly in the rest of that World Series, scoring just seven runs as they lost three of the four games that followed the breathtaking opener, that they had to answer to all of the theories and speculation of the national media. Had the wait hurt them? Had the "Gibson Game" thrown them into shock? Had the A's, a team Dave Parker described as a "monstrosity," underestimated the opponent? Were the Dodgers simply better for one week?

They stood up and answered the questions. The only one I remember as red-faced was Mark McGwire, who had gone 1-for-17 in the Series and then taken the public approach, "Everything gets blown out of proportion in the World Series." It struck me that the A's had taken such a solid, series-by-series approach to the season that maybe they had forgotten to remind the young players, "Now is the time to raise the intensity."

Said Carney Lansford, "I'll be in my rocking chair up in Oregon, and these guys will still be playing in the World Series... At their age, you think you're going to win every year for the rest of your career. But it's not that easy."

Lansford and those young players, of course, were back in 1989, sweeping the Bay Bridge/Earthquake World Series. But now they were making millions in, as Eckersley would say, iron, and Rickey Henderson had infected them with his dubious approach to the game. Fans pestered them everywhere they went. The media swarmed around, searching for new angles that simply didn't exist. The players became jaded, boring, and arrogant.

It wasn't nearly as much fun as 1988.

I think of Storm Davis, that spring, whispering, "It's just like '83." And I wonder if any of the A's will ever find themselves whispering, "This reminds me of '88," with that kind of reverence. I wonder if I will.

# 10

# A New Ballgame

Just as the 1988 season plays in memory like it's on a big screen with Dolby sound, 1989 seems like a collection of snapshots hidden away in a shoebox.

The A's seemed to hurry through the season, just so they could get back to the playoffs and World Series and right their wrongs of the previous October. There was little fun about it, except for the June acquisition of Rickey Henderson. Henderson added a terrorizing leadoff dimension to the A's that they had not had since he left them in 1985, and everything about his game said, "Pay me millions." He would make sure that the A's did pay up when the season ended, and would begin, during the 1990 spring training, to complain that they hadn't paid him enough millions. Give me Jose Canseco anytime.

I just wanted the 1989 season to be over as soon as possible. The less October, the better. I felt overworked and underpaid — the recession having already hit the newspaper business, which demanded more notes and sidebars and features of beat writers every week while crunching salaries and expense accounts. The work had doubled while salaries grew by single-digit percentages. My professional weariness was contaminating the rest of my life: Unable to stay home long enough to build a healthy romance or support network, I felt just plain lonely.

Besides, the conditions under which I had been hired had quickly changed. The originally prescribed travel quotient — one-half to three-quarters of the team's trips — grew to all the trips in 1987, and all but one each year thereafter. Now, when I came home from a roadtrip, my suitcase sat waiting in the guest room, unemptied and ready to make the next flight. I had visited most of the United States and concluded that the most beautiful part of the country is Northern California — yet, I kept leaving.

My sports editor, Dan McGrath, assured me I could remain in the Bay Area as a backup baseball writer and feature writer if I wanted to leave the A's beat, so I declared the 1989 season my "farewell tour" as a baseball beat writer and snapped pictures all along the way, from the desert to the Rose Garden.

The players, coaches, and writers smiled and posed for me and with me. And we toasted the "tour" in every American League city and many American League bars. But it was, both figuratively and literally, the longest baseball season ever.

The A's prolonged the agony by winning their division and then the playoffs easily; the San Francisco Giants compounded the agony of all of the Bay Area writers by also winning the playoffs. Covering a World Series is difficult enough when one local team makes it, but we had two local teams for the first Bay Bridge World Series between the A's and Giants. It would become known as the Earthquake Series, interrupted as it was by the Loma Prieta quake that rocked all of Northern California just before Game Three in Candlestick Park, at 5:04 on October 17.

I had been on the road for other earthquakes during my five years in California and didn't recognize this one at first. It began as a rumbling that sounded like the sellout crowd might have been getting antsy. Then the press box shook. Still, I did not know how bad this was until I looked up from the magazine I was reading in the press box and saw fear in the faces of native Californians. Then, I jumped out of my seat, probably more alarmed than they were.

The scoreboard was out, and the electricity was off, but people were amazingly calm. Maybe they were just grateful to be alive: The fans actually cheered. Jose Canseco said he thought it was one of his migraine headaches coming on, "But it was just an earthquake." Players sought out their families in the stands, and many of the writers checked on our friends in auxiliary press boxes. Soon, we all were asked to leave the stadium. Before I left, I called Baltimore to let my parents know everything was OK. Then I drove another sportswriter to his downtown hotel. He was from New York, and he was a nervous wreck. I negotiated us slowly through the traffic and damage.

Sports were put on hold; the next day, I visited Oakland and helped with news coverage. There was talk of canceling the World Series with the A's winning two games to none. Instead, at a candlelit press conference the next afternoon, Commissioner Fay Vincent postponed the World Series until San Francisco and Oakland had time to clean up the mess and mourn the dead. That meant that the A's and Giants had to bide their time with workouts.

I did not handle any of this well. My impatience over the never-ending season and my anxiety over the earthquake joined forces to turn me into baseball's biggest bitch for two weeks; I don't know how anyone could stand being around me. I even checked out for two days to seek refuge in a Sonoma spa — but that was cut short when the A's announced they were heading for Arizona, and my boss assigned me to go along with them.

I'm sure this was Mickey Morabito's idea — he loves Arizona. It had been raining for a couple of days in the Bay Area, and, besides, everyone was bored with waiting. So the travel director put us on a charter and took us away from the national media and league officials to Phoenix, where the A's worked out for two days in front of huge crowds who cheered them and left buckets of money for them to take home to the earthquake relief efforts. It was a great idea. I don't think many of the players really wanted to go — they had to leave their wives and families for this mini-spring training — but I think they all were glad they did. There was something about the annual spring rituals that refreshed and renewed everyone, and that seemed to work in October 1989. It was also a good opportunity for the players to talk to each other, instead of reporters and families, about how to handle the work (and, they presumed, impending victory) ahead.

The sun was shining back in San Francisco, too, on October 27, when the Series resumed. The stadium seemed quiet until the cast of "Beach Blanket Babylon," a long-playing cabaret show, led the crowd through the spirited song, "San Francisco." Then everyone cheered, and the public address system blared out Jefferson Starship's song, "We Built this City on Rock and Roll." The first "pitch" was tossed out by 12 earthquake heroes to 12 Bay Bridge series participants. And then the A's were back in business, clobbering the Giants 13-7 and 9-6 on consecutive nights.

Finally, it was over — a snappy four-game sweep by the A's over the neighbor they'd dominated since spring training. For once, it was OK for me to wear a brand new leather skirt (black, to the knee) and a silk blouse (fuchsia, buttoned to the neck) in a championship clubhouse, because, in deference to the earthquake victims, there was no champagne in the A's club-house this time, only affection and quiet celebration. A couple of my interviews ended with hugs, from Mike Gallego and Carney Lansford. Then there was the big hug from Dave Stewart, the Most Valuable Player of the series, who saw the tears in my eyes and said, "Don't you dare."

My favorite snapshot shows me sitting upstairs in the press box at Candlestick Park, having finished my final World Series story, my arm resting atop a closed computer. I felt no nostalgia, only relief. I was done.

Now that I was done covering the baseball beat, though, I did not know what to begin. I took all of the time off allotted me that winter and wandered for three weeks alone through the rain in Hawaii, reading fiction and studying for the law school entrance exam. Then I spent a sunny Saturday in a University of California-Berkeley classroom with a few hundred 22-year-old know-it-alls taking this test. By the time the score arrived to tell me, "You're in," I was saying, "Forget that." I thought about moving back to Baltimore and even inquired about job possibili-ties.

Does this sound like what they call burnout?

But spring re-ignited my sports spark. The *Bee* sent me to cover some baseball games at Stanford University, where the brightness of both the sun and the kids could usually set the sportswriters squinting. I rediscovered the pleasure of watching sports on television — something I had considered to be a sin when I was covering a baseball game every day. And I was reminded of the unique characteristics of other athletes in other sports.

Football players, for instance, probably give the best interviews. Most of them probably spent five or six years in college, which is bound to be educational even if you're not paying attention the whole time. But football teams, on the whole, are the most paranoid about the enemy's efforts to salvage from writers useful information or bulletin board material. That meant players were discouraged from talking too technically or too brashly. Too bad.

College kids tend to give the most candid interviews, if you patiently draw them out. Basketball players and hockey players tend to treat the press most humanely, which must say something nice about the tall and the Canadian.

Baseball players are the ones who sign autographs for money. No wonder they act like they're doing the media a favor just by answering a question. When the 1990 spring training season called me to Arizona for an invigorating couple of weeks instead of an exhausting six, and Rickey Henderson didn't want to play because the A's didn't want to tear up his contract, I knew I had made the right move.

Then, the baseball season brought new opportunities. For instance, I began scoring — *official* scoring. Official scorers distinguish base hits from errors, and they assign assists and putouts to defensive players. One E.G. Green did the scoring for the Chicago Cubs from 1882 to 1891; she was Mrs. Elisa Green Williams, who sat between two other ladies who did not even know she was the official scorer. So I was not the first woman official scorer in baseball.

I was the only woman official scorer in 1990, though, and I could soon see why. Other women must have been too smart to do this. It's a thankless job for which there is no real training or handbook — or even much pay (then, $65 a game, more recently, $75). The Official Baseball Rules scoring guidelines are so lame, there must be some missing pages somewhere in the Hall of Fame's massive library. Virtually any call could be made one way by one scorer in Oakland and a different way by a second scorer in Detroit.

And virtually any call made by any scorer in Oakland was going to make somebody mad. For this reason, some sports editors would not allow their writers to score; my editor and I agreed that I would not score any game I might have to cover in relief of our new A's beat writer, Ron Kroichick.

The A's were by now so spoiled that they were certain every call should be made in their favor — in other words, every time they swung their bats and reached base safely, they should be awarded base hits, even if the ball happened to hit the center fielder in the glove before it hit the ground. The pitching coach thought his team ought to field every ground ball flawlessly — otherwise, players ought to be charged with errors so that the runs scored off his pitchers would be ruled unearned. And the manager, who impressed me as the consummate professional except for when he condoned such immature knee-jerk reactions as these, led the league and his team in neck-craning.

Tony La Russa could spot the official scorer three decks up and reach him or her with a glare that said, "What's wrong with you? . . . Are you watching the same game I'm watching? . . . Do you hate me? . . . Better come see me later so I can chew you out." Often, A's coaches would call the press box during games to question calls, as if they had nothing better to do. Once, Tony even called an official scorer at home because, he said, that scorer would not come to his office and listen with patience and attention as he whined about a particular call.

This was not typical. Players, coaches, and officials of other teams, particularly the neighboring Giants, would apologize before they even politely inquired about a decision. I think maybe the A's had gotten so good at their game that their manager designed little chips for his players' shoulders, creating a "the whole world's against us" attitude to help his team keep its winning edge.

Most of the other scorers deferred to La Russa, changing calls when he asked them to, and I do not know why. I do know he can be fearsome, and I suspect that he could blackball a scorer who consistently irked him since scorers are approved by the league but assigned by the local baseball writers' chapter. I took my chances. Once, I complained about the team's attitude, officially, in a letter to American League president Bobby Brown. Tony La Russa and I argued later; he didn't like getting reprimanded on his conduct. But I didn't like hearing Rickey Henderson say, after one of my decisions, "If you ever made a call like that on me, I would kill you." This, to me, sounded a bit extreme.

I wasn't very solid in that first season, so I listened to all of the critiques, much of which sounded so much like intimidation that I ultimately opted to avoid the clubhouses unless I had a question for somebody. I wanted to be a good scorer, but I was doing the job primarily to drag my fanny out to the ballpark and fill my notebook with ideas for columns.

Sports column-writing, now there's a job for men. I don't think so, but they sure do. Sports editors attend conventions every year and meetings every day where they wonder, "How can we get more new readers into the sports section?" Of course, their vision of a new reader is a man who usually opts to read the Wall Street Journal rather than the local sports section, not a woman who would read the sports section if only it addressed subjects that interested her in ways that included her.

So, the sports editors make sure there's some 30-or-40-something white man's picture atop the centerpiece of their section, the main opinion column, every day. And he writes, like all of the other 30-or-40-something white male columnists, in praise of the courage of Magic Johnson for going public with the news that he has the AIDS virus.

"I think the reason we don't see women and blacks writing columns is the same as the reason we don't see them as sports editors: There's a large fear factor," said APSE president Sandy Bailey of the *New York Times*. "They're not accepted as mainstream. It's a risk. No one will say this, but there must be a fear that the black columnist will write nothing but black issues or that the woman columnist will not know what she is talking about."

Case in point: Helene Elliott had done beat work — on ice hockey, baseball, soccer, tennis, and college basketball and football — for 10 years when New York's *Newsday* began auditioning staffers for a column-writing opening.

"They even auditioned the horse-racing guy," she said, "but not me. I was very, very insulted. They said, 'We know you know baseball and hockey, but we weren't sure about the other sports.' And the only beats I hadn't covered were the NFL and the NBA."

She had acquired the multiplicity that is usually the hallmark of a columnist. No, it must have been something else that Helene was lacking — perhaps it was that something that we women sportswriters weren't supposed to look at.

Diversity ought to be a hallmark of every section of any daily newspaper wanting to be read by the multitudes, but it is not to be found in the sports pages. And I do not think that is so just because the media does not adequately cover women's sports, although it doesn't. The Amateur Athletic Foundation commissioned a study that found that major TV networks devote only five percent of their sports coverage to women and major newspapers about the same. This isn't much, and programming directors and sports editors rightly talk about increasing their allotment of women's sports stories. They do not wish to be considered promoters, though — they prefer to see signs of interest in women's sports, unsubtle signs like TV coverage or sellouts, before going out on their own diving boards. You can see the catch here — where do the cameras and crowds come from without newspaper coverage?

Cathy Henkel, sports editor of the *Seattle Times*, cased her region for women sports models when she joined the staff in 1988. There were none. "So we got in on the ground with women's basketball," she said. "The women's team (at the University of Washington) was outdrawing the men, so four years ago we started staffing them and using stringers for the men. Our high school coverage is about 50-50 girls-boys, excluding football, and I think that seeds interest locally.

"We did a survey of our sports readers a few years ago and found out that while we attracted more women than is the norm (38 percent of our readers were women), their interests were the same as the men's. They wanted the same things, the pro football, the baseball, the basketball, in the same order the men did. I was kind of surprised — the main difference was that they wanted more outdoor/recreational/participatory sports coverage. So we've done that."

I believe sports page readers are interested in superior women athletes and teams, which is why, in the fall of 1992, Stanford's national champion women's basketball team was garnering more column inches than its men's basketball team. But I believe it is a fallacy that women want to read about women's sports because that's what they play. And other fallacies are that women want to read about figure-skating, because a marketing study documented that figure-skating is the favorite spectator sport of women, or that women want to read about high school sports, because their kids might play.

"It is a large assumption of sports editors that everything directed toward making women comfortable with their sports sections must be related to women," Bailey said. "They'll say, 'We cover just as many girls' high school games as boys' high school games.' That isn't the point. How many games you cover isn't what draws women into the paper."

I think, as the *Seattle Times* discovered locally, women generally want to read about the same subjects men want to read about — the traditional men's sports of pro football, basketball, baseball, ice hockey, college football and basketball, plus men's and women's tennis and, more and more, women's college basketball.

But I believe women generally want different information than men do. My mother was my first model for this theory: She was not likely to look at the sports section unless a graphically well-designed feature caught her eye and was written with enough depth and range to sustain her interest. If the story was a good one, it didn't matter whether my mother had expertise in the sport.

Now, I can cite for evidence some marketing research produced by Matt Levine, who is currently the vice-president in charge of marketing the San Jose Sharks ice hockey team. He'd seat a man and a woman next to each other at a sporting event and then interview them about what they'd seen.

"It was like they went to two separate events," Levine said. "We're used to finding men into the technical and strategical aspects of what is going on. The women were more interested in the interrelationships between players and between the players and the coach, in the issue of dealing with pain, in how a player gets to be a great player — his nutrition, his training, his upbringing. Women were more into the overall feeling of the entire experience."

Hockey draws women in amazing numbers. From 35 percent to, in some markets on some nights, nearly 50 percent of the ticket holders are women. Some of the experts try to explain this by drawing some obscure correlation to women's interest in figure skating. "It's the grace and flow of the game," they say.

But the women fans I talked to said they liked the same features of the game — the action, the fights, and that bone-jarring, tooth-loosening macho — that the men fans liked. If there was any aesthetic element, it was that women were attracted to the helmeted, padded players. They found them tough, yet accessible. Pro basketball players wear no padding, no helmets, and little else, yet attendance at NBA games must be greater than 75 percent men. So perhaps when women say "accessible," they mean that hockey players look like average men while NBA players are so, well, tall — or, perhaps the accessibility has to do with race, since most hockey players are white and most NBA players are black.

Levine's theory is that women find everything about hockey accessible. "They don't feel intimidated," he said. "Most people in the building have never played ice hockey! So women find they can get into the action of the game and enjoy it."

A woman can go to a hockey game with her beau or her husband or her father or son and not feel excluded by not having played the game or been inside the locker room. She can go to a hockey game without feeling like she just walked into the wrong restroom. Elsewhere, that exclusive, big locker room attitude prevails.

On one autumn Friday morning, I awakened to my usual radio station. Sylvester Jackson's smooth voice sounded unusually excited today, though. He was raving about the packed sports viewing schedule of the upcoming weekend, and he was warning me. "Ladies," said Sylvester, "don't count on your men for much help around the house this weekend."

I was hardly even awake yet, but I was steamed. I got up, ate my bran muffin and headed for the gym to work it off. When I finished climbing stairs and lifting weights, I climbed back into the car and turned on the radio. There was Sylvester again with another sports report. This one began: "Fellas!" Off went *my* radio — he wasn't talking to me, I knew, and home I went to punch in the KBLX phone number to air out my radio friend.

"Sylvester, how could you?" I sputtered. "Did it ever occur to you that there might be some women in your audience who were looking forward to watching the weekend action on their television sets? Like, maybe, me?"

It simply hadn't occurred to him. Sylvester was no male chauvinist pig. He wasn't consciously excluding women from his broadcast — he was unthinkingly and automatically promoting a universal stereotype that may have accidentally alienated his women listeners. And I wasn't the only one: I had made plans to go to a sports bar that weekend with some other women to watch some of the action — sports action, not bar action.

Sylvester made me feel glad I'd called him. If only he'd seen me, standing there red-faced and mad, still drenched in sweat, he'd have laughed long and loud at anything I had to say. But he calmly said, "I see your point," and he offered to have me on the air one morning to talk about it.

And he did. He asked me, "Well, if the men and the women are all spending the weekend watching sports, who's cleaning the house and mowing the lawn?" I didn't know the answer to that, except that maybe our houses and lawns aren't as well-kept as they might be. Maybe people were having too much fun watching the games together to argue over who would mop and who would mow. Maybe sports weren't always and necessarily a point of contention between men and women, as the male-dominated sports media would like to believe.

And it's not just the media that's missing the boat on a large potential reader-listener pool out there — pro sports franchises are losing potential revenue by neglecting to expand their fan base. They do not reach out with much warmth, beyond the popularly targeted 30-or-40-something white male and the 12-year-old Little Leaguer, for the women who have a lot of interest in sports. They tailor their marketing and ticket sales strategies to target more of the audience they already draw, men.

I think their oversight is costing them money. True, in many markets, the local team does not have another seat to sell. If you want to buy season tickets for the Washington Redskins or the San Francisco 49ers, the Boston Red Sox or the Chicago Bulls, you've got to find your way into someone's will. Long waiting lists may foster an arrogance that precludes such teams-in-demand from expanding their audiences.

But there is more money to be made beyond ticket sales — money the franchises desperately need in order to stay competitive. The teams can make some of that money through novelty sales, which is why new franchises undertake detailed studies before they settle on a logo or colors. But they're going to make most of that money from television, which must be able to sell either the telecast (cable) or advertising in order to justify its payment to the teams or leagues for the TV rights. In either case, the potential size and scope of the audience could leverage the local team into a better TV contract.

In the case of cable or pay-per-view television, the team could only be helped by cultivating a female fan base in order to increase the volume of sales of the telecasts. But even in over-the-air programming, a documented female fan base could help sell advertising — or, in markets where every minute of ad time is sold out, inspire a bidding war. Manufacturers of goods and services spend their advertising dollars on the outlets they think will target their specific consumer profile. If the TV ratings consistently show that 80 percent of a particular viewing audience is male, Revlon is not going to spend money to advertise during that program. If pro sports franchises continue to foster the big locker room mystique about their businesses, Revlon is not going to spend money to advertise during their games.

The ability to urinate standing up is not a prerequisite for understanding and enjoying sports. The TV and sports marketing geniuses are failing to reach women only because they're not trying. The idea probably hasn't occurred to them because, like my friend Sylvester, they've been thriving for so long within the stereotype of "man as sports-viewing couch potato" and "woman as maid and waitress."

How could these men turn women on to sports? I don't think the answer is extremes — it's education. My friend Sabine King is a big baseball fan, yet, once, when one of her friends had missed a walk and asked, "How'd that guy get on?" Sabine's attempt at play-by-play commentary amounted to, "Oh, he balled him." Sponsor a businesswomen's lunch on the lingo of a sport, so Sabine can speak the universal language of sports with her male co-workers and bosses. Don't overdo that potentially demeaning hook of sex appeal, but do dispatch the best-looking and most charming players for daytime TV appearances. Design logos, uniforms, and apparel lines that gain the aesthetic approval of women. Hold special clinics directed toward the interests of women sports fans.

And keep in mind the results of the marketing investigations of Matt Levine, who found that men and women, even those who are side by side and maybe even holding hands, watch games not with an imbalance of interest but with a difference of focus. Men can already find the information they stereotypically want. John Madden draws them diagrams on television. The newspapers print baseball boxscores and how-they-scored details. So now tell the women what they want to know — about what the players do in all of those meetings and whether they go out for pizza afterward, and how frightened they are when a teammate is knocked unconscious, and what they learned from their parents and siblings.

"It's happening, gradually," said Cathy Henkel. "But there are still too many X's and O's in the sports section." If sports pages could find ways to communicate with both men and women, maybe they would be able to sell advertising beyond the typical, traditional, limited range of sporting goods stores and automobile parts suppliers. Oh, and let's not forget those other staples of the sports section, Bambi and her friends.

"It's a rare sports section that doesn't have the exotic dancer, all-nude, lap-dancing ads in it," said Sandy Bailey. "When APSE had its convention in San Antonio, Donna Lopiano appeared on a panel about coverage of women's sports, and the local newspaper did a story on Donna. The story jumped, and the jump ran right next to one of those ads — her name was "Suzy Boobies."

"So look what happened. No women read the section in the first place because it's normally geared to men, then this Donna Lopiano feature runs because stories about women supposedly are going to get more women into the section, and then the 10 women who get as far into the story to get to the jump page and "Suzy Boobies" are never going to read the section again!"

That's the reality. It's always been a fantasy of mine to have a perfume or a clothing designer call and say, "We want to buy an ad right next to Susan Fornoff's sports column." I tried, in my two years of writing columns, to reach the non-traditional sports page reader.

For instance, I interviewed a consultant who helps athletes deal with the media, and wrote about how image affects All-Star voting. A local college soccer team tied for the national championship one year and lost the following year in a tiebreaker, so I wrote about why we Americans are such sticklers for wins and losses that we go to extremes to create overtimes and shootouts. When Tony La Russa collected his 1,000th managerial victory, I wrote about how and why he someday would be fired. I wrote about how inflated salaries and guaranteed contracts tie the hands of managers and coaches. The San Francisco Giants held a Gay and Lesbian Day at the ballpark, for a charity that supports AIDS victims and their families, and I wrote about the integrity and bigness that required on the part of the Giants in the small-minded world of baseball. A black athlete emerged from a pistol packing neighborhood to attend a university considered white and rich, and I wrote about his experience.

I also wrote a couple of figure-skating columns. During the Clarence Thomas hearings, I wrote about harassment of women in sports. And I'm sure I presented views on games and athletes and trades that reflected something of my experience, not only as a sportswriter, but as a woman sportswriter. Sometimes I just chose the tack contrary to whatever the white males were writing and went from there.

I know by my mail that I reached a lot of women readers, and men, too. Other competing writers complimented my work. Other newspapers plucked my columns off the wires. Other sports editors called to inquire about my availability for openings. I loved where I lived, and I deflected their inquiries. Then, the spring of 1992, both of the *Sacramento Bee*'s full-time sports column positions opened. So I asked for one of them.

Do you know what I was told? The editor of McClatchy Newspapers, Gregory Favre, said, "You haven't found your voice yet."

Then the paper made a series of moves that appalled the women on the staff. It moved its 30-or-40 something white male sports columnist to news to write the lead column in the paper. Then it hired a 30-or-40 something white male lead sports columnist and promoted a 30-or-40 something white male basketball writer to second columnist. Three "voice" openings, filled by three white males of a certain age.

There is not a lead sports columnist at any large daily newspaper in this country who is a woman. I know of only two general interest full-time sports columnists at large dailies who are women. I do not believe I haven't found my voice. I believe my voice isn't masculine enough for most sports sections.

# 11

# *Readers Write*

The small sheet of paper and the plain postcard have turned yellow and crinkly. Still, they hang there at the top of my bulletin board, reminders of the scope of the First Amendment and the diversity of newspaper readers.

Both bits of mail arrived late in 1985, my first year as a full-time baseball beat writer for the *Sacramento Bee*. Both of them were addressed to my sports editor, Stan Johnston, who kindly passed them on to me. A guy named Bullet Bob wrote:

> *Now that you have relegated Susan Fornoff to someplace besides the World Series, what are you going to do with the best sports scribe in North California???*
> > *Male Chauvinist Macho fan*
> > *of a girl sportswriter . . .*
> *Never thought I see that day.*

And Dick (his real name, not just what I'd call him) had seen my off-season analysis of the team's trading season in his local newspaper. He wrote:

> *Fornoff has got to be one dumb bimbo. Every team and baseball man that knows anything has been raving about the A's steal of (Joaquin) Andujar. The guy is a jerk for sure, but it's still the deal of the*

*year. Please tell that dumb broad to go find something she can do and quit contaminating the sports wires. She doesn't know if it's stuffed or puffed.*

Stan wanted to know if Dick might be Kingman's brother-in-law. I'm sure they were related, by one thing (sexism?) or another (impudence?). At least Dick didn't attach his sentiments to a rodent. And at least Dick read my stuff.

This was always the bottom line, the answer to all of the letters, good and bad: At least they're reading. "Keep reading the *Bee*," I wrote to most of the readers who took the time to write to me. Some of them obviously required a great deal of time and effort to translate thought to paper.

Of course, I received my share of letters that deserved no reply. Most of *those* letters didn't carry a return address anyway. One that did responded to a column I'd written criticizing baseball's failure to sufficiently discipline some recent rules offenders. He wrote:

*That was an interesting article you wrote on Sunday about spankings and whippings. If you would like to meet a man on whom you could practice drop me a line at . . . and I'll tell you all about myself.*

I don't know any men sportswriters who received a letter like that one. Sometimes I wished I had initialized my byline; how would readers know "S.J. Fornoff" to be female? And sometimes I wished no photo had to appear with my columns, but then I would have missed out on letters like these:

*The picture at the head of your column does not do you justice. My source of information is the very occasional TV coverage of the press box.*

☙

*Beauty and thought (especially when the thoughts are of baseball) make for quite the combination. I enjoyed them both during your televised interview . . . What I would enjoy just as much would be meeting you. Didn't I hear you were single in the interview? Hope you don't get a lot of this — or maybe one of this is enough, too much?*

ॐ

*The good news is I love your columns... The bad news is your picture. It is really awful. Your hair looks like you had a blind beautician and then walked through a wind tunnel. Your smile looks like the photog said "smile" — and then waited 15 minutes to snap the shutter, while you froze in place. The top and pearls have no style! And to top it off, they cut off the top of your head.*

ॐ

*Your column today pounded another nail into the coffin of female sportswriters! Blame it on PMS? That's the legal female cop-out nowadays . . . (text about what a great team the Cincinnati Reds had) . . . Everyone knows women think more intuitively and emotionally than men, who rely on logic, but the sports section is no place for your complaining. You should marry (former* Bee *columnist) Tom Jackson, whose tunnel vision of the Series equaled your own!*

ॐ

*I have always had trouble with women sportswriters and (Susan Fornoff's) article sure did nothing to change my opinion. I say keep them out of the locker room and off the football field too.*

ॐ

*With women, everything has to be ritualized and sanitized. We men must bear that in everyday life (if we want a constant supply of sex, that is), but give us a break (in the sports pages).*

*When women get involved it invariably becomes feminized and its reason for being no longer exists. Why don't you hang your lacy curtins [sic] in your own clubhouse and let us alone to leave off our curtins [sic]. We like to see the world outside.*

And, from a couple of readers who sent me a package of Pepperidge Farm cookies:

*You may remember, you told us in a letter sometime ago, that you are not a good cook. (My wife) was going to bake you some cookies, but I told her maybe she better not because you might throw them away. After all, there are kooks who put needles and razor blades in Halloween cookies (and there are rats who send rats too!). So we thought maybe a sealed package would go over better.*

Yes, I ate the cookies. A sportswriter, male or female, turn away free food? Never.

The same gentleman whose wife had wanted to bake me cookies had written me one of the most meaningful letters I ever received regarding women in the locker room. This letter arrived after Dave Kingman had sent me the rat and I had become a news story. Thankfully, my office censored my mail at that time — and I say "thankfully" because some of the sick stuff found its way to me anyway and turned my stomach. But if you asked me how public opinion on the Kingman caper measured by my mail, I'd have to say it was almost all on my side.

I liked this particular letter because it was from a long-time sports fan in his 60s who had been, as he wrote "dead set against women in the clubhouse." But now he had changed his mind:

*Your writing is excellent. I have to admit that you probably could not do as good a job if you were kept out of the clubhouse. In particular, I liked your account of Jackie Moore the other day. . . The point is that you made a believer out of me. I am not at all a religious man, but I offer you some solace: "Give me the serenity to accept the things I cannot change, the courage to change the things I can . . . and the wisdom to know the difference..."*

The letters that appeared in area newspapers either ripped Kingman and the A's for being male chauvinist pigs, or they took one of two pro-Kingman tacks: Susan Fornoff cannot take a joke, or Susan Fornoff does not belong in the locker room anyway and so she's asking for it. The pro-Kingman letters that did not appear in any newspapers described in disgusting detail exactly what women are good for and then concluded that I got exactly what I deserved for crossing the boundaries of my sex.

Here are a few of the other letters that penetrated the *Sacramento Bee*'s censors and found their way into my mailbox:

When Kingman was a member of the Cubs, he dumped a bucket of ice cold water over the head of a male writer. Given the choice, I'd take the rat over the dousing any day. I have a feeling Ms. Fornoff would, too . . . Come on, face it. If the Chronicle, Examiner and Tribune had each supplied just one female sportswriter apiece for the past two years to provide Ms. Fornoff with some company and real support, the "rat prank" probably never would have been pulled. At least, if Kingman really is the tantamount chauvinist he's been portrayed to be, he would have been forced to buy four pet mice and (perhaps) had his fine quadrupled.

&

When will men of professional sport finally realize that women can do everything a man can and probably more? I was very dismayed to see Kingman come out of this the hero . . . I admire you a lot and respect your work. You are also a very attractive woman which really doesn't detract from your worth. Could you please send me an autographed photo? (I didn't send autographed photos.)

&

Don't let that bimbo get to you. He'll be gone soon and you'll still be writing long after he's history. Besides, he may be doing you a favor by drawing so much attention to you. It could pay off . . .

Sorry to hear Dave Kingman hasn't matured at all. I know it must be rough for you, but you're helping everyone by being so classy about it — tough in a good way that speaks volumes for women sportswriters.

&

Mr. Kingman's attitude has no place in today's sports world or anywhere else. Please do not let this one person's warped mind discourage you in any way.

&

Your arguments about going into the locker rooms aren't credible, but I'm sure you'll keep making them. Some people might even *be ignorant enough to believe them . . . I want you to know this is not a hate letter. You seem to be an adequate writer, but you let your feminism get in the way of what's fair . . .*

Aha: there it was, what I call the F-word of the sports section. Most general newspaper readers think the F-word had four letters, but most sports page readers seem to think it has eight (F-E-M-I-N-I-S-M). Any who wrote to call me a feminist meant it as an insult.

Later in the decade, as I began to write columns regularly, the scope of my subjects began to range beyond feminism and even baseball, but sometimes I didn't range far enough. And that's how I got into hot water with all of the bowlers of the world.

John Burkett, a pitcher for the San Francisco Giants, made his debut on the professional bowling circuit in a tournament in Pinole, California. He described bowling as a passion, baseball as a career, and I wrote a column that was intended to jab fun at Burkett's passion. It was the kind of fun you have in February, when the Super Bowl's over and spring training hasn't begun. At the risk of inviting more mail, let me say that bowlers don't seem to have much of a sense of humor. The irony was that one of my favorite spring training time-killers was, you guessed it, bowling. A sampling of the response:

*We all feel you no (sic) nothing about bowling or sports. My bet is that you have never bowled and have never played baseball. You no (sic) nothing about either sport but we have to read your crap when the Bee prints it. If you will write a column apologizing to bowlers for your story we will forget it ever happened. We are pissed off by your stupid column and want justice . . .*

❧

*I am a 15-year-old junior bowler who averages around 185. To me bowling is a sport. If you think bowling is easy than I will personally bowl 20 games against you at a bowling alley of your choice. Because to me bowling is my dream.*

*While all (bowlers) may not look like the physical specimens you imagine, I can assure you their arms, legs and upper torso are in extremely good shape. I could refer you to some golfers and athletes in other sports who also appear rotund, with baseball player Rick Reuschel coming to mind. When you demean a group of individuals who are working extremely hard to make a living in sports, and apparently condone the inflated salaries other athletes are receiving, it is not very good reporting. Hopefully you will be assigned another bowling event and see fit to look at it with broad strokes, not an opinionated view which you are going to get through at all costs.*

The bowlers were united. I did not get one shred of supportive mail from an anti-bowler. And only one pro bowler forgivingly excused my column for being, as it was intended, "tongue-in-cheek." But even he gave me his tongue-lashing.

The responses other columns elicited reminded me that sports readers come in all sexes and dispositions. Some of those readers, in fact, had stumbled over my work by mistake. Many letters began, "I don't usually read the sports section, but . . . " Or, "My wife isn't a big sports fan, but she likes your columns." I learned that women writers can present a unique perspective that draws readers out of other sections of the newspaper and into sports. We don't have to write about women's sports or women's issues to do this.

The example I use here is a column entitled, "Hey guys, how about just saying no?" I was writing about the perspective the male sports media had provided two recent issues: Magic Johnson's AIDS and Wilt Chamberlain's promiscuity. Chamberlain had claimed to have had sex with 20,000 women, an estimation that was met with lots of one-liners and laughs on the part of the male sportswriters. Then Johnson revealed he had contracted AIDS, and the male sportswriters reacted with this sentiment: "Those poor athletes. They're so good-looking and rich. Everywhere they go, women want them. They have no choice but to be promiscuous."

My view was that women learn to say, "No" to sex, and men — even good-looking, rich athletes — can learn that lesson, too. No law decrees every man must have sex with every woman who wants him to have sex with her, so we shouldn't feel sorry for athletes who take on and unload sex partners as if they were $20 bills.

A few days later, Martina Navratilova made public her more succinct view: If Magic Johnson were a woman, people would be labeling him a slut. Maybe in deference to his illness, they'd whisper—but the innuendo would circulate nonetheless.

My readers must have interpreted my "say no" column anyway they wanted. Could I possibly have received three wider ranging reactions than these?

*Hey Susan, how about just growing up? For every woman like you, there are a hundred others who accept life the way it is and enjoy sex and being a woman and the excitement of being a sports groupie! So what? Leave them alone! If (Chamberlain) had sex with only one woman or a million, it's none of your business! You're so blinded by your hate for men you can't think straight!*

*Women know how to say no, Susan. And men know how to say no too. Variety is the spice of life. You probably have a terrible sex life and are just jealous!*

ə.

*Thank you very much. It seems as though almost everybody wants to talk about safe sex, condoms and the like, but not the real problem, of rampant immoral behavior. I remember in the Bible it says "better is a man that controls himself than one that takes a city." I have always had an unfavorable attitude towards the women, feminist movement and still do to some degree, but I believe it has been a man's problem. A lot of women have been abandoned by their pleasure-seeking husbands. Again, I thank you for your honesty, for speaking the truth, even if it's not politically correct.*

ə.

*I found your article completely by mistake, but its contents so amazed and heartened me I felt compelled to write. Your courageous stance is to be given support and kudos, as your article expresses what many women, I am sure, are thinking. Perhaps since so many men read*

*the sports section of the paper, some of your keen (and yet obvious)*
*insights will filter down and make an impression...*
    *I respect your honor and courage to "tell it like it is" and your*
*seeming unwillingness to buy into the "boys will be boys" mindset.*


Of course, that last letter was my favorite. I don't hate
men and I hadn't meant to preach. But I was always hoping to
present a viewpoint that might represent some women *and* affect
some men. The reader/writer who typed letter number three
was a woman who thought I might have done just that.
    I believe I affected many other readers this way, because
my mail reflected their willingness to see a woman's face and
listen to a woman's voice in their sports section every morning.
Occasionally, I told other columnists about the positive mail I
received. They were amazed—first of all, that I received any mail
regularly, and, most of all, that I received intelligent positive
feedback on my writings about controversial issues. It's easy to
fire off a scathing letter when something you've read takes you
to your boiling point, less easy to sit down and write a calm letter
of praise. Human nature makes most of us quick to criticize, slow
to compliment.
    Maybe human nature accounted for my editors' willing-
ness to print letters that were critical of my ability. Maybe it was
sexism. One-third to one-half of the mail I received rated positive
marks, but probably nine out of ten of the letters printed in the
Sunday newspaper's mailbag department insulted me. One of
the letters that appeared in the *Bee's* Sunday sports section
included such cheap personal indignities that its appropriate-
ness for print was questioned later by staff members and higher-
ups.
    Now *I'm* calling the shots, so I include here a few of the
compliments that came from those I consider to be my more
erudite and insightful readers. And I didn't even have to pay for
these:

*Thanks for your sensitivity, for letting some of the best of who*
*you are come through in your writing, and for showing a lot of class in*
*a field that doesn't have much.*
    *Mostly when I read sports opinion, I feel like I'm being let in on*
*some ineptly sarcastic guy-thing that feels, really, like an advertisement*

*for the columnist. Ego and self-importance seem to get in the way of even good writers and otherwise intelligent people, who then take it upon themselves to demand Roger Craig's firing or declare the 49ers' season over after three games. Funny we didn't hear some of these cowboys suggest that Zeke Mowatt be arrested for sexual assault, or that Dave Kingman be fired on the spot . . .*

꙳

*A thousand and one cheers to Susan Fornoff for her insightful portrayal of the Washington Redskins' Art Monk . . . I have followed the Redskins for 25 years and am amazed that a sportswriter would have the insight and heart to praise a player for qualities that almost always go unnoticed. In this age of sports in America, we get too much coverage of egotistical loudmouths in the games. It's wonderful that Fornoff has the insight to praise a truly class act.*

꙳

*Your writing style is "reader friendly" and your knowledge of sports so professional and prolific. You point out the behind the scenes, interesting information, and make your reader so knowledgeable.*

꙳

*(From a woman:) I agree with you. I went (alone) to a game between Oakland and Boston in August. I was lucky in that I sat next to a 12-year-old boy; I am 77. We talked and discovered we both also choose Mike Gallego as our favorite player.*

꙳

*Yes, yes, and YES! Thank you for your article . . . Who says men all love sports and women put up with it? Many of my previous beaus have felt somewhat embarrassed they did not like football, and have relied on me to keep them up with the scores so they could keep up on the conversation with "the guys." Let's quit these stereotypes! Thanks for blowing the lid off women's love for sports. Maybe your next focus could be to boycott every station that interviews women in the mall on football day.*

꙳

*I finally got a copy of "Lending a hand to gay community" and wanted to thank you from all of us at (a local charitable project). The article is clear, sensitive and right on target. It helps us a lot to get this kind of coverage from the mainstream papers.*

ઋ

*I watch a lot of baseball, as do many of my women friends, and we think these guys should be more sensitive to their audience. If it weren't for such sexist attitudes, there probably would be some women playing major league baseball . . . I love your write-ups of A's games. I find them lively and fun to read, and it's obvious you have loads of knowledge about the game of baseball.*

(A postcard to broadcaster Jon Miller, forwarded to me):

*Highlight of 1986 season was your interview with Susan Fornoff. Invent a rain delay so you can have her on again.*

Let's return again, though, to my old friend Dick, who first wrote in 1985 to criticize my assessment of the Joaquin Andujar trade. I've often thought I should write to ask what he thinks of that deal now, because, even though I really didn't know what I was talking about at the time, I proved to be right — Andujar was soon washed up and the player traded for him, Mike Heath, enjoyed several more years of success. "Why rub it in, though?" I thought.

I wish now I had. In the summer after I left the newspaper, there came another letter, forwarded my way from the *Bee*, from Dick. He wrote:

*Giving Weiss an error in Tuesday's game proves once again you don't know your butt from second base. Why don't you give sports fans and the great game of baseball a break and go find a line of work you can handle?*

I didn't answer him. What was I going to say? Keep reading the *Bee*?

And, yes, it was so an error.

# 12

# Only Giants, Not Angels

In the spring of 1990, the assistant media relations director of the San Francisco Giants announced her engagement. It seemed akin to predicting Jose Canseco would strike out in the coming season, since everyone suspected she had been involved for several years with the man who had been the Giants' media relations director and was now working for another team.

"So, you and Dave are finally getting married?" people asked her.

"Nope," she said. "I'm engaged to Barry Locke."

Surprise! She had been secretly dating one of the team's sportswriters the previous season — keeping things quiet to avoid any appearance of conflict of interest for her or Barry, who covered the Giants for the *Hayward Daily Review* — and now Robin Carr was engaged, soon to become another favorite name of ESPN nickname champion Chris Berman, Robin Carr-Locke.

I didn't know Robin very well, since I had devoted five years to the Oakland A's, who annually observed a home-and-away schedule opposite that of the Giants. A Giants player could have shared a San Francisco apartment with an A's player and never crossed his path.

But Robin had been working for the Giants since 1985, when Duffy Jennings took her on as a public relations assistant. In 1988, Jennings sought to promote Carr to assistant director — but, first, he did some pleading with manager Roger Craig, general manager Al Rosen, and even equipment manager Mike Murphy.

"All of this, he had to do," she sighs, "just to make sure that I could go on the road four times a year."

Robin actually had to make five trips in 1989, the year the Giants won the pennant and lost the World Series to the A's. The media kept her busy at home with interview requests and live TV shots; additionally, substituting for public relations director Matt Fischer on the road, she wrote a four-page daily release on the status of the team and kept up with the day-by-day stats. If the team made any moves or official comments, it was her job to put them in print for the team's writers.

In other words, Robin had to know what the Giants were up to, on the field and in the front office, and make sure they communicated their intended message to the media.

"It went fairly well in 1989, and I attribute that to us winning and so we're in a good mood," she says. "Of course, the guys would be in the bar and I was never included in that. I didn't care, but I was *never* included and Matt always was. I'd wear pants to try to blend in on the field, but I'd still get the comments from Roger about the humm-baby hair and the humm-baby blouse. A bus driver in Pittsburgh tried to kick me off the bus. A stewardess asked me, 'Which one is your husband?' as if he'd be back there with his buddies in coach (where the players sit on team charters) while I was sitting in first class (where team officials sit) working on my computer.

"But things went well with the players, and I credit me and them for that. I can belt a few beers, throw out a few swear words. I was like a sister to them. If they ever called my room, it was to say, 'Hey, Rob, come down and have a beer with us.' And that was my goal: to be part of the team."

It wasn't just a goal — it was part of her job. But this did not stop one of the team's upper-management officials from telling her, "Keep in mind: men can go out, have a few beers, and carouse a bit, and that's considered macho. Women who do that are considered whores."

Robin thanked the man for his advice and, knowing this fun-loving friend as I do now, I'd guess she went out and put away a few beers. She went about her business much as I went about mine — doing her work, having her fun, and letting everybody else worry about any apparent overlap. Worry, they did — about her associations, her activities. Robin had to go into the clubhouses, too, and I learned from her that management's locker-room mentality created even more hostility toward women than the players' dressing room behavior ever had.

But in the spring of 1990, I knew her as just another of those blondes who wear leather — she would even wear lacy white leather for her black-and-white leather wedding that featured the campy musical artistry of cult star Bud E. Luv. Robin always seemed to be smiling and joking, so I extended my congratulations to her one sunny day at the Giants' spring training stadium in Scottsdale, Arizona, with the half-kidding editorial comment: "Ooh, I would never marry a sportswriter."

Well, Robin's father, Howard Carr, had been a sports-writer. She didn't find much humor in my remark, which I believe I amended with, "But Barry seems like a good guy." She didn't like me too much after that. She says that at the 1989 All-Star game, in Anaheim, I made matters worse by commenting on her outfit. Robin was wearing a favorite blue silk dress with a high neckline, and she remembers me telling her to "loosen up." Then we were assigned to the same roadtrip, an 11-day, 10-game swing in August of 1990 that began in Houston and ended in Philadelphia. I was filling in for whining, cigar-smoking Nick Peters of the *Bee*; Robin was covering for her insipid yet competent director, Fischer. And Barry was on the road with the team as usual.

I had been a sportswriter for 11 years and a baseball writer for five seasons, but I had never and would never again take a trip like this one. If they had all been like this one, I'd have wanted to be a baseball writer forever — except I'd surely have died after only a year or two.

The Giants were optimistic when they arrived in Houston on the night of August 5. The defending National League champions had hit last place by the end of May, falling 14-1/2 games out of first, but now they had climbed to second place in the National League West within 4 1/2 games of the Cincinnati

Reds. Their just-concluded homestand had started with a four-game sweep of the Reds, and the impending rematch between the teams — in the middle of this trip — was stirring both towns.

It was a thrill, for me, just to take a trip (any trip) with a team (any team) that was not the Oakland A's. The Giants promised access, not intimidation, starting with their manager. Roger Craig adopted a fatherly manner with the media, and, before games, he'd sit in the dugout and talk to the writers as long as they did not block his view of batting practice. (Tony La Russa always had to be cornered, and then he was off and running at the first pause in the interrogation.) Craig also was at his most charming with women: in the dugout, he'd clear the spots on either side of him for me or Robin or Jackie Krentzman of the *Santa Rosa Press Democrat*. I did not mind this kind of special treatment — I figured I could hear better sitting next to Roger.

Like Craig, none of the Giants' players seemed to much mind having women around — and I think that's because Robin Carr had trained them to relax with us. Will Clark, the team's star and big mouth, was always yelling some comment about my clothes, which often consisted of skirt-jacket ensembles now that I'd given up trying to blend in. But he answered my questions so courteously that sometimes I thought all of that yelling was Will's weird way of trying to make me feel comfortable.

Dusty Baker, the Giants' hitting coach, and outfielder Rick Leach emerged as my best connections for information and insight. Baker and I shared a friend, his former Dodger teammate Dave Stewart, and an attitude. He had spent his last season in baseball, 1986, with the A's, and was one of the unnamed players who disapproved of Dave Kingman's behavior. Later on he told me that he'd wished he had felt comfortable speaking more publicly.

And Leach, a former quarterback for Bo Schembechler at Michigan, had called loud and disapproving attention to the ridiculousness of Jack Morris's comments to sportswriter Jennifer Frey ("I don't talk to people when I'm naked, especially women, unless they're on top of me or I'm on top of them."). It was as if Leach wanted everyone to hear that he thought women writers ought to be allowed to do their jobs — a sentiment that, expressed so vocally, won him an instant fan . . . me.

I would be counting on Baker and Leach, I thought, as I stumbled and bumbled around mostly unfamiliar players in unexplored cities. I knew I wasn't out of my league anymore, as I had been on my first trip with the A's, but I still felt nervous flying into Houston.

On Monday, I worked out on the stair machine, ate at Neiman Marcus in the Galleria, and took the team bus to the Astrodome — once again trying to find my way around strange surroundings when all of the men were politely trying to let me go first. At least I knew these baseball writers well enough to say, "You lead me." Barry took me under his wing — he said Nick had done the same for him when he started — and showed me shortcuts through the Astrodome tunnels to the clubhouse.

We were quickly ushered out of the clubhouse, though. The team had scheduled a private pregame meeting about a matter we writers would not learn of until Robin issued a press release. We sat on the bench and gabbed, watching the Astros take batting practice as we awaited we knew not what.

Robin knew, of course, what had happened, and she was in the press box waiting for traveling secretary Dirk Smith to call from the clubhouse and say, "The meeting is almost over. Come down." After the long walk through the tunnels to the visitors' clubhouse, Robin arrived in the hallway just outside the dressing room area, where she saw that Roger Craig had not quite finished his meeting. So she waited, perhaps a minute, for Craig to wrap things up. When he did, she had a guard summon the media into the clubhouse. We entered raucously, thinking that Craig had just held a win-one-for-the-gipper pep talk. In fact, his news had so stunned Giants players that they told us reporters to shut our big mouths for once. Then Robin distributed the unforgettable opening act of the bizarre play:

Rick Leach, who was hitting .293, had been suspended for 60 days because, the weekend the Giants swept Cincinnati at Candlestick Park, he had tested positive for drug use, the announcement said. Then, Robin ushered us into a room to interview Ralph Nelson, Al Rosen's assistant general manager and mouthpiece, for specifics. I knew so little about Leach's prior problems under the commissioner's drug program that I fired question after question, just trying to catch up.

The Giants lost the game that night, 4-1. Ralph Nelson telephoned Robin's boss, Duffy Jennings, to tell him that Robin had walked in prematurely on Roger's meeting.

"As a consequence to my early arrival," Robin said, "Roger supposedly could not use the swear words he wanted to use, so the team did not get the full impact of his talk, so we lost the game. I actually lost a game for the Giants! Later I found out that Ralph was calling Duffy to complain about me throughout the trip."

I guess I got Robin in trouble later that night. Barry, continuing to extend hospitality, invited me to have a drink with them after the game. I went in the bar to find them, but encountered only a tableful of Giants officials — all of them men. Ralph noticed me, and I said something like, "I'm looking for my partners."

"Partners?" Ralph asked.

"Partners in crime — Barry and Robin."

I found them upstairs, where we enjoyed a bottle of wine and also a visit with Dusty Baker. We all liked Leach so much, I'm sure that's what we talked about. Meanwhile, Ralph was calling Duffy again to report on Robin being in the bar.

There was going to be a lot of that — Robin being in bars, and Ralph calling Duffy — on this trip.

The Giants lost two of three in Houston to stay within five games of the Reds, and then we boarded a team charter to Cincinnati. Traveling with the Giants felt humane compared to traveling with the A's: Wives and families were welcome (Will Clark's father boarded this particular flight), and alcoholic beverages were not. It seemed to me that just having families aboard would have offset the likelihood of players overdoing the alcohol, but the Giants played it safe.

Robin and I did not, however, play it safe on my first night in Cincinnati. We declared it girls' night out, since Barry had some work to do, and headed for the hotel bar.

It was, appropriately, a sports bar, packed with Giants and their friends and wannabes. Roger Craig was there, and so was pitcher Mike LaCoss, who had recovered from a knee injury and was about to rejoin the roster. Earlier in the day, I had told Roger that I wouldn't put LaCoss back into the starting rotation, I'd put him in the bullpen because that's where the Giants needed help. So, now, in the bar, Roger, drink in hand, was sharing my armchair-managing with LaCoss, who, drink in hand, argued with my theory. Actually, he thought it was valid — except that he wanted to be a starter, not a reliever.

I got into another conversation with Will Clark, drink in hand, about allegations that he was racist. I think I'd had a few beers by then, because I said, "How could a white guy growing up in New Orleans *not* be racist?"

Al Rosen, drink in hand, was in the bar, too, with Ralph Nelson, drink in hand, and Robin and I made some comment to them about it being, "Girls' night out." But it didn't end up that way. We were also joined by team officials Carlos Deza and Dirk Smith for a fun time that crossed the Ohio River to the Waterfront Bar, a barge that had been converted into an indoor-outdoor disco-reggae bar-restaurant partly owned by Bengals quarterback Boomer Esiason.

Lots of Giants players were inside the bar, and I asked Robin if we should move somewhere else, like onto the deck or down near the pool. But then pitcher Don Robinson spotted us and offered us some Dom Perignon — he'll always be Dom Robinson to me — and we were prisoners of the bubbly. The fun didn't even stop in the ladies' room, which featured a full bar tended by a Chippendales' could-be named Roger.

I do remember that as the night went on, I learned that Kevin Mitchell does not tell the truth about everything. He was the Giants' answer to Jose Canseco, the great hitter (Mitchell was Most Valuable Player in the National League, 1989) who comes across in police records as something less than a great citizen. Herb Caen, the wonderful three-dot (. . .) master of civic gossip, wit, and conscience for the *San Francisco Chronicle*, had cited Mitchell for ordering a round of a beverage called an "E.T." in a local restaurant. (The drink was supposedly so wicked, you'd be calling home after two of them.) When I lightly mentioned the column item to Mitchell a day or two later, he said, "That wasn't me. I don't drink." I dutifully recorded Mitchell's "I don't drink" defense at the end of that day's Giants' Update.

Now, here he was at the Waterfront, ordering test-tube shooters for me, Robin, and himself of — you guessed it — "E.T." He just laughed when I yelled at him.

I drank the thing, though — two, in fact. And I spent the next day recuperating, writing notes, and composing a letter to Rick Leach. He had checked into a rehab facility where no one could call him, but I wrote to tell him how much he'd been missed by his teammates — since I knew they were unlikely to tell another man anything of the sort — and to start a diary of sorts about what he'd missed on the trip. Giants trainer Mark Letendre couldn't tell me where Leach was getting treatment, but he relayed the letter to him at the end of the 11-day journey.

It was received and appreciated, as I learned when Leach returned to Candlestick on the last weekend of the season and warmly greeted me, in the middle of an impromptu press conference, with a kiss on the cheek. I was so red-faced, I felt I had to explain his action to fellow writers who politely asked, "Did you guys go to school together or something?"

I didn't mind, though — using my writing skills this way thrilled me more than covering a World Series ever had. Leach said the letter had meant a lot because (surprise, surprise) he had completely lost touch with his teammates and felt too miserable and ashamed even to listen to their games on radio. It had arrived, he said, at just the right time.

Ironically, by the time it landed in Leach's mailbox, I was probably a candidate for rehab. Our little band of merrymakers returned to Cincinnati's Waterfront, again and again, for five straight nights. We were celebrating: Robin, after all, had been born on that weekend 29 years earlier, and her friend Sabine, and Sabine's friend Mary flew in for the party weekend. They taught me that there may indeed be such a thing as "too much fun," and I savored the flavor of life on the road, mixed-gender style. It felt so much more natural to be part of a group that included men *and* women, I wondered if I would have wanted to leave the A's beat had there been more women on the road with us.

Soon, Robin and I were joking about my, "I'd never marry a sportswriter," faux pas. These were my friends now.

Ralph Nelson wasn't laughing, though. Ralph continued to call Duffy to report on Robin's activities — but he stopped calling Robin to report on the comings and goings of his players. One day, infielder Mike Laga arrived from the minor leagues, unannounced, in Cincinnati, and Robin literally had to run after Nelson to find out what Laga was doing there.

"That's when I noticed Ralph was trying to sabotage my job," she said.

The Giants lost the opener of the big series, 7-0. After the game, Roger Craig accused the opposing pitcher, Norm Charlton, of throwing a spitter. The Giants came back and won the second game, but Will Clark was booed for his hard slide into Reds shortstop Barry Larkin. In case the newspapers still had space to fill, afterward, the Giants released veteran pitcher Atlee Hammaker.

The Reds won the third game, on Sunday, prompting their manager, Lou Piniella, to guarantee a victory in the nationally televised fourth game Monday night. "No Humm-Baby. Nothing. We're just going to come out and beat them," Piniella said.

The Giants took a 4-0 lead but lost 6-5. Kevin Mitchell made a pair of misplays in left field that brought unwelcome criticism from his manager, who also had a few things to say about Piniella. "That's high school stuff—what he said and what he does," Craig said, starting a war of words that had reporters trekking back and forth between Craig and Piniella until deadlines finally intervened.

It was a thrilling weekend for us writers — we get that adrenalin pumping when the news is flowing, and there was so much happening in Cincinnati. But now the Giants trailed the Reds by 6 1/2 games, and we headed to Philadelphia sure to be soon bored.

Instead, we got 13 innings—in four hours and 28 minutes — the next night. And the Phillies finally won it when Giants relief pitcher Steve Bedrosian threw a first-pitch fastball inside that squiggled far enough past catcher Gary Carter to advance the winning run home from third on what was declared a wild pitch. Carter had caught every inning of five straight games, and he went straight to the full-body ice pack after this one. I waited to talk to him, but finally headed for the bus.

All of the seats quickly filled, except the one next to mine. Bedrosian finally took it. A team mainstay in 1989, Bedrosian had learned the following spring that his two-year-old son Cody, had leukemia. And he had pitched, all season, like a man with something besides baseball on his mind. Craig had relieved Bedrosian of the pressure-packed closing role, hoping that middle relief might provide a safer haven. But this wild pitch represented only the latest of so many failures, and I didn't have the heart to blame him for this latest loss in my story.

I could not imagine what I ought to talk to him about on the bus ride to the hotel, so I decided I'd let him brood. He had other ideas, though. His opening comment was something to the effect of, "Wow, your leg is really hot." So I moved. He said something else suggestive, so I tossed my compassion out the window and replied, "What was the pitch you had intended to throw Collins, anyway?"

"Huh?" Bedrosian said.

"Where was it supposed to be, that last pitch you threw to Collins?" I asked.

"You mean Cook?" Bedrosian said.

"Uh, no, the pinch-hitter. Collins."

"No, that was Cook, the pitcher, at the plate," Bedrosian insisted, looking at me as if I was a dumb broad.

I could not argue. Bedrosian had been pitching in the bottom of the 13th inning without even noticing that the Phillies had pinch-hit for their pitcher, and I could not even convince him they had done so. Nope, he wanted to know what I'd be doing later.

"We're having a little beer party," I told Bedrosian, who I thought to be friendly with Barry and Robin. "Give us a call if you want to join us."

He called *my* room well after the party had ended, and quickly separated himself from the phone when he realized that my invitation had been merely a gesture of friendly sympathy, not a proposition.

Meanwhile, I had discovered that I had indeed goofed on the identity of the game's final hitter. Carlos Deza read through Barry's story in the party suite and said, "There's a typo here." Barry, too, had written that the batter was Collins. It wasn't Collins — it was Hollins! The guy *was* batting for Cook, though, and I had to share with them the Bedrosian story. We marveled at the pitcher's apparent loss of consciousness, and shocked Roger Craig with the story the next day.

Craig was in for a bigger shock, though, the next day, and Robin was in for a no-hit pool. This was the day Terry Mulholland would throw a no-hitter at the Giants — the team that had traded him to the Phillies.

Mulholland was no Nolan Ryan, but the Giants were no Bash Brothers either. If losing two of three to horrendous Houston and three of four to successful Cincinnati hadn't entirely demoralized the team from San Francisco, maybe the 13-inning loss to the Phillies on a wild pitch the night before had finished the job and set them up for the ignominy of Mulholland's no-hitter. The stunned Giants stumbled out of Veteran Stadium into the hotel bar and proceeded to buy each other shots of concoctions to rival Mitchell's E.T.

Bedrosian was in the bar that night, and he gave me a strange look. I thought he must have realized by now (as I finally had) that Hollins had been pinch-hitting for Cook the night before. I thought maybe he was feeling a little foolish. So I said, "I was wrong, too — it was Hollins, not Collins."

Amazement filled his face, and, now, he turned to one of his teammates and asked, "Who was the batter when I threw the wild pitch last night?" He still believed it had been Cook!

The answer came to him from several players. "Hollins. It was Hollins."

Now the looks of amazement crossed their faces as they realized their pitcher didn't know who was batting. And a look of bewilderment crossed Bedrosian's.

Maybe he was realizing, as we just had, that his family's terrible hardship could not be stashed away in some remote chamber of his brain just because it was the bottom of the thirteenth inning — instead, it loomed in the midst of the central confrontation in baseball, blocking Bedrosian, the pitcher, from even identifying the batter.

The Giants finally closed the bar. Then they went out and lost again the next day and flew home now tied for second place, nine games behind the Reds. They never kicked back into the pennant race.

I hopped in a car and drove to Baltimore to cover the A's again, just for their weekend series with the Orioles. Back in San Francisco, Robin Carr was learning all about discrimination. Her boss, Duffy Jennings, demanded, "Were you seen in the bar on this roadtrip?"

Robin probably laughed. "Sure," she said.

Then Duffy asked her what happened in Houston. She told him how she had handled Rick Leach's suspension, and he told her that, according to Ralph Nelson, she had lost that game for the team because the manager couldn't swear in her presence.

Also according to Ralph, Robin had addressed the team's distinguished general manager, Al Rosen, as "Babe." I did not see this to be any big deal, since "Babe" had long been the greatest name in baseball, but Robin insisted that she would never have called "Mr. Rosen" anything of the kind.

"All of these stories came out!" Robin said. "I said, 'This is ridiculous — I know that Matt and Dirk go to the bars.' Duffy said, 'What you need to understand is that you need to be seen as little as possible.'"

"I asked, 'What should I do? Stay in my room?'"

"He said, 'That would help.'" And he made it clear that he was echoing the beliefs of upper management. And it was clear that I was not going on the road again."

There were no women in "upper management." Once, the team had hired a woman director, but she grew so tired of having to field the rumors that she had slept with Roger Craig — "This is absurd! He's like my father!" she'd say — that she resigned her post and renounced the sports business.

Carr evaluated the conservatism of the team's all-male upper management officials and finally decided to tell one of the team's vice-presidents, Corey Busch, what had happened. "He was appalled," she said. "And he made it clear that (Jennings' interpretations) were not upper management's feelings."

Five years earlier, Robin Monsky had sued the Atlanta Braves for sex discrimination when, she said, the team's manager and general manager told her, they didn't want a woman traveling with the team. Monsky settled out of court, presumably for money, but the suit cost her her job. Not surprisingly, Monsky has been unable to find a comparable job with any other professional sports team.

Carr probably could have filed suit, too, but she loved working for the Giants. At least she didn't have to kiss the owner — as Minnesota North Stars owner Norm Green admitted to asking of the women employees of his hockey team. So, she converted the discriminatory treatment into a raise and promotion, becoming director of communications — a job that made the most of her gifts of schmoozing and connecting and freed her from the mundane travel and statistics duties. It also freed her from Ralph Nelson's interference for the next 18 months, at which time Nelson finally was dismissed by "Babe" Rosen for reasons unspecified.

By then, we could define Nelson's treatment of Carr as "sexual harassment." He hadn't pinched her behind or grabbed her breast, but he had conducted himself with the apparent intent of "creating an intimidating or hostile or offensive environment." Women learned these elements of the legal definition of harassment in the autumn of 1991, when baseball playoffs in Toronto and Atlanta shared national television airtime with the Clarence Thomas-Anita Hill series on Capitol Hill.

Julie Fie, the publicity director for the Sacramento Kings basketball team, got a phone call that weekend from her mother, who told Julie, "I'm thinking about you, working in a man's world, and wondering what you're thinking about all of this."

Fie first answered: "Gee, nothing really shocked me, and I can't imagine jeopardizing a career over some of that."

Later, though, Fie reviewed Hill's explicit testimony and wondered, "What kind of an environment do I work in that it didn't bother me?" The big locker room had numbed her.

And, so what if she had been bothered? One woman who worked for a prominent sports agent learned that he was pitching her charms at the athletes he represented: Often, she had to escape the advances of their clients diplomatically enough to preserve her job. Once, the agent called her into his office, where, in front of three clients, he told her, "I think you would be taken more seriously in this business if you had bigger tits." The man offered her a loan so that she could have her breasts augmented, an operation the clients encouraged her to undergo. As tears of humiliation welled up in her eyes, this woman thought incredibly fast.

"I had a double mastectomy two years ago," she told them emotionally. "Do you think I enjoy having no breasts?"

The subject was dropped immediately — but, today, there are professional athletes out there who incorrectly believe this woman had cancer surgery! Why didn't she ever sue the asshole? She figured she'd never work in the business again, and she loved her job. Or maybe she thought, as another woman in the business of baseball told me when I tried to interview her on the subject of harassment, "I'd better not say anything — I haven't been an angel myself."

As if anyone had been an angel. As if any of us should have to be.

# 13

# Thanks, Dave

Kristin Huckshorn is blond and she wears leather skirts. So right away we had two things in common.

She also happens to be a wonderful writer and reporter. I knew her before I ever met her, through Ralph Perez. Perez was the adorable soccer coach at the University of Santa Clara when I was about to move to California in 1985. Ralph and I met at a coaches' convention in Washington, and he quickly disappointed me by talking endlessly about his wonderful girlfriend, the pro soccer writer for the *San Jose Mercury News*. When Kristin and I spotted each other one night in the Oakland Coliseum press box, we needed no introductions and greeted each other with hugs.

"Your boyfriend Ralph couldn't stop talking about you," I told her.

She waved her hand, saying, "But I broke up with him months ago."

So there we were already, moaning, "Men!" and beginning a friendship that was simply automatic.

It was Kristin who picked me up at the San Francisco airport when I returned — lonesome, exhausted, and even famous—from the June 1986 trip that had featured Dave Kingman's rat and Jackie Moore's firing. We commiserated for awhile over that one particular man, Dave Kingman, and then moved on to important things like lunch. I remember feeling fortunate to have access to this kind of empathy when there were so many women sportswriters isolated all over the country. At the *Bee,* I even had a woman assistant sports editor, Nancy Cooney. I had always been lucky, I thought, that I didn't have to start my career in the South or in the sticks, as I thought I would.

For me, the formation of the Association for Women in Sports Media began that day, over lunch with Kristin. I think it was the first meal I was able to enjoy — and even digest — since the rat arrived.

We didn't talk about the organization that day, though. There already had been plenty of talk. Michele Himmelberg of the *Orange County Register* had dispersed a questionnaire a year earlier to gauge potential membership and compile a mailing list. Unfortunately, Melanie Hauser of the *Houston Post* lost the painstakingly compiled list.

Eventually, it was Himmelberg, Cooney, Huckshorn, and I who got together for a casual dinner in San Mateo, California in the fall of 1986. We were shop-talking when Himmelberg said she'd been given the perfect suggestion for the group's name. It was and is pronounced, "awesome." By the time we finished dessert, we had toasted "Awesome" and assigned ourselves duties. Himmelberg was serving as a makeshift president, Huckshorn as treasurer, and Cooney and I worked with Jane Hughes-Yeung at the *Sacramento Bee* to produce the AWSM newsletter with the financial backing of our newspaper.

"The old-girl network branches out," screamed the first newsletter, featuring profiles on Mary Garber and Lesley Visser, a look at New Orleans (host to the NCAA final four that spring), and a guide to pro sports access. We requested $20 annual dues, and had received more than 50 responses with checks in time to produce the second newsletter.

Yvonne Terry White of the *Huntsville (Alabama) Times* spoke for the mini-masses when she wrote, "This is the best thing to happen to female sportswriters. It's nice to know I'm not the only one out there battling in a man's world."

And we weren't the only ones battling. George Solomon, the sports editor of the *Washington Post*, asked the Associated

Press Sports Editors to contribute seed money for our organization. We had nine original benefactors at $100 each, but these did not include Bill Dwyre of the *Los Angeles Times* or Dave Smith of the *Dallas Morning News*.

That seemed disappointing, because these two high-profile sports editors had been hiring, promoting, and encouraging women sportswriters for years. Dwyre had written me wonderful, enthusiastic letters when I job-hunted in college. His protegee with the *Milwaukee Journal* had been Tracy Dodds, whom he later hired at the *Times*. Smith had aided and abetted Betty Cuniberti in Washington and hired several women in Dallas — at one time boasting five full-time women on his sports staff. But Dwyre and Smith needed to be convinced that AWSM would help integrate, not isolate, women sportswriters.

Some of the women sportswriters, too, argued about this. Why form a women's organization when all we really wanted was to be accepted as sportswriters? Why segregate ourselves? Years later, Kim Boatman told me she knew that her job covering the A's was made easier by my trail-blazing with the team, but she never would join AWSM. Some women wanted to be women sportswriters, others wanted to be sportswriters.

I and my cofounders argued that we weren't segregating ourselves: that's why we called it the Association FOR (and not OF) Women in Sports Media. We wanted male sportswriters and editors to join, too, and many of them did. We extended invitations to women in sports public relations and broadcasting, and we welcomed just about anyone who would cough up $20. So many coughed up the money from their own wallets, and not some company fund or expense account, that we knew they profoundly felt a need for this kind of group.

All of these voices, we argued, could unite behind our primary goal: to render AWSM superfluous and obsolete. In other words, we had formed an organization to try to make the organization unnecessary. That was the premise that convinced Dwyre and Smith to jump on the bandwagon in time to serve as co-hosts for the conventions in 1990 (Dallas) and 1991 (Newport Beach, California), respectively.

At our first convention, 1988 in Oakland, we good-naturedly jabbed at APSE for starting its group with five guys who played golf the whole time. We started with 40 women who jabbered the whole time.

The session that really got us rolling was "Ethics," led by *Bee* sports editor Stan Johnston. We debated whether it was OK to accept a movie invitation from a coach, what to do when a fellow woman sportswriter acquires a sleazy reputation, and how we should handle an athlete who won't talk to reporters when there's a woman in the group. The movie invite got an automatic no. The sleaze, we thought, ought to get a few helpful pointers from us, especially since guys seem to have no trouble telling each other when they look like slobs. And when an athlete doesn't want to talk to a group of writers because the group includes one of us, we should stand our ground and force the athlete to choose between talking to all or talking to none.

But the debate was so polite and flat at that first convention, it was as if we were sipping tea with the Queen. We all wanted to agree on everything just because we were all women in sports media, and that didn't feel any more right than being excluded because we were women in sports media. I remember feeling somewhat self-conscious about telling the group, "I don't worry about appearances — I'll have a beer with *anyone*!" (And Stan nodded, joking, "I've seen her expense accounts.")

During less formal sessions, we got down to some really vital, important issues. Like, why do players sit around stark naked when they could so easily wrap a towel around their private parts? Most of us usually wouldn't have the nerve to ask, but there was safety in our numbers.

"I think it's a dare," Ronnie Lott of the San Francisco 49ers told us. "Athletes are intrigued by challenges . . . whether on the field or with the media."

"I wasn't raised to walk around naked!" protested Don Baylor of the Oakland A's. "We weren't even allowed at the dinner table without a shirt."

Baylor and Lott gave us our best show, along with support and advice, those three days in May. Kristin had recruited Lott, the 49er defensive back who had once saved Shelley Smith of the *San Francisco Examiner* when 300-plus-pounder Bubba Paris dragged her into the shower room yelling, "Isn't this what you wanted to see?"

I had originally invited/begged Glenn Hubbard, an A's infielder who had been a friend and supporter of Dale Murphy, to come talk to us. Murphy was the Atlanta Braves slugger who wouldn't talk to women in the clubhouse, the guy we talked about in our ethics discussion. He had told *Sport* magazine in 1985, "No matter how sincere a woman is about covering baseball, that's not the point. It's the men's locker room and there shouldn't be any women in there."

I thought it might be enlightening for us and for Murphy if his pal Hubbard would represent his views for us. But Hubbard told me, "They'd roast me. A few things you learn not to do, like criticize fans or speak out against women sportswriters."

Baylor shook his head in disgust when I told him Hubbard had RSVP'ed no. Baylor said, "I'll do it." Later, he told me he wished all of his teammates could have been in the room with him. "They would have learned a lot," he said.

So did we. Baylor and Lott — both of them veterans of their sports — told us, during one of the lighter moments, that we had raised the dress code for sportswriters. They noted that the male sportswriters don't appear to be such slobs since we came along.

That led us to another of those really important issues: Is it OK to wear a red leather miniskirt in a football locker room? Suzanne Halliburton of the *Austin American Statesman* became a legend over this one.

"Well, it wasn't red, it was black, and it wasn't a mini, it was very conservative knee-length," she said, years later. "But the story grew — Kelly Carter said she heard in Pittsburgh that it was red spandex!"

Reporters do hate to let those mundane facts get in the way of a good story. Black? Knee-length? Nah. Red leather/spandex and short.

Suzanne said she was visiting San Francisco with a few other women sportswriters during the first AWSM convention, and, naturally, talk turned to athletes. She had worn a leather skirt once in the Dallas Cowboys' locker room, and the Cowboys' great running back, Tony Dorsett, asked where she was keeping her whips and chains. When Suzanne told the other women about this, she said one of them spoke disapprovingly of her outfit, advising her, "Like it or not, we have to look like nuns."

The story got around, with embellishments, and so we debated. Everyone agreed that, no, it wasn't OK to wear a red leather miniskirt in a football locker room, but Kristin and I —

who did not know the actual facts of Suzanne's case — were left looking at each other, wondering, "Well, what about black leather to the knee?" We decided it was OK, in California, as long as you weren't fat. Then we went to dinner and ordered the chocolate whiskey cake for dessert.

But, seriously, what do you wear in the locker room? The fashion magazines never seem to get around to this. In the fashion magazines, women go to the office, women relax at home, or women go out on dates. The style options fall in line easily and categorically. But we encountered all of these tricky gray areas women who work in offices never have to address.

For instance, I responded to the newsletter question, "What do you wish someone had told you about your job before you had to find out for yourself?" with the reply, "I wish someone had told me what to wear to training camp on a hot day in July. I wondered why one player always stared at me — well, I was wearing sundresses to keep cool. Yeah, they looked pretty, but not professional . . . Now I'd wear a cool cotton skirt and blouse." But, two years later, I'd wear shorts and a tank top to spring training, just as the male sportswriters did.

Cindy Schmerler of *World Tennis* magazine remembered running down the stairs at Franklin Field, the football stadium at the University of Pennsylvania, in a skirt and high-heeled pumps. "Did I really have to dress that way?" she wailed. She thought so then because that's what the fashion magazines showed women wearing to work.

Some of these concerns, like Cindy's trip down the stairs, seemed practical enough. But we worried less about comfort, more about reputation. Cindy wore a skirt and pumps so players would see a woman working. That's why Joan Ryan was wearing a skirt the day a football player caressed her leg with a razor. Years ago, the Yankees had a problem with a woman reporter in their spring training clubhouse who protested the treatment she received. Their manager, Billy Martin, defended his team by attacking the woman's so-called provocative outfit. She reportedly was wearing shorts and a T-shirt — like the men sportswriters.

I once told one of my editors at *USA Today* how hard it was to dress for work thinking, "If Billy Martin wants to say I dressed suggestively, and I have on anything less than a turtleneck, what am I going to say?"

One woman at the 1989 Super Bowl wore considerably less than a turtleneck and reflected poorly on all of us. She wasn't a sportswriter, though. She was Elizabeth Snead, fashion writer at the *Fort Lauderdale Sentinel*, and she wore a black leather miniskirt to one interview and a miniskirt and low-cut tank top to another. Snead was widely filmed joking and posing with players.

The AWSM members at that Super Bowl reacted. "I think we all cringed," said Melissa Isaacson.

Then they debated. "If we're still judged as a group," wrote Kristin Huckshorn in the AWSM newsletter, "should we ever attempt to control someone else's dress or behavior when it reflects badly on our group?"

That attempt wasn't made, but the woman's attire and conduct were reported in the newsletter story. Kristin thought to call the woman's paper for a comment. A male editor there told her she had no business judging another journalist.

AWSM's (specifically: my) attempt to deal with the appearances issue included a not-well-received fashion show at our convention in Baltimore that spring. *Self* magazine made a valiant effort that elicited little but laughs among the conventioneers. It dealt with comfort and practicality, but I guess what we really wanted to learn was how not to be confused for bimbos.

Yes, there are bimbo women sportswriters! There was a woman in Oakland who would give players backrubs in the locker room and hang around for hours. Some of the players complained to *me* about her! Another woman falsely represented herself as a soccer writer (she was not) just to get a free ride back in the days when the New York Cosmos were wining, dining and transporting media members to their games. Yes, there were bimbos, and we did not want to be mistaken for them.

There were also women journalists who undermined the credibility of women sports journalists. Cindy Adams of the *New York Post*, that bastion of credibility, wrote a 1989 column headlined, "Bare facts about the Yank locker room," that ended with Adams describing a glimpse of a nude player as, "Nice. Very nice." It was a gossip column represented as a gossip column, but we worried that it reflected poorly on women sportswriters.

A British female journalist, Anne Barrowclough, used her press credential at a 1992 London Monarchs game to report:

"American football players look better with their clothes on than they do naked . . . (Naked) they are reduced to being just big men with huge thighs and overly fleshy stomachs . . . Some of the bodies could have done with the Hip and Thigh Diet." The team officially lamented her poor use of locker room access, and our newsletter agreed.

"Hardly AWSM behavior," we proclaimed. Adams, Barrowclough, Snead. . . We weren't them, and we didn't want them being mistaken for us. So we worried inordinately over appearances.

That's why Frank Deford caused such a stir at our 1990 convention. Deford was a writer at *Sports Illustrated* who had long ago discovered fashion. He wore a natty purple tie when he appeared before us in Dallas as the executive of the lively but short-lived *National* daily sports newspaper.

His remarks that night did not, however, seem stylish to us. First, he warned us that he would say a thing or two we might construe to be "sexist or patronizing."

Then, he told us that Sally Quinn of the *Washington Post* style section had been asked why she is such a good interviewer. "Because I'm blonde and I flirt good," Deford told us she replied.

Then he said, "You're young women dealing with young men. Don't be afraid to use that."

Deford made some other insightful remarks that night, but, of course, we all reported back to our co-workers later, "Frank Deford told us to flirt!" A few nights later, our president, Michele Himmelberg, dreamed that a major movie producer was filming our convention. Everything was running smoothly, except, Himmelberg said, "We were all wearing skimpy black miniskirts! And that's why we attracted the producer's interest."

See, stuff like this really gets to women sportswriters. We have nightmares over appearances.

A few days after her dream, Michele wrote an eloquent interpretation of Deford's pointed remarks. Or maybe it was a rebuttal, depending upon Deford's figurative intentions.

"My deepest fears about Deford's message lived in (my) dream — a fear that people believe his words too literally," she wrote. "We don't need to flirt to be good interviewers. We don't have to use seduction . . . Femininity isn't an asset . . . Something valuable that Deford did say . . . was this: "Don't be afraid to be yourself." Know your virtues and play on those."

Among Michele's virtues was a pair of beautiful blue eyes that I am certain coaxed out many a secret. I am sure that Christine Brennan of the *Washington Post* could fix her brilliant smile upon the Redskin of her choice and almost always get her question answered. And I have no doubt that many of my AWSM sisters honed their interviewing techniques on handsome Delta Upsilons at their college sorority mixers.

All of this seems, to me, only fair. At the same convention where Frank Deford told us to flirt, University of Texas women's athletic director Donna Lopiano told us, tongue in cheek, that we were sadly lacking in "testicular knowledge." Testicular knowledge she defined as man's chauvinistic belief that men are genetically and inherently more knowledgeable than women about sports. So if our gender would hinder us in this way, why not take advantage of the ways our gender could help us?

No, we did not have to flirt or seduce in order to succeed. But if we were going to be left out of what I call "guy talk" just because we were women, we should feel comfortable with the advantages of being a woman in a man's locker room. Athletes usually remembered our names long after they'd forgotten the names of the men writers. They heard our voices over those of the men. And often they showed us sensitivities that never emerge when men talk to men.

A male writer told me in 1978, "I tried to get Mike Morgan away from the park to do an interview with me and he wouldn't. How did you get him to sit down and have lunch with you?"

How did he think? I was 20, Morgan was 18, and I had called him and said, "I'm a rookie, too, and I've been assigned to do a story on you." It wasn't my Pulitzer Prize that got Morgan to have lunch with me and encouraged him to talk to me. And it sure wasn't my testicular knowledge.

Our big flaw as sportswriters — that we were not men — could turn into a virtue sometimes. For all of the Dave Kingmans and Dale Murphys of the world who refused to talk to women in the locker room, there occasionally were men who made themselves especially accessible to women sportswriters, especially the ones who were well-groomed, nicely dressed, and smiling.

But it was not politically correct for AWSM members to admit that sometimes we succeeded because of (not always in spite of) our gender/beautiful eyes/brilliant smiles/leather skirts.

Instead, we filled our valuable newsletter inches and precious convention hours with judgments and advice that rendered us fashion police and attitude adjusters: Don't wear this, don't do that. We never compiled a guide to help sportswriters approach subjects with a warm smile and a firm handshake. We did blast a TV woman who kissed a quarterback on his cheek.

Being a woman sportswriter was cause for complaint. But when it came to success, now we were only sportswriters. How confusing it was, this business of when to be a woman and when to be a sportswriter.

The confusion produced at least one extreme example, a woman who covered her beat well for a smaller newspaper, yet never could get hired for a bigger beat at a bigger paper. I had talked to her on the phone and couldn't understand why she was stuck. Then I met her.

She might as well have been "Pat," the "Saturday Night Live" character nobody knows to be man or woman. Oh, this was a woman. But her appearance was more boyish than girlish. I can imagine the consternation this produced among sports editors who really wanted to hire men, and among athletes who viewed women as sex objects. "Pat" didn't fit either of those molds — perhaps because she had her own style or perhaps because she was trying too hard to be considered a sportswriter.

The rest of us giggled about "Pat," and I joined in. I conspired with my sister sportswriters to trash women wearing red leather miniskirts or kissing quarterbacks. But now I think it's too bad. Maybe "Pat" was just being herself. Maybe the woman in red leather had wanted a skirt like that all of her life and had scrimped and saved so she could buy it and then lost 20 pounds so that it would look good. Maybe the quarterback kisser had played stickball with the fellow when she was eight years old. What did we know? Only appearances.

AWSM will have made progress when we exchange good leads and quotes and share our solutions to the tricky situations we encounter. That will happen when we stop worrying about appearances and accept, even revel in, both parts of the woman sportswriter label. I heard the women politicians in 1992 offering constituents a new voice in government. Why should we not feel free to offer a new approach in sports journalism?

We're getting there. I think of that first convention in Oakland in 1988 and remember the bonding that took place, mostly within quipping range of the very funny Lesley Visser, then with the *Boston Globe,* and Julie Cart, of the *Los Angeles Times.* They christened our hospitality suite "The Island of Peace," in ridicule of a stress management session that had gone awry, and engaged us all in watching the Miss Universe pageant and practicing the contestants' dainty waves.

We were all so polite and friendly that year, so eager to get along on the basis of our common exclusion from the big locker room, that some of the ladylike members got mad at the founders for conspiring to influence our first election. That wasn't lady-like.

Well, we were scared. Our new organization was an infant, and we didn't want it falling into the hands of a stranger. So we quietly — so as not to appear *un*ladylike — campaigned. Then we lined up the strongest candidates in the proper offices, all but ensuring that we would be run by Chris Brennan for the next two terms. As far as I'm concerned, we succeeded, because AWSM thrived in every department during those two years — even establishing a scholarship/internship that attracts interest annually from the finest sports departments in the country.

After Brennan, limited by our constitution to two one-year terms, retired, Tracy Dodds and Michele Himmelberg ran against each other for president. Two great, equally qualified candidates — yet neither of them felt comfortable campaigning openly. There was a lot of smoke-filled room talk about how to get this vote and that vote, but they seemed embarrassed about appearing too, well, unladylike by using the hospitality suite to lobby for support.

Tracy cried when she lost by a vote, but she may have been the lucky one. That year was AWSM's darkest hour, the year when Zeke Mowatt would expose himself to Lisa Olson and Sam Wyche, the Cincinnati Bengals football coach, would bar one of our members from his locker room. Michele had to write a ton of letters, make an earful of phone calls, and even arrange — in response to the NFL's fines of Mowatt and company — AWSM's first impromptu news conference. By the response she received, it's clear that she succeeded in placing our concerns within the NFL's inner circle of management men. But Michele, who had a job and two kids, did not want to run for a second term as AWSM president.

So, the next year, Tracy and I ran civilized campaigns against each other. Again, we were on eggshells so as not to appear to be campaigning. After Tracy's victory speech, some members came to me and said, "I think you'd be a great president, but I'm afraid Tracy really would have a` nervous breakdown if she lost again this year." Tracy and I huddled in the ladies' room, and she jokingly told me she probably *would* have had a nervous breakdown if she'd lost. I felt I'd lost to a worthy opponent, and she had a pleasant, uneventful year.

Finally, in 1992, it became possible to put aside personalities and elect on issues and qualifications. Cathy Henkel and Melanie Hauser ran for president in New York, and campaigning came out of the closet into the hospitality suite. It was fun — I campaigned for the winner, Henkel — and it was fair, and nobody cried or claimed bad sportsmanship. That election told us cofounders that AWSM could take care of itself now.

That was a landmark convention for AWSM in other ways. Three commissioners — Fay Vincent of baseball, Paul Tagliabue of football, and David Stern of basketball — accepted our invitation to a final-night banquet. Each knew the others had been invited, and none wanted to be known as the guy who didn't show up to talk to the women sportswriters. Tagliabue told us frankly that night that he had not been able to collect the fine he had levied on Zeke Mowatt, and feared the legal consequences of further efforts to do so.

Our keynote address, though, came from a woman — Melissa Ludtke, the plaintiff in the famous suit that opened baseball locker rooms to women 14 years earlier. But she, like her contemporaries Betty Cuniberti and Stephanie Salter and Jane Gross, was no longer a sportswriter. And she told us:

"I hoped the suit would open more doors for women. It has. I hoped that as more women entered, the prejudices and biases would diminish. How naive that vision seems today.

"We've all learned not to complain about the little crudities. We shouldn't look, talk too much, or dress too feminine. That took its toll.

"That's why I believe so many of us left."

The speedy progress of AWSM gives me hope that fewer of us will leave. Now, each of us can enter those rooms full of men knowing that she is not really alone.

# 14

# Strike Three

I thought I had finally found what the hitters call "a groove" in 1990. Leaving the baseball beat had spruced up my writing and my social life. I even bought my first home.

Dennis Eckersley might as well have been coming to the mound in the ninth, though. The big locker room was about to shoot me down.

In June 1991, as official scorer, I slapped a Detroit Tigers third baseman with an error when he did not retain possession of a ground ball hit very hard in his direction. The replay confirmed my call, but I did not consider that replays always make very hard-hit ground balls look not so hard hit, or that I had grown up watching Brooks Robinson play third base. The call stood. It was what we call a "tough error," but one that was not inconsistent with my scoring philosophy.

After all, how do we learn to distinguish between hits and errors? Reggie Jackson was saying — on the air, one booth down the hall, anytime I scored a game — that you have to be male to score baseball, which meant to him that you have to have learned the difference between a hit and an error by playing baseball. I say it's a subjective issue not related to gender. Anybody can learn to tell a hit from an error just by watching a lot of baseball, as I had.

Unfortunately for hitters, however, my subconscious had been trained in hit-error distinction by watching the Baltimore Orioles make baseball's best plays in the 1960s and 1970s. It was as if I had learned to answer the question "What is art?" by pointing to a Monet painting. Great fielders like Brooks, shortstop Mark Belanger, and centerfielder Paul Blair — even the reflexive Jim Palmer on the mound — had turned baseballs hit anywhere near them into outs. Watching them field so thoroughly and effortlessly had trained my instincts to declare, "error" when a fielder could not play a baseball hit to him. We all have our biases. Brooks Robinson himself, for instance, told me that he was much tougher on fielders than official scorers ever were, and I think it was clear that Reggie, for another instance, was reacting as a hitter and as Mark McGwire's friend.

Yes, it was McGwire who was the hitter — if you want to call him that — on the night of the fateful call. Barely hitting .200 through the worst season of his career, he needed all the hits he could get, and didn't get one from me, the official scorer. I heard he objected to the call, so when I arrived in Milwaukee a few days later to start my one A's roadtrip of the year and spotted McGwire in the hotel lobby, I approached him immediately. I wanted to give him a chance to air me out or say whatever he thought he had to say, figuring once he had done that we could just move on. We were, after all, two adults who had known each other for four years.

I remembered, two years earlier, getting into an argument with Carney Lansford. He'd had a few beers after a game when the team charter flight was running late, and he started busting my chops because I'd been making faces at him for not talking to the media. At the time, he was mad at us for quoting him directly (and correctly, I must add) for saying that Jeff Reardon, then pitching for the Twins, had lost something on his pitches. In protest, he decided to shut up.

Carney and I had weathered the best and worst of the A's since 1985, and I didn't feel right not talking to him at all, so I made faces at him. I guess the players' immaturity was contagious. Anyway, he yelled at me about it in the clubhouse — said he'd like a little more respect, if I didn't mind. The next morning, I get on the elevator to go to the health club, and who's the only other person on the elevator? Carney Lansford. We looked at each other like we hated each other, then, without saying a word, I stuck my tongue out at him. It was absolutely the proper gesture, because we both burst into laughter, and that was that.

The following spring, 1990, I almost started crying on Opening Night when Lansford, who had torn up his knee in a New Year's Eve snowmobiling accident, talked about not wanting to limp onto the field with his teammates for the introduction of the team that had won the 1989 World Series. He was in such obvious torment at not being able, for the first time in his career, to play in the opener, I thought he was going to cry, too. Sometimes these guys were such jerks, but sometimes they were such human beings. It was important to treat them as the latter, in the decent human hope that they would respond in kind.

That's what I hoped for when I approached the big red-headed first baseman. McGwire, though, was unresponsive when I said, "I hear you didn't like my call." So I searched for something light to say, and the best I could do was this: "Sorry that was such a tough error. I grew up watching Brooks Robinson play third."

He just stood there, blushing, obviously not interested in saying anything at all. The next day, at the ballpark, he continued to ignore me. The immaturity of his behavior shocked me. This was someone I knew well enough to have invited him and his girlfriend to join my friends and me at a comedy club. And now he could not even speak to me.

Reggie Jackson, however, approached me for a pregame chat on the bench. He sat very close to me, stuck his face in mine, and harangued me for about 20 minutes, saying things like: "You want people to like you, don't you? You're an attractive woman (he probably said girl, but I'll give him the benefit of the doubt), you have a nice personality. You don't want everybody mad at you. You don't want everybody thinking you're out to screw them. But that's what they think. They think Susan Fornoff hates the Oakland A's, she doesn't want them to get hits."

I took it. I wanted to throw up, but I sat there and took it. It reminded me of the time during the 1990 World Series when Tony La Russa ducked the media, all day, until he had showered and dressed in his suit and tie for the big gala that night. Many of us writers wanted to attend the party, too, but we could not even write our stories, much less go home to change, until La Russa had talked to us. So we stood around and took it.

Sportswriting had begun to feel demeaning. Some of the players called us leeches: from the way they and our editors treated us, I was beginning to think that maybe we *were* subhuman. The day after Reggie humiliated me, I went down the street to a bookstore and bought *Do What You Love, the Money Will Follow*. Teaching always had appealed to me, and now I thought that it would be more fun to work with schoolchildren than overgrown rich children.

McGwire had flipped my switch. I knew I was nothing but a bitch-cunt-sportswriter to Reggie Jackson, who spoke sweetly to me but sharply of me. McGwire, though, had always treated me like a person and I had always related to him that way, as I had related to most of the people I covered. The gap between athletes and sportswriters had been widening for years — the writers resenting the mammoth salaries paid to the men who lived lives so much like their own, the athletes concluding that they did not need good publicity to earn good money — and that fostered a relationship of mutual disrespect. And now Mark McGwire, supposedly one of the good guys, was acting like a petulant child.

The other writers said, "What do you expect? He's one of *them*." I expected him to act like a grown-up.

The big chill blew into Detroit as well, though, until I found myself sitting next to second baseman Mike Gallego one night in the hotel bar. He said, "You're really upset about this."

And I told him I was no more upset than I would be if he, after knowing me since 1985, decided not to talk to me — professionally or personally — because of some scoring call I'd made. I felt dehumanized, I told him.

The next day, McGwire gestured to me in the small visitors' clubhouse at Tiger Stadium. He still had the same locker by the door he had had as a rookie when, surrounded by reporters after a two-homer game, he'd looked up wide-eyed and said, "You guys all want to talk to *me*?" His face had opened and become friendly again — he told me he'd have liked to have had a chance to plead his case the night I'd made the error call, and my Brooks Robinson remark just made things worse for him. Other players had said, "You mean we're supposed to field like Brooks Robinson? He's in the Hall of Fame!"

I thought they'd missed my point, but at least the temperature had finally risen.

I sought out Gallego and said, "Thank you." He just smiled and answered, "I didn't say a word." There *were* some good guys.

But I already had begun navigating new career routes. The one I had chosen, I decided, simply wasn't meant to be mine for much longer. McGwire flipped the switch, and I could read the writing on the walls all around me. An essay called "The Death of Sportswriting," appeared in *GQ magazine* and affected me like a fiery sermon. Tony La Russa went berserk after a game in Chicago and threatened a sportswriter there. There were problems at work, where the new sports editor said, "Yes sir" to management and distanced himself from the staff behind do-this or do-that memos that mostly ordered us to save money.

In September 1991, my sports editor told me to move to Sacramento by March 1, because so much was happening there and we could no longer afford to keep an extra person in the Bay Area. I could not afford to move. I had bought a home 10 months earlier, with his approval, 100 miles away from Sacramento, and now he was asking that I take a huge loss and move or commute 100 miles. I remember catching sight of the San Francisco Bay on the way home — the Golden Gate Bridge, Mt. Tamalpais, the Bay Bridge — that day and feeling inexplicably elated.

Elated! I did not know what I was going to do — I just knew that I was not going to move to Sacramento, a fine town, I'm sure, but not *my* town.

It was as if Valerie had just knocked at my dormitory room door again, opening a world of possibilities that were as bound to re-energize as they were to surprise. McGwire had flipped the switch, and now light filled my future. I wrote my heart out for six months, then, in March, when I was supposed to be moving to Sacramento, I went to Arizona spring training — purely for fun — and never went back to work. I declined the so-called "transfer" to Sacramento. Then I fell in love. I traveled. I scored some baseball games. I went to others and cheered.

I still loved writing, and I still tuned in daily to A's and Giants games. But — with few exceptions like Dennis Eckersley, Mickey Morabito, and a handful of writers — I did not miss associating with the people and the business of sports. And I began to listen to what the women who had preceded me had said about why they left.

They *had* left, most of those women senior to me. Melanie Hauser was still at it with the *Houston Post*, but she had never seemed like a happy camper to me. And Michele Himmelberg still wrote, hoping to achieve a new career as an editor or columnist, but she described herself as "on the edge."

No wonder. All of the other veteran women sportswriters had moved out or up. Tracy Dodds had been bossed around enough: She became a sports editor. Kristin Huckshorn had said, "I'm too old to have some 19-year-old call me names," and switched to news, where, she kept telling me with wonder, people actually treated her as if she was an intelligent human being.

Stephanie Salter wrote news columns. Once, in 1988, she crossed back over the invisible line to do a story on Baltimore's record losing streak — and came away asking, "How did I do this for so many years? And *why*? Was I on a mission or was I just crazy?"

My mentor, Betty Cuniberti, had left sportswriting nearly 10 years before she wrote a column for the *National* explaining why she defected — a column I quote:

> Anyone who concluded we couldn't hack it is not much of a reporter. We "hacked" more covering any one season than men are subjected to over a lifetime career. Nonetheless, we certainly shed no tears over leaving locker-room hassles behind . . . When I left sportswriting, my feeling was not one of being beaten. I was just bored and fatigued by the battle. Who needs it?

Annette John-Hall of the *San Jose Mercury News* was in the process of transferring from sports to features as I interviewed her for this book. She told me she had once walked by the hotel bar and seen two other writers talking with the coach of the team she covered.

"I thought, 'I should be in there,' but I went to my room," she said. "Now, I'd go in there in a minute. I wish I knew then what I know now. But I'm 36 years old, and I don't want to cover sports anymore."

Claire Smith was still covering sports for the *New York Times*, but her beat had been sanitized into the business of baseball.

"These are executives, people in suits, I'm interviewing now," she said. "These are intelligent human beings who, for the most part, are dealing with me at face value, not on the basis of sex or race. The guys like (former baseball managers) Whitey Herzog and Dick Williams, you're never going to change them. And when they're gone, there will be someone else like them. I'm glad to be away from all that. I don't miss it at all. If this were 10 years ago and we didn't have the specialization and these national beats, I'd have probably moved out of sports by now."

Observed Smith's deputy sports editor, Sandra Bailey: "At some point in your life, if you're smart — and maybe I'm not smart and that's why I'm still here — you get tired of things that are going to look good on your tombstone. At some point, you just want to be comfortable. Sports editors are more comfortable as a group with women, but, individually, there are still some tremendous problems. The percentages are so bad, women are still an oddity."

"It wears you down," said Michele Himmelberg. "I like sportswriting, but the lifestyle and the travel and the pace and the demands wear you down as it is — then there are still all of these hassles you have to deal with because you are a woman. At one point, you accepted it. But, after 10 or 12 years, you just say, 'I'm sick of this — hopefully there's something else.' It's been one of my theories — perhaps it's arrogant — that the women who started doing this 10 and 15 years ago were not your typical sportswriters. They had to be so confident, had to have certain qualities that you need to succeed surrounded by all of these men."

Perhaps these bright and talented women had to be so exceptional in order to succeed in a business that didn't want them that, after a time, sportswriting no longer challenged their abilities, only their patience. They had asked that question before, written that quote before, seen that game before. They had heard they didn't belong there and proved they did, only to hear, again, that they still didn't belong and never would belong. They hit the ceilings in their sports departments and saw that they had hit glass — the men's ceiling was beyond their reach. Maybe they could get a better job in another sports department, but, tired of having to move across the country only to have to prove themselves again, they shifted gears.

They are thriving, but their loss to sportswriting saddens me. I wish I knew one 40-something woman sportswriter who had a happy family, a good salary, and a job she loved. I don't.

Then there is Lesley Visser, the most visible of us all. She gladdens me. She took time from her hectic television broadcasting schedule to write to me:

> After almost 20 years of covering sports, athletes rarely say anything demeaning to me anymore (unless you count the first time I interviewed Lawrence Taylor for CBS and he said, "Lesley, how old are you, anyway? Didn't you interview me 15 years ago?").
>
> Television is a different animal. There isn't the space to do lengthy pieces, but the impact is far greater. Sportscasters, particularly women, get letters from all kinds of fans (we're popular with prisoners!), and because CBS coverage runs all over the world, we hear from unusual places. I got a letter last week from a teenage boy in Czechoslovakia, who wanted an autographed picture and a New York Knicks schedule!
>
> I've always thought that covering sports is the ultimate passport. You meet everyone from the urban basketball player who grew up on the south side of Chicago to Prince Albert of Monaco. Sports is a topic that the cab driver and the king can debate with equal expertise. And the participants rely only on themselves — it doesn't matter where Michael Jordan's mother went to college or how much money his father has, if he sticks the jumper with time running out, he's done it on his own.

Lesley ran into one problem with a player, New York Jets tight end Mickey Shuler, and received written confirmation that times have changed for the better.

"Please accept my apologies for causing you any problems and embarrassment in your job covering the New York Jets. I personally believe from a male privacy aspect that women shouldn't be allowed in the locker room, but I understand that the rules of the New York Jets state that all members of the media are permitted in the locker room.

"Under any condition, I regret my actions to you and extend my apologies. Sincerely, Mickey Shuler."

Said the pleased recipient, Lesley Visser: "That might not seem like a big concession, but compared to where we were? It's enormous. It's important."

The reign of resistance has been falling, but slowly. Babe Laufenberg was a quarterback for the Dallas Cowboys in 1990 when he informally surveyed 10 of his teammates and learned that all of them agreed that women sportswriters want locker room access just so they can check out the naked bodies.

"I knew some guys felt that way, but I never would have guessed they'd ALL say that," Laufenberg told AWSM's Dallas meeting of 1990.

At that same meeting, though, Rolando Blackman of the Dallas Mavericks told us, "I never thought that's why a woman reporter was looking around. I just figured reporters look around to make sure one of my teammates doesn't dress quickly and leave before they can ask them questions . . . If I were you, I'd tell a guy to put on a towel if you want to talk to him. That's not too much to ask."

More men are vocalizing their support for women sportswriters. Sometimes it misses the mark, as it did when a male radio reporter dressed in drag for Cincinnati Bengals coach Sam Wyche's first game after barring Denise Tom from the locker room. Michele Himmelberg saw the pretty fellow standing in the group of reporters and finally asked, in exasperation, *"What* are you doing?" He said he was just showing solidarity — or was it sorority? Anyway, he meant well. At least, we preferred to give him the benefit of the doubt.

Other gestures cross the middle of the plate. Inside Wyche's locker room, several of his players were telling Himmelberg, "This is crazy." A black player, Himmelberg said, told her, "I know what it's like to be left out, in a minority situation. You guys shouldn't have to go through that."

One of my former fellow A's road warriors, Bud Geracie of the *San Jose Mercury News*, stood outside the University of California-Berkeley's locker room last year waiting to talk to Cal point guard Milica Vukadinovic. Cal had just been eliminated from the NCAA tournament; Vukadinovic had fouled out with 14 minutes left. Inside the locker room, Joan Ryan of the *San Francisco Examiner* talked to Vukadinovic. On her way out, Ryan spotted Bud shuffling his feet. She said something like: "How nice to see a man standing here waiting for a change."

Geracie wrote a column from the viewpoint of somebody usually on the inside now standing outside. "I'd never given much thought to the importance of locker room access...," he wrote. "(Being an outsider) is an uncomfortable, inequitable position, I know."

Another Bay Area sportswriter, Ira Miller of the *San Francisco Chronicle*, regularly took up for women sportswriters in his role as president of the Professional Football Writers of America. He wrote NFL commissioner Paul Tagliabue a letter declaring that "the issue of women in the locker room is bogus." And more coaches validated Miller's stance than Wyche's stance. Michelle Kaufman was first alarmed and then thrilled when, at the end of her first Detroit Lions training camp practice, head coach Wayne Fontes asked his players to go down on one knee and then asked Michelle to stand in front of the group.

Said Kaufman: "He put his hand on my shoulder and said, 'Men, I'd like you to meet Michelle Kaufman — she's a new reporter at the *Free Press* and she's going to be out here regularly. I want you to know she's here to do interviews. She's not here to get dates. She's not here to get autographs.' Then he said to me, so they could hear, 'If anyone here doesn't treat you with respect or treat you the way they treat the other reporters, I want you to call my office directly.'

"I never had any problems with the Detroit Lions."

Himmelberg loves this story. She remembers Fontes as an assistant coach for Tampa Bay when she lived her worst horror story, covering a game in Minnesota where the Vikings closed their locker room to all media and pointed the finger of blame at her.

"Wayne was a real outgoing, gregarious, fun-loving guy, and I remember him being in the bar with (head coach) John McKay and some other coaches," she said. "They talked me into having a kamikaze, and Fontes and I ended up dancing and talking about the whole idea of being professional, yet not being one of the guys, yet not having to hide in your room because you're afraid of what people might think. So, 12 years later, there he is a head coach, passing his open-minded attitude on to a whole new group of players . . . "

Players . . . who might someday became coaches themselves.

In New Jersey, a hockey team president passed his open-minded attitude on to a whole group of radio listeners. Lou

Lamoriello invited Sherry Ross, a long-time hockey writer for *Newsday* and the *Bergen Record*, to do color commentary on the New Jersey Devils' broadcasts. She's now into her second season of forgetting all swear words.

One night in spring training of 1990, I lounged on my bed, writing, with ESPN telecasting an NCAA basketball tournament game in the background. The game soon took center stage in my room, when I heard a woman's voice calling the action. This would not have been unusual, except that it was a men's game, not a women's game. The voice was that of Mimi Griffin, who had been assigned the game with no advance public notice whatsoever. Bully for ESPN: There was none of the aren't-we-enlightened preening one might expect from an all-sports network. Griffin was good, too — she called a game for CBS the following year.

With every Wayne Fontes and every Mimi Griffin, every Lou Lamoriello and every Sherry Ross, the crack in the locker room door widens another inch. And, someday, Helene Elliott won't have to answer the question, "What's wrong with you, Helene — why are you still doing this?"

Elliott has been a sportswriter for 15 years, and I believe she has set a record in beat reporting for a woman. No column-writing or cushy takeout jobs for Helene — she's been covering the nuts and bolts of team after team after team, most recently baseball's California Angels but currently the Los Angeles Lakers, her first NBA assignment.

She was half-thrilled and half-terrified at taking on something new after 15 years of proving herself in other venues. "I guess I'm still trying to get it right," she says jokingly. "I can't sing or dance or draw or sew, or do anything socially redeeming like ditch digging. This is all I know, and I have a mortgage.

"Seriously, though, I still like the idea of being on deadline. I'm a journalism junkie — I still get excited by the day-to-day pursuit of a story."

Elliott certainly cannot attribute her longevity to any shortage of harassment. "It's every day," she said. "You face it every day. But now I'm going onto the Laker beat, where there's already a woman, Kelly Carter of the *Orange County Register*, who really knows her stuff. Now, all of a sudden, the attitude is, 'Oh, another woman sportswriter. If she's anything like Kelly — and

maybe she is, because she's a woman — she could be really good
to deal with.' Here, it's a plus to be a woman on the beat.

"The things that bother me now are the little things —
things like having your credential checked seven or eight times
a day when the men never have their credentials checked once,
like walking into a pressbox and getting asked, 'Are you with
him?' No. I'm here. I'm a real writer. I covered a football game at
the University of Illinois, and at each seat in the press box was a
packet of press notes and little goodies, like a matchbook in the
shape of an Illinois helmet. My place was empty — not even any
press notes. It's those little things — going into the Detroit Tigers
locker room and still having to have a security guard go in first
and announce you.

"But it's not really small stuff to me. It's a sign of a lack of
respect, and (the establishment's) need to reinforce second-class
status when we've fought so long not to have second-class
status."

Someday, though, the small stuff that makes sportswriting
tedious for women is going to go the way of the big stuff that used
to make it impossible. I know this by the large pile of scholarship
applications, from would-be women in sports media, sitting on
top of Kristin Huckshorn's dining room table. I know this by the
decision of yet another NCAA conference to provide constant
and unconditional equal access for all credentialed media. I
know it by the addition of a women's room to the U.S. Senate and
the election of a president whose wife is an attorney.

I know it by the scattering of the Oakland A's — who
know it, too — to the four corners of the baseball earth for the 1993
baseball season. Dave Stewart will police the deportment of the
Toronto Blue Jays, and Jose Canseco will be talking as openly to
the women of Texas as he talks to the men anywhere. Rene
Lachemann will teach his young Florida Marlins that press is
press, and Willie Wilson will show the Chicago Cubs what a class
act is all about. With ambassadors like these, the so-called small
stuff is doomed.

And I know this especially because Helene Elliott tells me
they finally hung a shower curtain across the visitors' clubhouse
shower/urinal area in Cleveland Municipal Stadium. Future
women sportswriters there can carry small notepads if they want
to — they won't need to erect their own personal paper walls as

they hurry through the accidental peepshow into the manager's office. And the most modest of athletes no longer has to wait until he gets to Chicago to take a long, carefree, private shower.

A shower curtain in Cleveland. Imagine that.

See, it can work, this business of being a woman in a man's locker room. A shower curtain here, a bathrobe there, and a little common sense everywhere. The athletes and sportswriters who are making it work every day know — like the male patient with the female doctor or the men's minor-league hockey team with the female goaltender — that it is possible for men and women to cooperate under even the most awkward circumstances.

Their bosses, I am afraid, will be more slowly persuaded to allow women in their own locker rooms. Ensconced in their offices and meetings, writing memos and eating power lunches, they are missing the world of possibilities that diversity and commingling bring to the workplace. A different viewpoint is not yet an acceptable viewpoint — much less a plus — to the sports editor hiring a columnist. A different social style is not an acceptable social style — hardly a pleasure — to the sports executive looking for a publicist to travel with his team.

This resistance is not one of the "little things," it is the big, thick wall at the heart of the "woman in the locker room" debates.

It wasn't those little locker rooms that drove me away from sportswriting. It was that big locker room.

# Epilogue

On December 18, 1992, Dave Stewart joined several of his former teammates for the annual A's performance in the Oakland Ballet's *Nutcracker*. All of them appeared as soldiers in Act One, and Stewart danced a solo in Act Two's Arabian Dance.

He was a Toronto Blue Jay now, but he said that Oakland would always be his home. During curtain calls, he hugged his former manager, Tony La Russa, who also had danced. Then, afterward, he struggled to harness his emotions for the post-performance reception, but he decided not to go. He was feeling too sad about leaving the A's, no matter how many millions he could make to the north. By spring training, though, Stew seemed enthusiastic about the chances of his new team—and, especially, about the power he was feeling on the mound.

The Oakland A's that Stew and I knew are, in essence, gone now. Their trade of Canseco was, it now appears, a fiscal move — an omen of the off-season decisions that would retain Mark McGwire and Ruben Sierra, but decimate the pitching staff to a roster of, and I quote David Bush of the *San Francisco Chronicle*, "Welch, Witt, and the wusses." Oh, they still had Dennis Eckersley, the winner of the Cy Young and Most Valuable Player awards for 1992. But a closing relief pitcher can only save games when his team leads, and I am not sure how many opportunities the 1993 A's will present him. Maybe the cycle begins again for the A's, who can now start rebuilding their talent and attitude—if they could only dispense with whining Rickey Henderson— so that they can, someday, once again enjoy the surprised, almost innocent pleasures of a season like 1988.

The media pack that had surrounded the A's since 1988 already had disappeared by spring training, most of it wandering up Scottsdale Road to see the San Francisco Giants. There, a woman was stealing the headlines from the Giants' $43 million man, Barry Bonds. Her name: Sherry Davis. She had emerged from a throng of 500 at open auditions to win the Giants' public address announcing job. A long-time Giants' fan who has been keeping a scorebook since 1987, Davis is the first woman in the history of major professional sports to earn the honor of announcing, "Good afternoon, fans, and welcome..." I say "honor," because it is hardly an occupation: Davis's salary is just $75 a game.

It was a good publicity move for the Giants, but maybe mere window dressing. By spring, the new owners had not hired or promoted any women executives—and they had, in her view, demoted Robin Carr Locke to "publicity coordinator," and hired a man as media relations director. Robin says she was told she wasn't "strong enough" for the directorship and was not even interviewed for the position.

But the new season of baseball did bring some signs of a new season of attitudes. Three nights before the *Nutcracker*, I sat on the floor in the living room of Robin and Barry Locke's townhouse in North Beach, munching on pizza and looking up at the new manager of the Giants, Dusty Baker.

Baker had been named manager that day, and Robin had been hustling him and his girlfriend, Melissa, from interview to interview. When they finally had a break, they said they just wanted to unwind for a couple of hours at the Carr-Locke household.

Only Dusty never unwound. He sat there on the couch, still wired and energetic, talking — somewhat hoarsely by now — about the changes he wanted to make and the philosophies he would bring to his new job. He will clearly be a different, open-minded kind of manager, one who, he said that night, would be growing his hair into Rastafarian locks if he weren't trying to rise through the conservative white ranks of baseball. And Melissa might be the Hillary Clinton of baseball's significant others—she has a job, which is unusual enough, and is not a model or flight attendant, but an accountant.

Since I had the opportunity, I asked Dusty if he wanted his players to side with each other as the Oakland A's had in 1986, when Dave Kingman sent me a rat and teammates would not speak out against what he had done. Dusty said he wanted his players to have a strong sense of team, but to also have the integrity and maturity to stand up for right against wrong.

I look forward to sitting in the sunshine and watching these new A's and Giants, and, of course, my beloved Orioles, play their game.

But, most of all, I can't wait to see men like Dusty Baker infiltrate baseball's big locker room and infect others with tolerance and integrity. Someday, maybe, it will be everybody's game.

***Marge Schott...Unleashed!:*** Explores the controversial tenure of Marge Schott as owner of the Cincinnati Reds, and what really led to her suspension. Available June 1993.

***Pittsburgh Pirates: Still Walking Tall:*** Takes an exciting look at the team that won the last three National League East division crowns, and is picked by many experts to do it again this year. Available April 1993.

***Glory Jays: Canada's World Series Champions:*** The Blue Jays are the first team to take the World Series trophy north of the border. *Glory Jays* details the highlights of their exciting season, and gives a preview of this year's team. Available April 1993.

***Lou Boudreau: Covering All the Bases:*** Boudreau tells the story of his exciting career in this autobiography. His years as a player manager with the Cleveland Indians, and his nearly three decades of announcing for the Chicago Cubs. Available June 1993.

***Phil Rizzuto: A Yankee Tradition:*** Tells the story of Rizzuto's rise to baseball stardom, including his years in the minors, four All-Star appearances, and 1950 MVP performance. Available June 1993.

***Down for the Count: Investigating the Mike Tyson Rape Trial:*** This controversial new title gives an in-depth description of the trial of the year; including the numerous miscalculations by Tyson's defense team, the testimony of Desiree Washington and of Mike Tyson himself. Available May 1993.

**Please call Sagamore at 1-800-327-5557 to order any of our spring sports titles or to receive a free catalog of the best fall sports titles.**

*Against the World: A Behind-the-Scenes Look at the Portland Trail Blazers' Chase for the NBA Championship* ISBN 0-915611-67-8 $19.95

*Best in the Game: The Turbulent Story of the Pittsburgh Penguins' Rise to Stanley Cup Champions* ISBN 0-915611-66-x $19.95

*Blue Fire: A Season Inside the St. Louis Blues* ISBN 0-915611-55-4 $22.95

*The Fighting Irish Football Encyclopedia* ISBN 0-915611-54-6 $44.95

*Hail to the Orange and Blue* ISBN 0-915611-31-7 $29.95

*Lady Magic: The Autobiography of Nancy Lieberman-Cline* ISBN 0-915611-43-0 $19.95

*Lou: Winning at Illinois* ISBN 0-915611-24-4 $18.95

*Metivier On: Saratoga, Glens Falls, Lake George, and the Adirondacks* ISBN 0-915611-60-0 $19.95

*Stormin' Back: Missouri Coach Norm Stewart's Battles On and Off the Court* ISBN 0-915611-47-3 $19.95

*Take Charge! A How-to Approach for Solving Everyday Problems* ISBN 0-915611-46-5 $9.95

*Undue Process: The NCAA's Injustice for All* ISBN 0-915611-34-1 $19.95

*William Warfield: My Music & My Life* ISBN 0-915611-40-6 $19.95

*Winning Styles for Winning Coaches: Creating the Environment for Victory* ISBN 0-915611-49-x $12.95

*Woody Hayes: A Reflection* ISBN 0-915611-42-2 $19.95